BI 0785305 X

M9321487
£10·88
MDAA

Checher

Information Management

Opportunities and Risks

5

Information Systems Management

Opportunities and Risks

Ian O. Angell
Steve Smithson

Department of Information Systems
London School of Economics

St. Martin's Press   New York

First published in the United States of America in 1992

Printed in Hong Kong

ISBN 0–312–07941–9 (paperback)

Library of Congress Cataloging-in-Publication Data
Angell, Ian O.
Information systems management : opportunities and risks / Ian O.
Angell, Steve Smithson.
    p.   cm.
Includes index.
1. Information resources management.   I. Smithson, Steve, 1949–
. II. Title.
T58.64.A44   1992
658.4'038—dc20   91–46131
                                            CIP

Contents

v

Preface

Managers of Information Systems (IS) are being pulled in two directions. On the one hand within much of the information technology (IT) industry, the 'Spirit of the Age' is still one of unbridled hype and optimism, where computer-based systems are seen as a first response and an instant solution to any problem. Information technology is promoted as an agent of change that can deliver competitive advantage in terms of better quality products, enhanced control, reduced costs and increased flexibility. On the other hand, there seems to be no sign of any let-up in the 'horror stories', and the consequences of faulty computer-based systems still grab the newspaper headlines. In Paris, in September 1989, the Court computer mailed out 41,000 summonses for parking violations. Due to a mistake, or perhaps to a deliberate act of malice, the actual summonses sent were for prostitution, living off immoral earnings, burglary, even manslaughter. Pandemonium resulted from the embarrassment and family recriminations heaped on these victims of circumstance. We should not be surprised, such examples are legion: a few weeks later a British bank inadvertently transferred two billion pounds in less than half an hour to various international institutions; luckily the money was returned.

IS managers have to steer a difficult course between the 'hype' and the 'horror'. It could be argued that this situation is not new, it was the case ten (or even twenty) years ago; computer salesmen were just as plausible then and information systems failures also made the headlines. However, we would contend that the situation is rather different today. Firstly, the risks are much greater as systems become larger, more integrated, and thus more complex, so that it is very much more difficult to isolate particular failures and to limit the 'knock-on' effects. Furthermore, organizations have become more vulnerable; many depend crucially upon information technology because their basic transactions and much of their more sensitive information is now held on computers. Secondly, information technology is no longer 'new' and, whilst past mistakes could be written off against experience, we should now be seeing organizations using the technology in a mature fashion. The 'stage' theory (Gibson, C.F. & Nolan, R.L., 'Managing the four stages of EDP growth', *Harvard Business Review*, Vol.52, No.1, Jan-Feb 1974) suggests that by now most organizations should be managing their 'information resource', rather than trying to control errant application programs. Many IS managers, who were told that they would be managing change, find instead that they are managing crisis, a crisis of control.

We will try to give substance to the often unexpressed fears and uncertainty felt by many user managers and IS managers, and by laying the issues before them, guide them towards sensible decisions. We will question the limits of this technology in the managerial context, but leave it to individual managers, in their own particular situations, to decide what is appropriate and inappropriate for their organization's specific needs. Our aim is to encourage the 'thinking manager' towards a more critical evaluation of computer-based IS. Notwithstanding the countless books and articles emphasizing the benefits of IT, our message is that decision-makers must re-examine the assumptions under which systems are justified, and they must become aware of the risks inherent in the introduction of information technology and balance them against the many benefits.

Above all, this book is about balance. It is about recognizing the 'pros' and the 'cons' of applying computers. Managing computerized information systems will involve capitalizing on the many opportunities made available by IT to the benefit of the organization, while at the same time avoiding the risks that can be detrimental to its well-being. In this respect, and as a general principle, the management of IS is little different to other areas of management. However, where it does differ is in coping with the all-embracing systemic nature of information, and with the effective use of this resource in dealing with the uncertainty that pervades every aspect of the commercial environment.

With this message of balance, we have organized the book into twelve chapters, starting with an introduction that lays out the scenario of opportunity and risk in information systems. In Chapter 2, we propose a theoretical basis for understanding and managing this opportunity and risk, while Chapter 3 describes the concept of strategy as a sensible approach to the management of IS. The organizational issues of IT are considered in Chapter 4, and the effects on, and maintenance of, the integrity of an organization and its information systems are outlined in Chapter 5. Chapter 6 examines the promises and pitfalls of information technology in the context of information systems. Chapters 7, 8 and 9 discuss the key infrastructural technologies of databases, networks and office information systems. Chapter 10 considers questions of the development of information systems, and Chapter 11 discusses the evaluation, monitoring and control of operational systems. In Chapter 12 we culminate with a look at the need for people amidst all this automation, and finish with an unequivocal recognition that the successful implementation of computer-based information systems is totally dependent on quality human intervention.

Top quality management and staff, well trained and highly motivated, can harness the power of the technology to provide a range and quality of services, undreamt-of a few years ago. Without such people, and without the technology, organizations are on a road to nowhere.

1   Introduction: the need for balance

- *The crisis of confidence*
- *Systemic risk*
- *Complexity*
- *Uncertainty*
- *The introduction of information systems*
- *Measurability, Predictability, Rationality*
- *Coping with the crisis*

The crisis of confidence

Throughout a large number of very different industries, IT decision-takers are confronting a growing crisis as the time approaches to authorize new computer-based information systems. Here, we use the term 'crisis' advisedly. The Oxford English Dictionary defines crisis to be: *A vitally important or decisive stage in the progress of anything; now applied in times of difficulty, insecurity and suspense in politics or commerce.* To psychologists a crisis is: *when the individual is in a situation where past experience and old reaction patterns are no longer adequate. A time of danger and suspense.* In medicine it is: *a point in the progress of a disease when a development or change takes place which is decisive of recovery or death; a turning point for better or worse.*

The backdrop to this situation is a widespread faith, throughout much of industry and academia, in the inherent virtue, almost omnipotence, of the technology. Despite a whole catalogue of incidents, businesses are still encouraged to seek the 'Holy Grail' of competitive advantage through the employment of this seductive technology [1]. Yet, they are rarely warned that they may be unwittingly gambling with their futures. Since the earliest days, there has been criticism of the self-proclaimed benefits of computerization (Ackoff [2], Roszak [3], Weizenbaum [4]), but these have largely been ignored. Newspapers, television, radio and film stress, explicitly and implicitly, the merits of computerization. Governments invest huge amounts in computer education and in high-technology industrial collaboration. But computing has often not lived up to expectations and there is a sense of irritation, even dissatisfaction, in the business community. Is it right that this self-evident certainty goes unchallenged,

1

or have we reached that decisive stage in the development of information technology, a time of difficulty, insecurity and suspense, a time of crisis?

Is this a turning point, for better or worse? Much will depend on the recognition of many more variables and marginal issues within information systems. The recognition of this crisis and its implied new behaviour patterns will not be easy for managers of information systems, who have been trained in the technologies and machine-centred requirements of the past. Awareness of the crisis is vital, even for those that are at present successful users of information systems. For the indications are that organizations cannot rely on past experiences and old reaction patterns for future success: a totally new mode of IS management is needed.

Systemic risk

It is not enough to apply traditional cost–benefit analysis to IT projects. As well as to appreciate the opportunities attached to the project, it is important to analyze the risks. These risks are usually associated with systems' failures or unforeseen adverse consequences of the introduction of new information systems. Such risks seem to be endemic to information technology. For example, American Airlines clearly gained a major commercial advantage and substantial income with their SABRE Reservation System. Unfortunately together with this success is the possibility of major unforeseen legal battles over unfair competition, with huge financial liabilities. The airline also lost fifty million dollars by flying planes well below capacity, when customers were transferred to their competitors after a software bug incorrectly informed booking clerks that aircraft were full!

Systemic risk is a result of the complexity implicit in all large systems, but particularly in socio-technical systems where people interact closely with the technical system. This realization is not new. Murphy's Law *"if it can go wrong, it will go wrong,"* and the accompanying lemma *"Murphy was an optimist,"* sums up the situation succinctly. No technology always behaves in the way we expect and believe it should; instead it almost appears to have a destructive purpose of its own: 'Gremlins'. Gall, in his highly amusing book *Systemantics* [5], gives many examples where blind optimism and a lack of understanding of the way that systems function have led to devastating conclusions and, with tongue in cheek, he outlines a number of profound 'laws' relating to the misbehaviour of systems. It is a surprising side of human nature that we treat the inevitability of uncertainty with humour. Perhaps this is the mechanism that has made the human race so successful in dealing with these dilemmas. And we have been successful, although, to listen to some proselytes of artificial intelligence and decision analysis, we would gather that humans are somewhat inadequate in this respect.

Complexity

Sheer complexity, not just in the technology itself but in its interaction with any application environment, throws up inevitable, yet unpredictable, emergent phenomena, many of which are likely to cause problems. The KISS advice, *Keep It Simple, Stupid*, is too often ignored in the grandiose schemes of managers who seem to be chasing the glamour and kudos of advanced technology. In both the USA and UK numerous large military 'command and control' systems have run into severe problems. Barclays Bank in the UK abandoned two multi-million pound projects. Perhaps, as has been suggested, we should emulate successful Japanese companies and use information systems that are simpler and more selective than those presently used in the West.

Previously seen only in terms of its many benefits, the convergence of computer and communication technologies could very well be 'an accident just waiting to happen'. Rather than a communications network spanning the world, with Open Systems Interconnection (OSI), we could be building a spider's web, a trap of unimaginable complexity; a tangled web that the manufacturers seem very keen to promote. *"Communications is the heart of AT&T's business. And technology is our lifeblood. We see our job as connecting people to people, machines to machines, systems to systems, unhindered by geographic and technical barriers"* (AT&T advertisement). Technocrats, businessmen and politicians are launching technological monsters into our society, in the arrogant belief that because they initiate a system, they somehow control its evolution and its resultant effects. The short-sighted leading the blind!

Commercial and social pressures, cultural incompatibilities, chaotic changes, resistance to change, unpredictable accidents, criminal intent, malice and sabotage add to the already excessive complexity, and can have surprising effects on what are usually considered technological decisions. For example, electronic mail has many benefits, yet it has well-documented negative effects: the danger of reduced social interaction; magnetic disk stores filled to capacity with multiple copies of unread messages; hours wasted reading 'junk mail'; and possibly worst of all there is 'flaming', where carelessly phrased messages on trivial matters precipitate aggressive responses, and a feedback of antagonism that can cause major social disruption within an organization.

Another aspect of information technology that is rarely fully appreciated is the sheer scale and complexity of the administration needed to maintain an information system, including everything from maintaining the integrity of a file-base to satisfying the requirements of data-privacy legislation and safeguards. Taken to excess, a rigid electronic bureaucracy prepares fertile ground for Parkinson's Law: *"Work expands so as to fill the time available for its completion"* [6]. A rigid bureaucracy can enforce a straitjacket of short term thinking that is blind to the opportunities and risks within information technology. It can even introduce a mind-set that rejects both commonsense and innovative thinking, with ludicrous consequences. In 1990, despite the proximity of increased trade within the European Community, over half the computer systems in UK banks could not cope with European currencies, and European character sets!

Uncertainty

In times of stability decision-takers may be justified in extrapolating the past onto the future, but in turbulent times, times of crisis, this limited way of thinking is invalid. Yet, it is in times of extreme uncertainty, when managers do not have a clear intuitive picture of the future, that they are tempted to reach out for formal computer-based tools (statistical models, spreadsheet analysis) in an attempt to reduce this uncertainty. Such tools can readily give comforting, quantitative answers, as well as reassuring managers that they are acting in a rational and scientific fashion. However, all these tools require some numerical input, which in times of uncertainty are likely to be very arbitrary 'guesstimates'. The software then performs highly sophisticated calculations (in a statistical sense), usually without warning the decision-taker of the crucial dependence and model sensitivity on the data input; whence 'garbage in – garbage out'. It is too easy for managers to be blinkered by a false sense of security, engendered by mathematically sophisticated models that fail to consider the real unmeasurable uncertainties of the situation; and the uncertainty remains, perhaps even made worse, by the arbitrary application of computing technology.

There is a need to forecast the future business environment to answer the demand for estimates of the costs and benefits of introducing a new system and for predictions of technological trends. Particular technologies may be fashionable today, but may quickly become unfashionable. Fledgling technologies, such as artificial intelligence, emerge from laboratories amidst extravagant claims of effectiveness and relevance to organizational needs. Grandiose claims are made as to their widespread applicability, and many organizations attempt to develop sophisticated systems on the basis of these claims. Few systems become operational and current opinion among some influential IT commentators is that such systems will be of marginal relevance at best. One example of companies jumping onto a particular technology bandwagon, only to find 'that the band was getting off', concerned the six thousand users of British Telecom's System 4 service. This VHF-based cellular radio system was prematurely closed down in July 1990, rather than continuing well into the next decade as was originally anticipated, to the great annoyance of customers who had invested in the hardware and developed business applications around it.

The introduction of information systems

Bearing in mind the fairly evident risks and perennial horror stories, it is pertinent that we examine the assumptions underlying the justification and approval processes for the introduction of any new information system, on the grounds that many of the problem systems should have been aborted at the planning or feasibility stage. Many difficulties result from a failure of imagination in these early stages of the system's development. The problem seems to be a failure of forecasting: if the failures had been foreseen, then they should have been avoided. Forecasting is a difficult process (or art) in most areas of business, and is especially so with information technology because of the failure to appreciate the unknown and unknowable consequences of introducing large-scale information systems, and because the current conventional wisdom is an unquestioning acceptance of the desirability of state-of-the-art IT.

The decision to proceed with or to cancel a new computer-based information system is normally taken as a result of some form of feasibility study. All too often, however, what should be a wide-ranging investigation of the implications of the new system turns into a much narrower cost–benefit analysis. If the technology can supply an idealized system and if predicted benefits of this system exceed the costs with an appropriate return on investment, usually perceived from the perspective of short time-scales, then development of the system commences in earnest. While the dominance of such an approach appears to reflect a laudable and economically rational concern with the 'bottom line' of profitability, it entails a number of critical assumptions that simply cannot be justified without a far deeper examination. We will consider only three such assumptions.

Measurability

The measurement of deliverables, costs, benefits, and risks is certainly the 'Achilles' heel' of this approach, as has been widely recognized in civil engineering when dealing with the social costs of large projects, such as the nuclear plant at Shoreham, New York, whose final cost was $5.1 billion, twenty times the original estimate. With most information technology projects, the main difficulties are in measuring the performance of both the new technical systems and the workforce that they ostensibly support, and also in predicting the effect of the projects within the organizational context. Such projects are often justified on the grounds that they will increase the productivity of 'knowledge workers' (management and clerical staff), even though measuring that productivity is extraordinarily difficult compared with measuring productivity in manufacturing industries. There is the temptation to take trivial and arbitrary performance measures based on activities (for instance, the number of telephone enquiries dealt with per hour) or computer hardware (the number of disk accesses per hour), and then to fit these numbers into a simplistic cost model. However, there is an element of choice in all measurement; not only in which parameters should be measured, but also in the accuracy to which each measurement is made. Such choices can cause major problems, because even the smallest differences in the measurement of a parameter can make a substantial difference to the solution of the most elementary deterministic mathematical equations.

Granted that no organizational administration can function without a sensible means of measurement. When properly used they can be a valuable aid to understanding the behaviour of systems. However, a regime of unquestioned compliance with naive performance measures creates perverse innovative systems which in turn distort the original intention behind those measures. Automation of these measures is likely to make things worse. All the creative energies of the organization may become geared to maximize the measure scores but, rather than accomplishing the original purpose, they achieve the exact opposite (so-called system inversion). During this process, insidious properties may emerge, which can remain inconspicuous until they have a firm hold within an organization; a hold that is then impossible to dislodge. Such measure-driven practices can have short term advantages, but they are likely to create long term problems and even systems failure. Of course, performance monitoring of systems is essential but the limited quantitative measurement achievable must be seen within the overall context of the organization's objectives and the intuitive qualitative observations of management.

Many expected impacts of IT are very difficult to evaluate in terms of monetary value or time: these are the intangible costs and benefits. Managers have the unenviable choice of excluding such impacts in their calculations or placing an arbitrary value on them. It is easy to understand why key aspects, such as staff morale and customer goodwill, are placed on the sidelines. A British Building Society (Savings and Loan Bank) provides a good example of the failings of optimizing short term performance measurement. The Society was using IT in an attempt to measure customer satisfaction and staff efficiency, by counting customer throughput. When asked a simple specific question about mortgages, clerks in three different branches provided three different answers (all of them wrong!). Each clerk appeared to give the first answer that came to hand, in an effort to improve throughput and hence their personal performance measure.

Predictability

Computerized models based on data from the past cannot be expected to predict an ever more complex and uncertain future, a future of crisis made more complex and uncertain by a lack of understanding of the phenomenon of information technology, paradoxically the very technology developed to ease the situation. Uncertainty is compounded by the mistaken identification of correlation among the measures of real events with causal relationships between events. The wishful reflection of past trends and structures onto an uncertain future virtually guarantees a misinterpretation of novel emergent realities and innovations that could suggest real commercial openings.

Thus, computer-based systems, used either as part of the process of prediction or as part of the 'solution', may actually make things more complex and uncertain. Perhaps it is an incorrect theoretical comprehension of complexity and uncertainty that is causing the problem, the very concepts central to the definition and application of effective management. Perhaps it is the restrictive mathematical view of complexity and the statistical/scientific view of uncertainty, both reliant on the concept of measurement that is wrong. Perhaps it is the diminishing of confidence in man's decision-taking and his relegation of problem resolution to machines that is exacerbating the uncertainty, and causing a feedback of dissatisfaction and a feeling that human values will be superseded by those of the machine and of the 'bottom line'.

Some models may permit the consideration of alternative rational futures: perhaps a 'best case' and 'worst case' scenario. This is fine, although further in the analysis there is usually an unfortunate tendency to collapse these into an 'average case' or 'most likely outcome', using highly dubious estimates of probability. Such arithmetic is often meaningless, since in practice the best and worst cases will be alternative achievable futures which are based on different assumptions, and on averaging could create an irrational compromise worse than the worst case. Risk analysis is one 'rational' attempt to predict and deal with dangers and adverse consequences. In theory we would support this move but, regrettably, the recognition of real risks is obscured through the use of simplistic probability calculations. In order to calculate 'exposure', the possible losses are multiplied by the estimated probability of their occurrence, a fatuous calculation when considering highly unlikely yet potentially fatal risks.

Rationality

It is too easy for those involved to become totally lost in the mathematical logic that seems to permeate information technology. Arguably, computer enthusiasts, who are currently in the ascendent, are more likely to subscribe to a deterministic, positivistic view of the world. This view cannot adequately cope with the subjectivity, the uncertainty (which transcends probability values), and the political action that are the distinguishing features of most organizations. 'Bureaucratic rationalism' may lead to a naive, simplistic view of the organization and its future environment. For too long the state-of-the-art has been the self-serving logic of computer solutions looking for problems, and a belief that most problems can be modelled and have programmable numerical solutions. These solutions are created in insulated software laboratories and ignore the realities of emergent complexity within the open human environment.

A rarely stated assumption of 'scientific' analyses is that the analyst has a good understanding of the complex situation. However, the problem may not be one of attaching values to predictable consequences but rather one of failing to comprehend the range of possible consequences. This includes the common assumption that the consequences will be solely benign and that there will be positive benefits although the level of such benefits may be hard to predict. In practice, there may well be unforeseen adverse consequences, with the benefits claimed for IT more than counter-balanced by risk and danger; perhaps *"there is no choice that results in no harm"*. The introduction of new technology may solve some simple problems but may actually cause more complex and costly difficulties. For example, few organizations would have predicted the health and safety problems of anxiety attacks and of repetitive strain injury (RSI). We may well be seeing just the tip of the iceberg with the cases of RSI that have already been reported, including about a hundred journalists afflicted to a varying extent at both the *Financial Times* and the *Los Angeles Times*. Computerized 'Just-In-Time' stock control systems have clear advantages for customers in manufacturing industries but, on the other hand, they both increase firms' vulnerability during times of labour unrest as well as pushing the problem of stock control down to the suppliers. The solutions adopted by these suppliers, terrified of losing contracts, may not be socially acceptable; for example, easily accessible storage in old and rusting trucks permanently stationed on roads near customers' factories.

Coping with the crisis

Only now are some users beginning to accept that the effects of systems can be chaotic, disruptive, and unpredictable; simplistic mathematical models are not enough, and scientific, statistical, and technological methods may be inappropriate. It seems clear that a rather different approach is needed in place of the current orthodoxy; we would disagree with James Martin's comment: *"it is technology that has created the dilemmas, and yet the only way out is more technology"*. We must change the focus away from the technology towards people, as it will be people, high quality people, who will be able to understand and cope with the impact of the technology. Success will not be gained by machines, but by that very scarce commodity – the excellent individual. Instead of regarding the machine as central to information, managers need to shift their focus to viewing information systems as social systems, in order to understand the fundamental place of people: employees, customers and suppliers. Their perspective should begin with the context, the purpose and the meaning of information. Such an approach is inherently multidisciplinary, implying that, although communication and computing technologies were born in the natural sciences, engineering and mathematics, their effective use is based firmly in the social sciences. The use of this new technology cannot be separated from human intellect, aspirations, culture, philosophy, and social organization. To link information technology solely to a mathematical and scientific theory, leaving no room for intuition, insight, inspiration, and lateral thinking, would be to ignore the most important subjective human connection in this symbiotic technology.

The major impact of information technology will not be in software or hardware, or in computerized decision-taking, but in the linking of information technology to a more efficient industrial and commercial base, in enhanced human–human communication, in the application of solutions to problems that lend themselves to calculation, and in the application and sale of expertise and of information itself. For it is the human factor, not technology, that makes the difference between commercial success and failure, and between acceptance and rejection of a system. Hence the true asset of a company is its educated employees supported by IT; the real strategic resource essential for commercial growth and the real stuff of competitive advantage. Finding out who the 'best' people are, how to attract them, how to train them, how to employ them, how to motivate them, how to support them with technology and, just as importantly, how to keep them, requires major investment by forward-looking organizations.

Investment in people does not necessarily imply hiring and training yet more programmers, even though some estimates have suggested that ten million programmers will be needed in the 1990s, at an annual cost of 250 billion dollars. Considering the evident growth in end user computing and the simplified information systems development offered by software packages and fourth generation languages, we would argue that careful consideration is needed before embarking on the mass recruitment of programmers. Perhaps a comparison can be made with the early days of the motor car, when corresponding predictions placed limits on car production because of a shortage of chauffeurs! The reality is that we have absolutely no idea how many programmers will be needed in the next century, and fatuous 'guesstimates' based on extrapolating present trends are likely to be very misleading. Many believe that programming is a low level task, and that programmers will be the 'car-mechanics' of the next century. Vocational skills lead into the cul-de-sac of a closed technological environment, whereas it is education that gives an intellectual platform on which to base decisions about the management of crisis, complexity and change, which are essential in these turbulent times. Rather than programmers, we need broadly-based well-educated 'thinking managers' and knowledge workers who are confident when using and managing the technology, but who also know when not to use it.

Advances in computer and communication technologies are rapidly out-stripping our ability to use and manage the resulting products, and this can prove highly counterproductive. It is no use treating computer systems as static objects, we must recognize the need to study their behaviour. Even well-engineered designs can fail when there is poor training, when the context changes, or when the unexpected occurs; this is all part of systemic risk. Its counterpart, systemic opportunity means that even poorly designed systems can work well 'in the right place at the right time with the right people'. The emphasis should not be on which systems can be built with the available technology, but on whether they are appropriate and relevant. A major question for the future is whether the right people will be in place to manage information systems after they have been intro-duced into organizations, and into society in general. Will information technology produce environmental, intellectual, cultural, or social pollution? When we look at the values behind this technology, rather than synergy will we find entropy, and our future mortgaged for short-term gains? We must concentrate on the concepts which stand behind the use of information technology, by focusing on the human and organizational problems of the development and management of information systems. We must invert the hitherto unsuccessful mind-set of technology, and only then will it be possible to find a more effective approach.

Discussion issues

Newspapers and magazines are a ready source of up-to-date as well as historical information on business applications of computers. Check the reference libraries in your locality for the published indexes and microfiche back-copies of major newspapers (*New York Times*, London *Times* etc.). Many of these newspaper articles will name important books, reports and reviews about the IT industry worldwide and give leads on both 'horror stories' and 'success stories'. The major problem in this exercise is knowing what key-words to search for in the index; however, once you find the first few articles then you will soon formulate a 'problem-domain vocabulary' that should help you with further searches.

Divide your group into two debating teams, so that one team will be supportive of the benefits of information technology while the other will be antagonistic. Research material for class discussions on the following topics: the rapid growth of the 'IT consultancy industry'; forecasts about the future needs of US, Japanese, and European industry with regard to manpower and equipment; the failure and misinterpretation of the warning information system at Three Mile Island; advantages with 'fly by wire', and its problems, using data on the BA320 Airbus crashes at Hohenheim and Madras; the advantages and disadvantages of the American Airlines SABRE system; computer viruses and worms; insurance of computer centres; computer fraud; the impact of IT on the stock market crash of Black Monday, 19'th October 1987; the use of expert systems in production industries; trade unions calling strikes in carefully selected computer centres to force companies into negotiation. Simply searching under the key-words 'computers', 'software', 'electronics', 'IBM' ('Digital Equipment Corporation' or any other computer company), 'workstations', 'information technology', and 'communications technology' will give you many more ideas for discussions.

References

1. Porter M.E. & Millar V.E., 'How information gives you competitive advantage', *Harvard Business Review*, Vol.63, No.4, 149-160, July-August, 1985.
2. Ackoff R., 'Management Misinformation Systems', *Management Science*, Vol.14, No.4, B147-B156, December 1967.
3. Roszak T., *The Cult of Information*, Lutterworth Press, Cambridge, 1986.
4. Weizenbaum J., *Computer Power and Human Reason: From Judgement to Calculation*, Freeman & Co., San Francisco, 1976.
5. Gall J., *Systemantics*, General Systemantics Press, Ann Arbor, 1988.
6. Parkinson C. Northcote, *Parkinson's Law*, Penguin, London, 1986.

2 Understanding information systems

- *Information systems as social systems*
- *Analysis or interpretation?*
- *Systems thinking*
- *Models and mechanisms*

Information systems as social systems

In order to account for the situations outlined in the previous chapter, it is necessary to understand more fully the nature of information systems. This chapter aims at developing a relatively straightforward theoretical perspective from which to view the information systems phenomena that appear in practical situations. We shall use this viewpoint to explain why information systems issues are inherently problematical. The perspective should assist IS managers in understanding the inherent opportunities and risks, but at no time does it recommend specific approaches. The appropriateness of an approach is largely dependent upon the unique environment, and thus generalizations are likely to be meaningless. Thus, rather than postulating rules, we shall merely suggest certain general principles that, suitably interpreted, should prove to be useful in practice. Ultimately, 'thinking managers' must not shirk their responsibilities by delegating decisions to rule-books implemented on mere machines.

It is first necessary to distinguish between computer systems and information systems. Computer systems consist of the complex interconnection of numerous hardware and software components, which are primarily formal, deterministic systems, such that a given input will always result in a particular output. A computer system is a mere sub-assembly of an organizational information system, which will also include the users, their information, policies, procedures and organizational structures. Information systems are social systems whose behaviour is heavily influenced by the goals, values and beliefs of individuals and groups, as well as by the performance of the technology. As such, the behaviour of information systems is not deterministic and does not fit into any formal algorithmic representation.

This can be seen by considering the difficult situations faced by managers of information systems in organizations. While some technological problems remain, we would argue these are mostly the preserve of research laboratories; the majority of opportunities and risks thrown up by information systems are largely concerned with organizational, business, social or human aspects, and not with technical detail. Concisely summarized, managers must concentrate on the 'appropriate' strategic and tactical application of information systems.

Even the self-evident benefits of word processing need to be properly managed, where of course management must: choose the best hardware and software; estimate and budget for the expenditure; decide on the most effective distribution of the hardware across the organization; standardize the file-base to optimize applications; deal with consumables, maintenance and training etc. But they also have to deal with organizational situations that deny any form of rational optimization. They should seek to gain 'competitive advantage' from the package by for example novel use of mail-merging customer address lists, and decide whether to subcontract document production or to bring it in-house. Management must cope with 'vanity computing' - politically powerful individuals, who insist on their own workstations, even if they never use them, and request state-of-the-art software which is surplus to their requirements. They must limit resistance among staff to the introduction of new technology, and convince newly-trained staff not to leave for higher-paid jobs in other companies. They must prevent poor quality or careless use of word processors, such as text errors perpetuated across large numbers of different documents, letters sent to addressees on the wrong list, a customer name inadvertently replaced by a similar dictionary entry through misuse of a spell-checker program; and avoid over complex back-up and archiving procedures that cause old versions of documents to be retrieved instead of the up-to-date ones. Such a list can go on and on; of course it is further extended by all the other hazards that are unique to the particular organization.

Thus, as computer-based information systems become more central to the life of the organization, the role of information systems managers becomes more oriented towards organizational and business aspects and away from the narrowly technical. However, the reality of general management demonstrates the marginal nature of a management science obsessed with quantitative representation. Mintzberg (in Quinn et al [1]) groups the various management roles under three headings: interpersonal, information, and decisional. Interpersonal roles include those of leader/motivator and liaison (maintaining a network of contacts outside the particular function), while the information roles are concerned with passing relevant information between their group and the rest of the organization. Finally, decisional roles are associated with internal trouble-shooting and resource allocation as well as with the negotiation of tasks and resources that enhance the status of the group within the rest of the organization.

Analysis or interpretation?

An approach for coping with typical organizational situations cannot be found within any scientific conception of the management process. The scientific approach that was so successful in creating the technology is inappropriate for application within organizations. Computer systems are a triumph of traditional physical science; however, organizational information systems require approaches that recognize a different type of complexity inherent within organizations.

Numerous writers from the field of organization theory have emphasized that organizations cannot be considered as machines. Organizations comprise individuals and groups with different objectives, beliefs and value systems, interacting together within a business context. The objectives of each group are likely to be highly rational, in an individual sense, in that they will be associated with increasing the prestige of the group, but they may not be compatible with those of the organization as a whole. There is likely to be a pattern of conflict and coalition as groups squabble over scarce resources. In this respect, an organization can be seen as a complex political system, rather than as a team with a unanimity of purpose centred on the stated mission of the organization.

Information technology offers a remarkable opportunity to support the information processes within an organization, but it also contains the germ of technological determinism. The rigidity and bureaucracy implicit in the methods and techniques associated with the technology may be inadvertently imposed upon the organization's social system with horrifying results. The natural inexactitude and informality of organizations may become replaced by a bureaucratic rationalism that only recognizes predefined quantitative problems. People are not mere processes, waiting to be programmed; organizational phenomena are not susceptible to the sort of complete specification required by computer programs: *"I can't define an elephant, but I know one when I see one"*.

The acceptance of the predominance of human characteristics, together with the complexity and uncertainty of the organizational environment implies the rejection of techniques based on the principles underlying traditional physical science: reductionism, the identification of general laws of causality, and the neutrality of the observer. Reductionism, whereby a problem situation is broken down into its constituent parts in order to render it susceptible to analysis, is likely to lose the essence of the organization: *"... every organization must be both more and less than the sum of its parts. It is less, because organization constrains. ... It is more because, when organized, [components] are enabled to do together what none could do alone, or if unorganized, even together"* (Vickers [2]). This is the phenomenon of synergy, that an assembly of parts and their interrelationships are *both more and less* than the sum, and that its manifestation cannot be predicted, even given the fullest knowledge of each component. To a certain extent it also depends on who is counting, and how and what they are counting. Too often businessmen see synergy purely as the sum being more than the parts, and thereby they lose the balance between opportunity and risk that go hand in hand with this phenomenon.

Similarly, in complex social situations, where there are numerous factors and influences upon the people involved, the notion of general laws of causality is meaningless. Physical science relies on controlled experiments that can be repeated and refuted. Social situations are intrinsically singular, and too dynamic and complex to permit repeated experiments. Thus, general laws are often misapplied; inappropriate use of the same technology can lead to widely differing effects when introduced into different organizations.

Finally, the notion of an independent, objective observer is inappropriate in social situations. All observers (managers or researchers) are conditioned by their particular values and biases. These determine which elements of the complex situation are recorded and how they are interpreted. Thus, in social systems, subjectivity will obscure any attempt at objectivity. This implies that objective analysis, in the tradition of physical science, is impossible with social systems. Rather, we must try to interpret the meaning of the situation, recognizing the subjectivity and complexity that this involves. However, in certain highly constrained circumstances, reductionism may be applicable and we must be careful to avoid an approach that is redolent of mysticism: *"As the anti-analytic bandwagon has begun to roll, advocates of Zen Buddhism, Jungian mysticism, and extra sensory perception have climbed aboard, and the young student of management must now wonder whether to head for Harvard or the Himalayas"* (Dreyfus & Dreyfus [3].) We would stop short of this strident rejection of the non-analytical approach, in an attempt to be more balanced and open minded.

Systems thinking

In this situation, it is tempting for both academics and managers to shrug their shoulders at the messiness of organizational reality and to deny the relevance of any theory. Similarly, it is very easy to treat the management of information systems as a series of half-remembered anecdotes, frameworks and voluminous lists of guidelines. But such an approach is basically inert and, taken in isolation, fundamentally futile, as it fails to provide any explanation or rudimentary understanding of the dynamic nature of information systems in organizations.

While there are a number of approaches in organization theory that explain, to a greater or lesser extent, the behaviour of organizations in practice, a particularly useful approach for understanding the use of information systems in management is to consider not only the information system, but also the organization, in *holistic* or *systems* terms. Such an approach emphasizes the limitations of reductionist thinking, but far from rejecting analytic, mathematical and engineering principles, some aspects of the systems approach wholeheartedly absorb them. By balancing the application of analytic frameworks, against the use of certain 'systems principles', metaphor and analogy to compare the wholeness of their behavioural properties with the functioning of generalized abstract systems, it is possible to provide a limited comprehension of the operation of commercial organizations and their information systems. But it can only be limited, because of the paradoxical non-systemic and often arbitrary nature of elements within each system, that identifies it as different and unique.

It is all too common that schemes, based on a grand vision, are proposed and accepted within organizations, in an atmosphere of belief that only 'dotting the i's and crossing the t's' is needed for successful completion of the programme. Of course nobody accepted that they were making choices, nobody considered the ambiguities, and nobody directed the other systems in the environment to stay away. The joke is that these schemes may even solve the problem as intended, only to create worse problems. Industrial pollution, carcinogenic food colouring, asbestos, 'killer bees' and starlings in the USA, rabbits in Australia; the 'road to hell is paved with good intentions'.

We even have the situation where a system not only fails to solve a problem, it actually achieves the exact opposite: *system inversion*. One uniquely perverse example is from Professor Glass of the University of Oklahoma, who gives dire warnings in respect of toothbrushes: intended to help oral hygiene, they can actually spread diseases. Mouths are full of bacteria, which are transferred to the brushes where they breed among the bristles. Vigorous brushing often causes the gums to be scratched allowing the bacteria to enter the bloodstream directly, bypassing the natural mucous defences in our mouths. So why should information systems behave any less perversely than other systems? We will describe here some of the more common properties of systems, and then use them as a basis for explaining, in part, the behaviour of information systems within organizations, although we would stress that such holistic analogies must be treated with great caution.

The systems approach stresses the need to treat any system as a whole, hence the need to go beyond *systematic* thinking (that of using an analytic approach) to *systemic* thinking (that of interpreting from the systems viewpoint, which is both analytic and synthetic). An intuitive understanding of information systems in management will, explicitly or implicitly, need to go beyond systematic thinking to the systemic, but it must also embrace the limitations of both approaches. Successful systems thinking will involve the ability to grasp the essence of the idea, whilst accepting the implied vagueness and limitations of definitions such as [4]:

a system is a set of two or more elements that satisfies the following conditions:
1) *the behaviour of each element has an effect on the. behaviour of the whole;*
2) *the behaviour of the elements and their effects on the whole are interdependent;*
3) *however, subgroups of the elements are formed, each has an effect on the behaviour of the whole and none has an independent effect on it.*
A system, therefore, is a whole that cannot be divided into independent parts.

Another useful definition of a system is [5]:
1) *an assembly of parts or components connected together in an organized way;*
2) *the particular assembly has been identified by a human being as of special interest;*
3) *in general, the parts are affected by being in the system and they are changed if they leave it;*
4) *our assembly of parts does something (but remember that behaviour may be **not** doing something when the outside world changes.)*

From these definitions it is possible to see that while an analytic approach to systemic phenomena can provide information on their composition and knowledge of their structure, a synthetic approach can yield understanding in terms of their purpose, function, or role in the environment where they operate. A yet more meaningful comprehension of the phenomena can only be obtained through the combined application of analytic and synthetic approaches - this is the goal of 'systems thinking'. Von Bertalanffy [6] postulated a *General System Theory* (*GST*), in that a general model, principles and laws apply to the notion of system (not just specific examples such as biological organisms or social systems), irrespective of the particular discipline, the nature of components and the interrelationships between them. The intention of GST is to derive the transdisciplinary language and set of concepts that relate these different disciplines, although doubts about GST have nowadays led many of the 'systems community' to prefer the less imperious concept of '*systems thinking*'.

A system is understood to have a *boundary*, chosen according to the human observer's particular purpose and priorities, which separates it from its *environment*. Given this understanding of boundary and environment, systems may be classified as *closed*, where nothing from outside, except pre-chosen parameters, can cross the boundary, or as *open* where possibly unknown elements from the environment can have an effect.

There are two pairs of concepts, or *provenances* [7], that are fundamental to the systems approach: *emergence* and *hierarchy (organismic provenance)*, *communication* and *control (technological provenance)*. Within a system of organized complexity that is an organization, there is a hierarchy of levels of stable sub-systems, each (*macro*) level being chosen to introduce a simplifying interpretation of the complex behaviour of sub-systems at the (*micro*) level below. The elements at each macro-level are identified by emergent properties that do not exist at lower micro-levels. "*New levels, new laws*"; the complexity of components at micro-levels cannot, on their own, explain the emergent properties of macro-levels. Thus the laws of physics and chemistry, considered at the micro-level, cannot explain biology at the macro-level. In turn, biology at the micro-level, cannot explain the macro-level behaviour of animals or societies. An example from information systems is the emergent all-pervasive phenomenon of unsolicited (junk) mail. Without the technological micro-phenomena of computerized mailing lists and word processing, the societal macro-phenomenon of junk mail would not exist. But in themselves they do not explain junk mail. That requires much more subtle emergent economic concepts such as marketing and cost-effectiveness. Automating the mailing process reduces the cost to the sender, but at the price of inconvenience and annoyance to the receiver. Adding yet more sophisticated technology makes it even easier for the sender, but correspondingly more expensive for the receiver. Low fax charges now make the cost of junk-fax negligible even compared with mailing, and it has the added advantage of targeting higher socio-economic groups. Apart from the problem that junk can delay the receipt of important faxes, to add insult to injury the receiver even has to pay for the paper on which the message is printed. Perhaps it is not surprising that suppliers of fax-paper are some of the biggest senders of junk-faxes! This problem, could not be explained solely in terms of the Post Office, or of computers; both were needed, in conjunction with the need in the marketing community. Similarly, computer viruses can be viewed as an emergent phenomenon. Of course from an analogy with biological systems, it was only to be expected that certain general forms of parasites and diseases would emerge as computer systems got more complex. However, the specific forms could not be predicted and these are only apparent in hindsight.

Communication between elements of a system is needed in order for it to regulate itself and to control its actions and reactions, to maintain its identity, to renew and to repair itself while interacting with its environment. It is information that is perceived as the stuff of this meaningful communication, and an information system is the view of the system from this perspective. A proficient information system is one that collects and communicates sufficient information concerning events in both the environment and the system itself, to enable a timely and effective response by the system. The *raison d'être* of computerized IS is the belief that computers can enhance the effective communication of information, that in turn puts managers in command of their actions so they can make sensible decisions, and hence run their organization successfully. Much of the confusion and misapplication of information systems is caused by the attempt to over-computerize the control function to the detriment of communication.

Both deterministic and non-deterministic *causal mechanisms* for control and communication are at work within any system, and *multiple feedback* from a system's own outputs continuously modify, and amplify, elements, processes or sub-systems within itself. Such feedback is termed *positive feedback* when it amplifies processes that carry the actual state away from some 'reference state' that was chosen to identify the system, and *negative feedback* when it counteracts such processes. It is also claimed that some systems have the ability to anticipate a discrepancy: *feedforward*. Confusingly, the term feedback is often mistakenly limited to deterministic causal loops, and so we highlight the difference between, on the one hand, the causality of algorithms and predictable mechanisms, and on the other, non-deterministic and emergent processes working within uncertainty and ambiguity that are only apparent in hindsight. It is too easy to treat uncertainty and ambiguity naively, as either misunderstanding or a degree of randomness. We should differentiate between the deterministic (predictable cause/effect relationships linking input and output), the probabilistic (with some degree of statistical uncertainty in predicting outputs, which nonetheless aggregates to a statistical distribution), and the 'truly' random. Even the word 'random' has connotations, which may be invalid or misleading when considering arbitrary non-systemic situations, and it certainly cannot be used to describe the genesis of unpredictable emergent properties; phenomena that are ordered, far from random, and yet totally unpredictable.

In a deliberately vague way, we consider a mechanism or installation as an 'initial state of the system'. A system is what it has become, what it will become. Therefore, we would say that an information system is far more than just a computer system of hardware and software; it is everything that emerges from the existence of the computer and its relationship with its environment. This means rejecting the traditional computer science view of systems; both information systems and the organizations they serve are far from being closed, mechanistic, deterministic systems made up of manufactured components. Nor are they comparable with biological systems of interconnected living cells; they are social systems. Furthermore, the accrual of other components and sub-systems, feedback, the reality of emergence and synergy, the development of new systems and the breakdown of old systems from interactions within the environment, imply that there can be no permanent control over a system that is continuously evolving and emerging. There is only a limited form of control, that of purposefully directing a system's procedures as they exist in their present state. These control procedures will have evolved along with the system, but they are as much a consequence of relative stability of the environment, as of the system itself. Deterministic and probabilistic mechanisms, programs and procedures are designed; systems, in particular information systems, are not! Mechanisms and installations can be engineered, information systems cannot!

By the very nature of a consensus demarcation of a boundary, any system will have an identity, which must be maintained in a dynamic yet recognizable state. For most mechanical devices and biological organisms it is not problematic to achieve a consensus on the choice of boundary. However, in social systems, sub-systems can be simultaneously part of the system and part of the environment. This immediately introduces doubt about an agreed perception of a boundary between the organization and its environment. Thus the choice of boundary can be a source of doubtful classification, signifying that social systems are intrinsically ambiguous. Within an organization (a system, perceived to have its own purposes), IT professionals (sub-systems) often form peer groups with individuals in other companies, perhaps within trade unions, to compare notes and experiences, and to optimize career opportunities. It is not uncommon that their loyalty is to their 'trade' (an emergent system with totally different purposes) and not to their employer. And of course these individuals have family ties, political, philosophical and religious beliefs, so-called lateral loyalties, all adding to the ambiguity. Recognizing the inevitability of such ambiguity means that even the very identification of the coherent whole we call 'system' involves purpose-driven choice. So there can be no absolute analysis, design and implementation of systems; managers are left only with perpetually changing questions of appropriate or inappropriate choice.

The maintenance of a stable state, *homeostasis*, does not imply rigidity, and the negative feedback that stabilizes a system in one environment can turn to positive feedback and become destructive in another. In some companies (such as Hewlett Packard) workers have agreed to cuts in pay in order to help it through a bad patch, whilst in others workers will aggressively push the company to bankruptcy. Environments are continuously changing, and to be effective a system must be capable of a variety of responses to match those changes in the environment (Ashby's *Law of Requisite Variety*): *"only variety can destroy variety"*.It is because of this dynamic situation that we insist on differentiating between deterministic and probabilistic mechanisms (with parameters based on sufficient information) that can be the basis of planning and *tactics*. Unknown processes in the environment, apparent only in hindsight, have to be catered for *strategically*. An effective information system can help to steer an organization through its environmental turbulence, taking tactical advantage of the environment and avoiding risks, but only within the constraints of strategies that will enable it to deal with the unknown; but more of this in Chapter 3.

Systems can be seen to have distinct *life cycles*: systems are born, they grow, stabilize, mature, age and finally die. The characteristic bell-curve of the life cycle and its cumulative S-curve counterpart are well known symbols in many disciplines: marketing of products; economics of organizations; engineering of components; software cost-estimation; biology of organisms; learning and experience curves. Nolan [8] uses this concept of systems when describing the development of information systems within an organization, categorizing their cycle into initiation, contagion, control, integration, data administration and maturity. From this he advocates management techniques to deal with the information system at each stage of development. All too often the ageing of systems and their demise are not considered in the IS literature. Without the requisite variety, information systems will die like every other system. The long term costs of the inevitable phasing out of system components, or even whole systems, are not included in calculations. Rarely is obsolescence allowed for in the construction of applications, nor is there any recognition that non-productivity at the obsolescence stage of a computer-based information system (CBIS) can be destabilizing to an organization. Indeed Joseph Weizenbaum [9] goes as far as to say that information technology is itself a missed opportunity to replace outdated organizational and societal structures. It prevents competitive progress by prolonging these obsolete structures behind a protective facade of computerized efficiency.

It must be appreciated that although there is substantial empirical evidence for the existence of life cycles, the concept is basically a *post-hoc* analogy of a biological phenomenon, and it can only be valid when the environment is stable and consistent. Being struck by a fast car puts an abrupt end to many a life cycle! Thus decisions based on life cycles must presume that short term survival is not in question – a presumption that is highly suspect nowadays given the uncertainty, turmoil and crisis faced by information technology. In fact many of the prescriptions given in Nolan's paper themselves soon became badly unstuck, with the economic downturn of the early 1980s and the increased importance of the microcomputer against the mainframe.

Many other biological analogies have been brought to bear; Darwinian evolution is a very popular theme. Lloyd [10] uses this phenomenon to forecast the impact of new technologies on large organizations, and supports the stance that 'small is beautiful'. Because of the way large organizations (dinosaurs) have evolved, their *exposure* (relative impact) to any new innovation must be marginal, and this in turn limits their enthusiasm to innovate and to cope with rapid changes in the environment: the result – extinction! The problem with all such metaphors is that the links are highly tenuous, and they take a very self-selecting and restricted view: where are the analogies for other mechanisms and processes, such as reproduction, within this organizational evolution? They are all based on the highly questionable presumption, that the observed phenomenon is behaving in a biological or even systemic manner. Nonetheless, interpreting such behaviour, as the general properties of systems, does add to our understanding.

Models and mechanisms

The construction of a model of any system necessarily places an artificial boundary around that system, and freezes it with a restricted interpretation based on a mechanistic classification that is at best a good analogy of past performance. The recent theory of *deterministic chaos* [11] implies that even physicists no longer accept the universality of 'similar systems in similar environments will undergo similar changes', and they, after all, work in a reasonably well-behaved universe of discourse where the meaning, measurement and choice of a particular 'similarity' can be justified. The problem is exacerbated as deterministic and probabilistic mechanisms deny the dynamic nature of systemicity, and misrepresent its inherent uniqueness born of uncertainty. This highlights the fallacy of creating a machine/model to simulate a system. The implied ambiguity and incorrect emphasis, the arbitrary extra components that, even if perceived, are taken to be non-systemic and irrelevant, the uncertainty and emergence, mean that the model ends with just one of an infinity of possible universes.

Paradoxically, we must not fall into the trap of assuming that now everything is systemic; there is a danger of imposing systems thinking at levels where ambiguity and disaggregation make it inappropriate, just as the arbitrary application of scientific thinking is unjustifiable. To a certain extent, every organization is disorganized and unorganized, every system is disturbed by 'noise'. But self-fulfilling 'tidy minds' could impose organization or system where there is none. Joseph Weizenbaum [9] tells a highly relevant story. *A policeman sees a drunk scrambling around on his hands and knees, under the street lamp. "I'm looking for my keys, I lost them over there", the drunk says, pointing into the darkness. "So why look here?" asks the policeman. "Because this is where the light is!"* The particular light (scientific or systems thinking) may not be capable of illuminating the problem.

Much of the present-day interest in the *theory of chaos* stems from the understanding developed in the science of complexity, especially the mathematics of chaos, that the behaviour of certain computerized deterministic models, even though relatively straightforward, can only be explained in hindsight. An initially marginal event can be the major cause of long term dramatic events: the Lorenz *butterfly effect,* named thus because weather forecasters have come to realize that even the 'insignificant' flapping of a butterfly's wings, through complex feedback, could trigger a major weather feature, implying that their forecasting techniques are limited to 'stable' weather conditions and to the short term.

Too often, management deals with mechanisms and functionality, and not with the systemic nature of business. It does not take into account the magnifying effect of positive feedback in ill-structured and turbulent environments such as the business world, and so ignores the 'butterfly effect' where the marginal and insignificant trends of today become the major business opportunities/risks of tomorrow. Furthermore, management techniques based on rigid deterministic thinking can precipitate further problems. The tension between rigid control mechanisms and the dynamic emergence of systemic phenomena from the fluid environment, is itself a source of many problems. Modern management must learn to live with this, and not deny the inevitable ambiguity and vagueness.

The automation of such deterministic and mechanistic management processes may introduce a further level of complexity that can obscure our lack of understanding, and serves to deny our uncertainty in those processes. Computer models can only be a pale shadow of what actually happens, they cannot emulate 'being there', with all the subtle, and not so subtle, checks and balances, and the unknown and unknowable interactions. Many technocrats fail to comprehend that their simplistic data structures searching for *"Perfection of planning*[,] *is a symptom of decay"* (Parkinson [12].) Uncertainty is not just a matter of incomplete information. It thus makes little sense to submit the decisions that affect commercial success to simplistic rules and measurement, all implemented on a 'glorified adding machine'! When used to enhance (rather than replace) intellect, information systems can be useful tools, and can form an opportunistic framework for coping with future innovations, trends and requirements, as well as minimize dangers. But unquestioning acceptance of their models and simulations of open-ended human experience is sheer folly.

Every mechanism and measure we use, deterministic or probabilistic, has limitations and a hidden agenda of choice. Their interaction with components in a system reflect an act of faith in the existence of the element, the property and the system. This existence has to be perceived, a boundary imposed, and no emergent property can be measured or manipulated before it has emerged from the unknown. Measures are *ergodic*, they are just numerical samples of an apparent property of the system. The numerical value must reflect a consistent behaviour of that property through the system as a whole, and it must conform to some sense of *statistical distribution*. All measurement involves sampling and choice; see the 'tipping' exercise below. In order for systemic properties to be measurable, the system itself must be relatively stable within a given time scale; it cannot be in an unpredictable or chaotic state of flux. Just because these techniques have found widespread acceptance in physics and biology does not mean that any of the assumptions are self evident in social systems. And so the behaviour of measures and mechanisms must be well understood and seen to be relevant and appropriate to the problem at hand, before they are applied.

Accepting the existence of systems and their behaviour can cause major problems with the standard ways of dealing with information systems within organizations. An IS manager must accept that operational systems are messy, vague and, more often than not, demonstrate the marginal relevance of any mechanistic interpretation of information. Much of the management of information systems is about dealing with change, and that change must be seen as a systemic reality and not necessarily as systematic. Thus IS management should be driven by an understanding of the behaviour of these systems, and by an avoidance of the pitfalls of the anthropocentric view, where human intent is seen as the ultimate driving force. The only sensible long term stance is to deny the omnipotence of efficiency and effectiveness and learn to recognize information systems within the business environment for what they are. They may start off with pre-programmed causal mechanisms, as installations, but the outcome when introduced into the wider business environment is often uncontrollable. Because so much of uncertainty must be recognized as emergence, IS managers must learn cope with it.

Facing uncertainty is a matter of accepting that the unimaginable can and will happen and being prepared to deal with it on the level of personal choice. Responses based on mechanistic feedback and other systemic constructs will have little meaning in a context that is not systemic or where the existence of systems is not even perceived. Emergent phenomena are only apparent in hindsight, and give no prior indication of emergence. This leads us to advocate a treatment of dealing with uncertainty by *steering* with appropriate tactical responses. All actions are situated, and only in a manager's self-determined reality do they acquire their meaning. In any other context they will acquire a different interpretation. Thus, a manager has to steer in the flow of events as they appear meaningful to him. This must entail a disposition to act, that is free of the organizational guidelines and of preconceptions of problem solving and planning. When the ambiguity of the situation cannot be resolved into some, possibly systemic, pattern, then the jumping to the application of methods is merely impulsive stress-relief.

Conclusion

Today we are at the end of that stage of development, when organizations, in a feeding frenzy, have bloated themselves on information technology. In the future, they should be more careful in their choice of IT diet. Given the uncertainty they face, management must now question whether the use of IT is an appropriate universal response. Much of the remainder of this book is geared to give the reader a broader understanding of information systems within organizations, from the perspective of applied technology. For a knowledge of the technological context is needed before the analytic or synthetic approaches of systems thinking can be applied by management. A knowledge of technology and systems should give managers a basis from which to recognize the opportunities and risks they face. However, this will not be enough. Ultimately it will be the quality of management, and that of their staff, to observe, interpret and innovate, that will be the major factor in taking decisions appropriate to the commercial environment.

P4

Discussion issues

1. Imagine you are working in a bar, restaurant or nightclub and you depend on tips to supplement your income. Do you leave a plate where patrons can leave money, and do you 'salt' it with your own coins (or banknotes) to start the ball rolling. Why not do a scientific experiment? Salt the plate with a random collection of coins (a mixture of both large(ish) and small denominations) and watch how many people give, and also note the distribution of the size of the tips. Then put only large denominations on the plate and repeat the process. Would you dare to duplicate the experiment with only small denominations, or does an *a priori* expectation of loss stop you? You can scientifically optimize your tips, but which measure do you use; is it important that everyone gives, or is it only the total income that matters?

    Then approach the situation with systems thinking. What will a pompous management ("We are a People Company!") say to you treating customers as a statistical sample for your own personal gain? Would they act differently if it was for their gain? Will a plate of high denomination coins give an up-market image for the bar? Will customers give once, then in annoyance refuse to return? Dare you put up a notice asking for tips? What effect will video-recording the experiment for greater accuracy have on the way people give? How do the social norms within the bar effect your experiment – will your colleagues resent your 'smarty-pants' approach? How do you feel about sharing tips between staff? Discuss among yourselves other issues that this example could raise. If you are working your way through college in such a bar then why not put this into practice, rather than just talk about it.

2. Discuss among your group the systems issues we have raised. Find examples
    of systems inversion. Use biological analogies to interpret other aspects of
    introducing information systems within organizations. Consider the devel-
    opment of Computer Centres from the early mainframe days to the present
    trend for end user computing. Interpret their initial rapid expansion and
    present-day defence strategies in terms of systems behaviour. Other behav-
    ioural properties of systems must be considered in using this approach to the
    study of IS in organizations. Every theoretical approach has its own
    specialized vocabulary, if for no other reason than to ease conversations,
    among the initiated, regarding previously agreed-upon complex concepts. The
    study of systems is no exception. The following paragraph will expose you
    to some systems 'jargon' gleaned from many different disciplines, so that
    you can discuss the issues we have raised using the correct terminology.

    By the very nature of a consensus demarcation that is its boundary, any
    system will have an identity, which must be maintained in a dynamic yet
    stable and recognizable reference state; a property named *homeostasis*. A
    system needs to receive energy/material/information from outside its bound-
    ary, or to be *negentropic* in order to be homeostatic; negative entropy
    (negentropy) is perceived as contrary to entropy – the thermodynamic princ-
    iple that systems run down to ultimate disorder or death, to the state of
    maximum entropy. The system must maintain a relatively stable state, but it
    must be adaptive to the continual changes in the environment, both predic-
    table and unpredictable, and to survive, reproduce, be purposeful and *teleo-
    logical* (where developments are due to the purpose or design that is served
    by them), grow, colonize, cooperate, achieve results in different ways and
    from different initial conditions (*equifinality*), and do any of the things that
    physical, biological and social systems do. That the environment itself
    contains a thriving bubbling mass of systems often means that there is
    conflict between the individual processes that maintain communication and
    control, emergence and hierarchy within any given system. Some sub-
    systems will combine with others from the environment to form new
    systems. Systems may co-exist peacefully or they may be involved in conf-
    lict; either way the environment will be perpetually changing because of the
    interaction. In this way disorder and death can be seen as systems in conflict,
    and not as entropy in the strict thermodynamic sense. Finally we consider
    here the unpronounceable *autopoesis* and *allopoesis*, although within
    'systems thinking' there are many, many more concepts for you to discover.
    Autopoetic systems are self-creating, self-repairing and self-perpetuating, and
    they maintain a coherent unity; examples of such systems are biological
    organisms. An allopoetic system is the product of other component prod-
    ucing systems, but different from them. As such they have no autonomy, and
    examples are hierarchical and bureaucratic systems, and crystal structures.

3. The Darwinian model describes just one of many different mechanisms that have been proposed for evolution. It happens to be the best one so far that fits biological evolution. The Lamarckian theory, of organic evolution by the inheritance of acquired characteristics, has now been generally rejected for biological evolution, but it could be more suitable than Darwinism when dealing with the evolutions of organizations, which do, after all, have institutionalized memories. It is also important to realize that biological evolution is about 'The Origin of Species', and not about individuals; think very carefully about the confusion between the evolution(?) of a single company, and that of a type (species) of company in a particular market sector. Discuss the relative merits and demerits of each theory, and in particular consider the role that could be played by operational information systems within the evolution of companies. Also consider the evolution of information systems themselves, considering not only the general situation, but also that in particular industrial sectors (e.g. banking) and in specific examples, say in your own university or company.

Suggested reading

The distinction between analysis and interpretation is discussed in more depth by.
> Burrell, G. & Morgan, G., *Sociological Paradigms and Organizational Analysis*, Heinemann, London, 1979.

Information is a most misused and misunderstood word. A very good introduction to the subtleties of its interpretation can be found in:
> Liebenau, J. & Backhouse, J., *Understanding Information*, Macmillan, London, 1990.

For those who want to find out more about 'systems thinking', we can highly recommend the books by Ackoff, Beishon & Peters, and Checkland (particularly those mentioned above), and of course the works of Erwin Laszlo, including:
> Laszlo, E., *The Systems View of the World*, Braziller, New York, 1972.

Information Systems Management

References

1. Quinn, J.B., Mintzberg, H. & James, R.M., *The Strategy Process*, Prentice-Hall International, London, 1988.
2. Vickers, G., *Responsibility - Its Sources and Limits*, Intersystems Publications, 1980.
3. Dreyfus, H.L. & Dreyfus, S.E., *Mind over Machine*, Blackwell, Oxford,1986.
4. Ackoff, R., *Creating the Corporate Future*, Wiley, New York, 1981.
5. Beishon, J. & Peters, G., *Systems Behaviour*, Open University Press, New York, 1972.
6. Bertalanffy, L. von, *General System Theory*, Braziller, New York, 1968.
7. Checkland, P.B., *Systems Thinking, Systems Practice*, Wiley, Chichester, 1981.
8. Nolan, R.L., 'Managing the crises in data processing', *Harvard Business Review*, Vol.57, No.2, 115-126, Mar-Apr 1979.
9. Weizenbaum, J., *Computer Power and Human Reason: From Judgement to Calculation*, Freeman & Co., San Francisco, 1976.
10. Lloyd, T., *Dinosaur and Co., Studies in Corporate Evolution*, Routledge, London, 1984.
11. Gleick, J, *Chaos*, Sphere Books, London, 1988.
12. Parkinson, C. Northcote, *Parkinson's Law*, Penguin, London, 1986.

3   Strategy and tactics

- *Definitions of strategy and tactics*
- *The disposition of systems*
- *The IS environment*
- *Strategy frameworks*
- *IS within the organization*
- *The way forward*

Definitions of strategy and tactics

The contagion of both local and global change is generating severe insecurity among managers. That information technology will come to the rescue is a vain hope; on the contrary IT is now seen as just another agent and source of this change. The present use of this technology is inappropriate for coping with this situation. Without coherent ways of thinking about the place of information systems in respect of the perpetual changes around them, companies can no longer place their faith in technological solutions. For in doing so, they surrender responsibility for IT to technocrats, who all too often indulge their fascination for irrelevant technology, without considering the wider needs of the organization. The necessary way of thinking must not be just a token tribute to philosophical problems and questions of meaning. The present emphasis on simple functional issues and short term advantages of IT, must be balanced against the application of information technology both to simplify and to enhance a company's long term competitive position in the light of profound uncertainty and complexity. But how successful are these attempts to introduce information technology? We can be sure that the integration of an IT strategy with a corporate strategy requires a sensitivity to issues far broader than the merely technological: 'The IT tail must not wag the organization dog'.

Organizations must be flexible in the face of the unknown while at the same time make the best response to the opportunities and risks at hand. We have seen that decisions must not be based on seductive technological fashions and simplistic mathematical models. Aggrandized management information systems, that are little more than computerized executive toys, must not be allowed to replace effective qualitative management with an alien quantitative imperative.

The real benefits of systems simplification must not be overlooked in a confusion of complexity, supported by an explosion of facile classification, as decision support systems vie with expert systems, which vie with expert decision support systems and executive support systems.

In times of change, uncertainty and transition, 'thinking management' should emphasize flexibility and recognize the *equifinality* of different starting points and alternative routes to achieve their objectives. As well as considering such aspects as the avoidance of tying in the organization to the whims of a single supplier, the emphasis on flexibility provides further justification for strategies based on the development of human resources, and tactics based on informed decisions. Of all organizational resources, the workforce is arguably the most flexible, and that flexibility can be encouraged and exploited through the provision of education and training schemes. Unless the social context of information use is fully appreciated, and unless organizations become aware of the true nature of crisis, risk, complexity and uncertainty, the benefits of strategic and tactical applications of IT will remain mere wishful thinking.

Before considering the relationship between strategies and information systems, we should really ask, 'what is a strategy?' Is it just another trendy buzz-word, like 'synergy', that is sloshing around in the international business community? Can it be defined, or is it another of those nebulous concepts, and the more we try to understand it, the less we grasp its essence? The Oxford English Dictionary says that strategy is *"the art of the commander-in-chief; the art of projecting and directing the larger military movements and operations in a campaign. Usually distinguished from tactics, which is the art of handling forces in a battle or in the immediate presence of the enemy"*. Military strategy has been the source of numerous books from time immemorial, and the business world has zealously taken up the military metaphor. Most business writers agree with Von Clausewitz's observation that strategists do not achieve certainty, they only have an edge on the opposition; and with Napoleon's notion of strategy as 'planned flexibility', although they may shy away from his policy of selecting only the 'lucky' generals. Tactics on the other hand are considered not nearly as important; they are *"the arrangement of procedure, the action to be taken, in order to fulfil an end or objective"*. Tactics are what lieutenants do, but strategy is the work of generals; a most peculiar attitude since it is the appropriateness and quality of tactics that separates success from failure in the short term.

The vagueness implicit in the military meaning of 'strategy' has transferred into management theory with numerous observations and taxonomies. Strategies are *"aggregates of philosophies or agglomerations of programmes"*; they are abstractions, *"concepts in the minds of interested observers"*. According to Quinn *"a strategy is the pattern or plan that integrates an organization's major goals, policies, and action sequences into a cohesive whole. A well-formulated strategy help to marshal and allocate an organization's posture based on its relative internal competencies and shortcomings, anticipated changes in the environment, and contingent moves by intelligent opponents"*. This definition leaves plenty of scope for interpretation; it dallies with systems ideas, but falls short of emergence and hierarchy. Yet in the same article, Quinn does claim that strategic decisions are those that determine the organization's viability in the light of *"the predictable, the unpredictable and the unknowable"*. Ansoff (in Quinn et al [1]) differentiates between the grand large-scale corporate strategy, and the more competition-driven business strategy. Mintzberg (in Quinn et al [1]) concentrates more on the classification of strategies as *plan, ploy, pattern, position* and *perspective* (the 5-P's) discussed below. He hints at a limited form of emergence, observing that strategies are not only formulated, they can also evolve.

The disposition of systems

From our systems theoretical basis, it is possible to give an interpretation of the terms 'strategy' and 'tactics', as well as 'strategic information systems', and thence outline a mixture of views on the concepts, both descriptive (what we understand is happening) and normative (how things ought to be according to our understanding). We should stress at the outset that our theoretical meanings of these words will vary to a greater or lesser degree from the normally accepted definitions that are based on functionality. For this we make no apology.

To prosper, a system has to evolve a *disposition* that will satisfy the Law of Requisite Variety; it must have the facility, by sufficient internal variety, to respond to perpetual changes in its environment, and hence to survive and flourish. Such disposition is in no way fixed and inflexible. It is inherently ambiguous and constantly being refined and redefined via feedback from its interaction with the risks and opportunities within its perpetually changing environment. A disposition to act is an implicit property of every system, perhaps even the very essence of being a system, and the clue to the identity of its reference state by which we choose to classify it as a system. Naturally, examples of systemic disposition are everywhere. Bureaucratic systems seem to have the disposition to grow no matter what is happening in the organization they serve (see Parkinson's [2] classic example of the British Admiralty). Motoring gets more and more popular despite road deaths and pollution. Industrialization seems unstoppable, despite the damage it is causing to the planet. And, of course, IT is dominating business thinking, despite numerous horror stories.

From this basis, we can introduce our use of the words *strategic* and *strategy*. We use the adjective *strategic* to describe any influence that has a lasting effect on the disposition of a organization. This influence will have emerged from human actions, but not necessarily human designs. It will be perceived as a benefit if it increases the system's ability to generate variety, and a loss otherwise. The optimization of short term or even long term results is not strategic, but the ability to optimize within the system under varied conditions is. We consider a *strategy* to be purposeful human decision and action that is intended to be strategic. But, not all strategies are strategic and not all strategies achieve their intended strategic aims. Just as importantly, not all strategic effects are the result of strategies – they can be the consequence of unintended actions. There can be no guarantees – with its disposition, a system may prosper in its environment to a greater or lesser extent – failure may eventually mean extinction. Time constraints cannot be imposed on a strategy – the time factor only refers to the duration of the effect on the disposition. Thus, strategies should not be equated with long term plans. Nor should they be identified with beneficial changes, but only with intended change, and that may not be achieved. Strategy is not the sole domain of management, it is not just purpose expressed by the powerful; the actions of everyone in the organization will influence its disposition to a certain extent. Strategies may increase or decrease internal variety, ultimately they may or may not achieve success for the organization; a strategy is not the panacea many textbooks make it out to be.

We do not see strategies as the conscious attempts of strategists to change, to influence and to graft preconceived notions of 'generic' strategies onto the apparently blank sheet of an organization. However, organizations have complex predispositions even before the strategists start, and these dispositions will evolve and emerge from human actions, with or without, even contrary to, the considered attentions of these strategists. System inversion is probably the most extreme situation, where the emergent disposition of the system will finesse and even diametrically oppose the original intentions of the strategists, designers and planners. A proposed strategy will only be accepted when the receiving system is well disposed towards it, and even then it seems reasonable that the more radical strategies should be introduced incrementally (Quinn [1]); evolution rather than revolution is needed to avoid the ill effects of a 'shock to the system'. Design only works if it is not contentious to the present disposition. Misapplied and inappropriate strategies may result in tension, disruption, and both constant and perpetual change within an organization, with highly detrimental effects. A deliberate strategy, with all its camp-followers, emerges as a sub-system of the organization, and the problem of its implementation is exacerbated by the conflict and the dubious classification of other internal sub-systems, each with their own dispositions, which can be ill disposed to and resist the expansionist intentions of this new strategy (*"not on my turf"*). In Britain some trade unions decided on a series of selective strikes in the computer centres of the Department of Health and Social Security (where they believed they could quickly hurt the employers) over wider pay demands in the public sector. The management responded rapidly by out-sourcing their computing requirements.

By its disposition, an organization attempts to profit from its environment. To do this it senses, interprets and reacts to events observed in the environment. Data on these events are transmitted by an information system to the control centres of the organization. There the management treat it as information, and then formulate forecasts of trends, model the data, derive *plans* and transmit *tactics* to systems components (via the IS), in order to take advantage of the circumstances. It is innovation that affords a greater store of tactics, and variety that is the potential to innovate. So, from this interpretation, competitive advantage is seen as primarily tactical and not strategic. Not that this diminishes its importance in any way, since the immediate survival and expansion of a system will depend directly and essentially on tactical success. However, the tactics used to achieve competitive advantage may coincidentally turn out to be of lasting effect on the organization's disposition, but whether this strategic influence will be beneficial is by no means certain. It is perfectly conceivable that a tactically advantageous approach, of concentrating on previously successful procedures, will reduce internal variety and so restrict future capacity to innovate. All tactics lead to crisis if they are not abandoned in time. Exactly because they are meant to exploit confidence in the circumstances of an enterprise and prescribe specific and potentially successful moves, they falter as soon as doubt springs from a change of circumstance. If tactics are continued despite change, they effectively prevent the manager from being innovative, and introduce an organizational inertia that ignores new environmental conditions. Furthermore, if information systems, which are supposed to administer tactical goals, become ends rather than means, then they change from a competitive resource to a competitive burden.

In addition to their inertial influence on decision-taking, tactics may allow emergent problems to arise. These can, even over a short period of time, acquire such prominence, that managers are compelled to concentrate much of their energy on the system that was designed to support them in their initial enterprise. As mentioned above, many of the bureaucratic structures, that stifle so much of modern business, have emerged in the self-defence of bureaucracy. Our interpretation of strategy, not as a plan or method, but as an intention to cause a lasting effect on an organization's disposition, should be taken as a matter of common sense. Naturally tactics, plans and methods have their place in day-to-day management and administration. However, action under conditions of uncertainty is essentially where the tried and tested methods do not inspire enough confidence in the application of tactics.

Information systems, therefore, can be used for both tactical and strategic applications, but they can be mutually contradictory. Putting it somewhat over-simply, we see strategies as aimed inwardly at the system itself, whereas tactics are aimed out at the environment; competition is tactical, the ability to compete is strategic. Given the uncertainty and continual change in the environment, any tactical gain will be transitory; consequently, changing trends will require chang-ing tactics. The ability necessary to change perception and tactics will require much internal variety, supported by an effective strategic information system. Just as tactics cannot fulfil a strategic task, strategy does not replace tactics. A tactic responds to its environment with a certain 'syntax' of answers, or with certain 'moves'. The more variety in the business environment, the less control the organization has over the course of events. A resilient environment has a potentially unlimited variety of moves in store. This demonstrates the paramount importance of strategic management over short term tactical manoeuvring. Without continuous innovation and generation of the required internal variety, in the long term, an organization will be in a permanent state of crisis management.

We can apply our approach to the business situation, and interpret and extend many of the standard functional explanations of strategy. The principle of strategy, as we describe it, can have many forms, but also we must recognize that the disparate use of the term strategy in the literature will turn out to be a mixture of our interpretation of both strategy and tactics, as for example in Mintzberg's 5-P's approach. He sees strategy as *perception*, the consensus world view (*Weltanschauung*) within an organization, of the variety in its environment and in itself, and the interpretation of this variety as communicable information. As *pattern*, it is a perceived consistency or trend (a system perhaps?) in this information which feeds back into the organization. As *plan*, a purposeful action, consistent with the system's predisposition towards perceived patterns in itself and its environment: feedforward. As *ploy*, a manoeuvre (a tactic?), the projection of a false pattern intended to outwit or deceive intelligent protagonists, created after prejudging patterns in their disposition, tactics and strategies. As *position*, the choice of an advantageous location and posture for the system within the environment. We have extended the idea of strategy as pattern to recognize that disposition does exist beyond human intention. Mintzberg's view still takes an anthropocentric (or is it a manager-centric?) stance, which falls well short of a full understanding of properties that emerge from a history, presence and organization of human action, but not necessarily from human purpose.

With our interpretation, we can look at both the use of IS in tactics and strategies, and tactics and strategies for IS. An organization and its environment are both seething broths of interacting systems and, in order to formulate tactics, it is necessary for management to choose, observe, systematize, measure and interpret the environment. This will involve the mapping of observations onto analogies and models based on previous personal experience or onto formal methods. Each system, measure, model, analysis and analogy is based on choice. Each is a distorting and distorted filter, and any structure we sense in the 'filtrate' can just as easily be a product of the filter as of the observed event. It may even be a sensed transient phenomenon which biased the choice of filter in the first place. Every model will involve arbitrary and simplistic measures, comparisons, classifications, and syntheses; every analogy will involve a conscious association between different events; and all compounded with layers of the chosen systematic analysis. But they will ignore the debris of detail in the unfolding history of a system being modelled and in its environment. These memory fragments, when reconstituted by a particular contextual significance and relevance, have the potential of changing the disposition of systems and environment, as opportunities and risks. In their models, designers can only see a tidiness that is a limited snapshot of an ordered functionality and utility. Although we have no alternative but to use this approach, we must nevertheless be aware of, and question, its appropriateness, relevance, flexibility, validity, consistency and permanence.

Is it any wonder then, that the interpretation of words such as 'organization', 'strategy', 'tactics' and 'system' are so vague and confusing, and that the end product of systematic thinking about strategies and tactics so often results in no more than recipe lists, agendas or grids. Lists such as the 7-S framework which perceives an organization in terms of *structure*, *strategy*, *systems*, *style*, *staff*, *skills* and *superordinate goals* (or *shared values*) (Waterman et al, in Quinn et al [1]). Or two-by-two grids, which classify our complex world with just four metaphors. Grids have been very popular since 1970, when the Boston Consultancy Group brought out their product portfolio grid (on which is superimposed a highly subjective scale) to compare the growth rate of a product against its market share, with *dogs* (low,low), *cash cows* (low,high), *problem children* (high,low) and *stars* (high,high).

Can we expect such 'frameworks' and 'methodologies' to show anything other than the palest shadow of organizational complexity? This dynamic and ambiguous complexity of an organization's future just cannot be reduced to such simplistic data structures, which imply a tidy and convenient homogeneity in organizations that is just not there. But the framework concept itself carries the weight of meaning and authority that is derived from the dominating position of 'hard' science and technology in the mind-set of Western society. It is easy to be seduced into believing in an equivalence between the functionality of framework models and the behaviour of 'real problems', where control over the framework becomes control over the underlying problem. The installation of a framework shifts the validity of decision-taking from objective knowledge to a numerical justification based on a consensus authority within the business community. Knowledge has been replaced in favour of mutual understanding by means of an agreed explanatory framework, which assumes for itself the position of a superior interpretative power. What we can know about a problem situation is replaced by what we can explain within the limitation of the framework. Initial success of installations then ensures that the validity of the framework goes unquestioned in the community, and reinforces its authority.

When implemented, frameworks focus on specific, unambiguous features of systems, and so they are necessarily restricted and restrictive. In the process they lose all sense of the true complexity, of wholeness and endemic uncertainty. Ultimately all of these approaches are merely guidelines. That they are guidelines is not meant as a criticism. If frameworks are used sensibly, that is to help focus on consequences and not just on intentions, then they can help formulate tactics that will be appropriate within strategic and organizational constraints. For it is a truism, as with for example the concept of Myth, that an approach does not have to be valid (logical, tenable, sound, verifiable or based in truth) to be useful. However, an approach, valid or otherwise, will come to nothing without the input of a quality individual, the 'thinking manager', who can fully understand the disposition of the organization and can relate to the compromises being made within the system, and thereby cope with its inherent ambiguity.

The IS environment

Information Technology is an increasingly important factor in contemporary management. Information systems are being set up in business explicitly to accommodate the new opportunities of this technology, and these are having a lasting effect on managerial practice. However, the full implications of this technology-driven development have not been appreciated by organizations. For in absorbing technological systems, they are tolerating a great drain on their resources. Because an information system cannot assess its data critically, the manager is called upon to make the connection between numerical data and its relevance to a decision. In addition the manager also has to worry about the efficacy of the information system. This can be a serious burden on the manager, who now has to face an increased professional load placed upon him by the restricted validity of the numerical system, and aggravated by the technical task of managing the machinery.

Nevertheless, we do have to consider the place of an information system within an organization, given the very real advantages that are available and that so much time and capital is tied up in this new technology. It is important to stress that an information system is itself a semi-autonomous system, which has the organization as part of its environment, and so it will evolve a disposition towards the organization, as well as to the rest of its environment. We must also consider the dispositions of the environment, the organization, and its sub-systems, with all their intrinsic ambiguities, towards the information system. We cannot assume that either disposition will be harmonious; this may have been the original intention, but the result can just as easily be one of major disruption.

"*Today, information technology must be conceived of broadly to encompass the information that businesses create and use as well a wide spectrum of increasingly convergent and linked technologies that process information*" (Porter and Millar [3].) Information technology is changing the very structure of industry, and with it, the basis of competition. It spawns new products and even new businesses, often from existing operations, but it also kills off old products and companies. It changes the balance of power and creates ways of outperforming or being outperformed by rivals. It creates and destroys 'barriers to entry', raises and lowers the costs of switching between suppliers, and it highlights the possibility of both competitive advantage and disadvantage. Information, the very stuff of systemic communication, is essential for the cohesion and the control of the organization facing a future of perpetual change and uncertainty, which is itself exacerbated by the introduction of IT. An understanding of the value of information within an organization should be fundamental to any corporate or IT strategy. Recognition of this fact in the business community has spawned a large consultancy industry. There is much nonsense around, masquerading as strategy; for strategy is trendy. One well-known consultancy claimed to have produced "*a five-year strategic systems development plan for a leading investment fund manager which justified a doubling of its spending on IT*". A strategic plan may require a certain time for its formulation and implementation, but time constraints cannot be imposed realistically on the effects of development on a disposition.

Ashby's Law of Requisite Variety implies that an IS manager should ensure that his organization has enough internal variety of responses to be able to react tactically in an appropriate manner to changes in the business environment. This calls for strategic management, a recognition of short term tactical thinking, and the preparation and disposition of information resources within an organization, enabling it to function and to contend in a preferred way with, not only the commercial competition, but also the uncertainty, complexity and ambiguity inherent in an unknown future. The concept of predisposition within an organization, *feedforward* in systems terms, will involve alertness, patience, tolerance, perseverance, imagination, innovation, inventiveness, quality, commitment, motivation, productivity, experience and many of the other unmeasurable human aspects. Unless the strategic context of information is fully appreciated, and unless the managers of information systems are aware of the true nature of crisis, complexity and uncertainty that awaits them, then strategies will become mere wishful thinking. Then the proponents of 'proactive management' will launch deterministic mechanisms into the unknown, without being able to recognize what emerges, or to react sensibly and sympathetically, or to follow the feedback effect of these reactions. Grasping the place of information systems within the business reality is a never-ending process.

Strategy frameworks

The evident importance of information systems to business, and the implied but unarticulated need of planners to understand the disposition of IS towards organizations (and vice versa), has engendered a confusing number of strategy frameworks to approach the problem. Given the uncertain nature of the problem, it should come as no surprise that they all have different emphases and perspectives. Recommending an eclectic approach, and in an attempt to help clarify the situation, Michael Earl [4] collected many of them together under a *framework of frameworks* (figure 3.1). His three-by-three matrix compares classes of framework (for awareness, opportunity or positioning) each with their own attributes (of purpose, scope or use) to give nine 'strategic classes', and is intended to ensure that 'the right framework must be used for the right purpose in the right context'. The awareness frameworks are more conceptual than prescriptive, and are used to increase the recognition of the potential and impact of IT among executives. Opportunity frameworks are tools which indicate or clarify strategic options. Positioning frameworks identify the character of IT within a given sector.

Framework / Quality	Awareness	Opportunity	Positioning
Purpose	Vision	Ends	Means
Scope	Possibility	Probability	Capability
Use	Education	Analysis	Implementation

Figure 3.1 Earl's "Framework of Frameworks"

Many of these strategy frameworks proposed by the IS community are based on the work of Michael Porter [5], who focuses on the five competitive forces between rivals in the industry, and on new entrants, suppliers, customers and substitute products. His advice is that the strategic use of information technology should be aimed at creating a disposition within an organization to diminish the power of customers and suppliers, to create barriers against new entrants into their market, to minimize the possibility of substitute products by building in switching costs, and so gain a competitive edge over rivals. He compares competitive advantage against a range of target markets, and derives three alternative generic strategies: cost leadership, differentiation, and focus (on cost or differentiation). Such a classification leads to an idealized but somewhat limited perception of the competitive environment; it can help reduce the complexity and apparently resolve some of the inherent ambiguity; it does give clear directions for strategic intention. But, with a restricted understanding of the disposition of the organization and of the marketplace, its mechanistic application can be misleading or counter-productive. Any company, tendering for a contract with the aim of using an information system to tie-in the potential client, will be at a disadvantage against a competitor system based on international standards which leaves the client with flexibility of choice. Clients may not like being tied-in, and they have read Porter's books too! The competitive advantage of American Hospital Supply rapidly disappeared when talk of its takeover by one of its large customers, Hospital Corporation of America (HCA), reached the attention of other major customers who were rivals of HCA [6].

Porter, with Millar [3], highlights the importance of IT in a company's ability to compete, by reference to the *value chain* concept which considers the position of IT within the organization and its relationships with the commercial environment. They classify a company's interdependent *value activities* as *support activities*: infrastructure, human resource management, technology development and procurement, interlinked with *primary activities*: a sequence of stages connecting inbound logistics, operations, outbound logistics, marketing and sales, and service. At each stage of the value chain, the organization should take the opportunity of adding value to its products and services. Porter and Millar identify opportunities for IT to optimize the linkages between value activities, and thereby list ways for companies to achieve competitive advantage, at the same time highlighting how the nature of competition is changing through IT and how new industries are emerging. They recommend that managers take five steps towards taking advantage if IT.

- First, senior managers must *assess information intensity*, and identify priority business units for investment.

- Second, they can use an *information intensity matrix*, to compare the 'information content of a product' against the 'information intensity of the value chain', in order to classify the potential role of information technology in the particular industrial sector.
- Third, managers must identify and rank the ways in which IT might create competitive advantage. They must look for new linkages, identify activities most likely to be affected by cost and differentiation, and recognize how IT will effect Porter's five competitive forces. At this stage managers must also consider if they can include more information technology with their product, or bundle more information along with it.
- Fourth, managers must investigate how IT can spawn new businesses, thus identifying opportunities and risks. Checking whether they have saleable information, whether their IT capacity can form a new business, or if IT makes it feasible for them to create new products.
- Fifth, the previous steps must lead to an action plan to capitalize on the new technologies, ranking likely investments in hardware, software and 'wetware' (people). It must lead to organizational changes that make the most of value chain linkages, and so distribute the responsibility beyond IT professionals. The plan must aim at integrating IT into company strategy.

Porter's understanding, of a flow of interdependent activities from the perspective of the product and customer, has encouraged a positive shift of emphasis for many IT analysts. However, it can be misleading, given the secondary role that it places on human resources, public sector and social issues, internal and external politics, research and development, and economics and finances. But, by moving the emphasis away from treating the organization as a management pyramid, a structure that filters out most detail except for chronic failure, he has given insight into the real opportunities for applying information technology.

A variant on the value chain perspective is the Customer Resource Life Cycle (CRLC) of Ives and Learmonth [7]. They stress the importance of the customer to an organization's disposition by listing stages in the life cycle of a product (or service) from the customer's perspective. Customers:

- *determine a need* by establishing their requirements for a product, together with its attributes;
- *acquire the product* by locating, ordering, taking possession, testing, accepting, authorizing and paying for the resource;
- *manage the product* by supporting the inventory, monitoring, upgrading and maintaining the resource;

- finally they *retire the product* by transferring or disposing of it, and then accounting for the total 'spend'.

A supplier of a product can gain an advantageous trading position, by using IT to help customers with handling that resource throughout its life cycle. But there are no guarantees. From this perspective, they give a number of illuminating case studies of suppliers, some of whom gained an advantage in this way, and some of whom were disadvantaged.

Nolan [8], in his Stages of Growth approach, gives a useful life cycle frame for understanding the disposition of an organization to the development of data processing systems. *Initiation* and early successes increase interest and experimentation, are followed by rapid and uncontrolled *contagion*, before they are brought under *control* to minimize waste. Then the emphasis shifts towards data and information and away from machines. Systems can then be *integrated* until they form part of an organized *data administration*, before finally entering the stage of *mature use*. Each stage has to be managed differently, because each involves different requirements, objectives and implications for the company. For example, responsibility for IT moves higher up the organizational hierarchy as the life cycle progresses. Similarly the position of the user moves from non-involvement, through interest, active involvement, to being accountable for applications. This general treatment is theoretically highly questionable, as the use of IT is very rarely homogeneous across an organization. Nevertheless, when it is linked to recommended actions at each stage, it can in fact prove highly beneficial for organizations trying to manage the confusion caused by the introduction of an information system.

Most articles in this area recognize that IS managers are searching for the confidence of measurements that will illuminate their position in the competitive environment, and which will show them how computers can 'nudge them in the right direction'. McFarlan and McKenney ([9] and with Pyburn [10]) develop their *strategic grid* by comparing the strategic impact of information systems against the potential dependency on and criticality of information systems, to understand how companies change their structure and control mechanisms in order to take advantage of the new technologies. Individual firms and industrial sectors are identified as progressing through particular quadrants: support (low,low), factory (low,high), turnaround (high,low) and strategic (high,high). Thus the banking industry, by using automatic teller machines (ATM) and electronic funds transfer (EFT), can be seen to progress from being a data processing factory, through turnaround, to the strategic quadrant. This enables management, at national and organizational levels, to focus on important issues, to prioritize investment towards achieving strategic goals, and to prescribe management action.

STRATEGIC GRID

Strategic Impact of IT

Dependency on IT

	Low	High
Low	**SUPPORT** Textile/Wood Storage/Warehouse Real estate Services Allied to Transport	**TURNAROUND** Education Retail Advertising Precision Legal Market Research Engineering Land Transport Publishing Postal Electrical Engineering Medical/Health Consumer Architectural Robots Electronics & Technical Industrial Heavy Services Machinery Engineering Hotel
High	**FACTORY** Accounting/Auditing Air Insurance Speciality Chemicals Petroleum Refinery Petrochemicals Pharmaceuticals	**STRATEGIC** Printing Computer Services Financial Telecoms Industrial electronics

Figure 3.2   Developed by the National Computer Board of Singapore. Based on a model described in [9]: used with permission

This approach has been fundamental to the national plan of Singapore (see figure 3.2), which is undoubtedly the most extensive *per capita* national commitment to date. Their prime minister, Lee Kwan Yew, made the strategic decision to charge ahead and totally transform the whole commercial, legal, governmental and educational infrastructure of the City State, with an ambitious computerization programme. The sheer scale of investment reflects their national aspiration, commitment and belief in the ultimate value of information technology across all industrial sectors.

In their *Strategic Opportunity Matrix,* Benjamin et al [11] choose instead to compare the market for IT (internal or external) against product novelty (traditional or requiring major structural change). Their matrix is presented as an aid to refocusing, and thus changing, a company's attitude towards, and its awareness of, information technology; thence gaining the company significant competitive advantage by improving its approach to market forces and to internal systems. Charles Wiseman [6] gives a *Strategic Option Generator* which requires the manager: to identify the *strategic target*, supplier, customer or competitor; to choose the *thrust*, differentiation, cost, innovation, growth or alliance; to settle on an offensive or defensive *mode*; and then to decide the *direction* of whether to use or supply the IT product.

The standard SWOT analysis, 'brainstorming' on the Strengths, Weaknesses, Opportunities and Threats of using CBIS within an organization, is another commonly-used approach in decision-taking. Its value is predicated on the belief that a broad and frank discussion of the systemic risks and opportunities of IT in an organization's disposition toward its commercial environment is essential for strategic management. A similar, but more formally structured and sophisticated, technique is Rockart's [11] *Critical Success Factors* (CSF) method. This concentrates on what must go well, or may go badly (and so need most concern), for the overall success of the organization. Here, interviews with CEOs identify the factors that need special and continual attention:

- factors critical to all companies in the industry;
- issues related to the company itself and to its position in the industry;
- environmental factors (legal, political, economic and social trends, etc.);
- activities within the company that are proving to be short term problems;
- monitoring procedures, the ability to keep track of operations; and
- building for transition, necessitated by changes in the business environment.

By identifying the information needs of executives, such critical factors give focal points at which to aim information systems. Unfortunately, the successful synthesis depends heavily on the quality and experience of the interviewer. It is a lesson well learned that expertise (in using a framework) should not be separated from experience. Rockart and Crescenzi [11] take the CSF method and include it in a process for the planning and development of strategic systems. Their approach is to start with a workshop at which the method is explained, commitment is sought from the management, and the information needs and system priorities are established. This is followed by CSF interviews, and then brainstorming at a focusing workshop, leading to an analysis of priorities, and the proposal of decision scenarios. Then a prototype design is developed, culminating in an information system to be continuously monitored and modified along the lines indicated by further CSF analysis.

The 14-step IBM Business Systems Planning (BSP) method [12] is a similar practical procedure for designing the company's overall information resource. It is typical of such prescriptive methods, and so it is worth giving a brief outline of its steps. BSP starts by setting up the project team, and gaining commitment, support and perhaps membership from senior management (1). Then in preparation for the study, schedules, lists, rooms and references are prepared (2). At the start of the study, the team reviews objectives, preparations and schedules (3), before identifying the key business activities (4). Data is categorized into 'data classes' such as customers, suppliers, orders, parts etc. (5), so that the organization's information architecture can be designated by relating data classes, procedures and information systems (6). Then the support for current systems can be analyzed (7). The senior executives of the organization are interviewed to verify assumptions, information needs, problems and priorities (8). From all the information collected the team can list their findings and conclusions about changes to old systems and new systems (9), before determining the criteria and priorities for development (10). The team is now in a position to review the management of the organization's information resource (11), and recommend and develop an action plan (12). There must be regular reports of the results (13) and an overview of follow-up activities (14).

There are many, many more methods for recognizing IT needs, and for designing and implementing systems. The questions who? why? where? what? which? when? whither? whether? and how?, are all approached by one method or another. Managers can be swamped with these similar but subtly different prescribing and proscribing frameworks, and so they should be made aware of the severe limitations and their dubious theoretical validity. Like the icing on a birthday cake, these methods provide an attractive topping to the content which, in the case of IS strategies, should be a good comprehension of the company's business, organizational and information systems. But, given the complexity, uniqueness and lack of uniformity of each situation, can we really expect to map experiences, history and culture, or to sense similarities, or to justify comparisons and classifications, basically to perceive dynamic structure and changing pattern? How can we justify the systematic approach, when these methods, based on a very doubtful choice of classifications, are wide open to 'garbage in – garbage out'? Multiple perspectives, synthesized from various cases, can only produce vague generalizations. Being systematic and methodical, will have uncertain consequences dependent on the dynamic context, and so will neither resolve nor avoid the ambiguity.

Good business ideas do not come from these frameworks alone, but require a profound understanding of the specific context in which they are applied. Many beneficial strategic influences are not produced by intention and decision, but by the creation of a positive disposition, and a recognition of the importance of culture, trust, quality, motivation, inspiration, enthusiasm, encouragement, reconciliation; qualities that just cannot be input as parameters to methods based on systematic procedures. The often quoted case of American Hospital Supply is a case in point [6]. Their competitive advantage did not derive from an idea that appeared spontaneously with IT; an efficient manual system was already in place, and there was a spirit of enthusiasm and innovation ready to take advantage *of* the technology. But competitive advantage does not grow from the seed of a generic approach that is identified in these methods. Competitive advantage is the result of the potential and unique disposition of an organization. An appropriate application of these frameworks can be thought provoking and, therefore, can help focus and enhance a manager's understanding.

IS within the organization

Consequently, there is a need for managers to concentrate more on information than on technology (Information technology with a capital 'I' and a small 't'), and to recognize where the application of technology is appropriate to their needs. This must colour their attitude towards IT expenditure in relation to products and services. Managers must decide whether, in business terms, expenditure is: a cost that must be controlled; a necessary expense; a necessary investment; or a priority investment on which the long term future of the company depends. They must consider whether to gear the organization's computing towards transaction processing or towards office information systems (OIS), to use mainframes or minis or micros, to centralize or to distribute the computer resources, to be strict or flexible with users, all depending on the specific situation and available resources (human and machine). Managers must be experienced in both the business and the technology, be highly sceptical of the claims made for hardware and software, and be eclectic in their use of the above strategic methods when taking decisions. Their goal must be to develop a sense of vision and mission, a sense of wonder, judgement, and an understanding that they are dealing with complex issues that are forever changing.

Thinking IS managers recognize that information systems are more than just closed technological and functional systems, and that they are dealing with other interrelated and interacting systems, each with its own unique and dynamic disposition. So they must keep well informed about, and be in tune with, their own system and organization, and must concentrate their resources. Strategic management requires that they keep the initiative and follow their own judgements and disposition wherever possible by reducing the number of times they are forced into decisions or confrontations. There is so much misinformation and misunderstanding about IT that all too often the organization has totally unrealistic expectations. Managers have to understand what they themselves might do, can do, want to do and ought to do (Andrews [1]). They should only adopt projects that are technically feasible, that are consistent with the potential of the information system to increase variety, and that are tactically well disposed to the commercial and organizational environment. It is also important that managers be aware of the danger of overplanning. Announcing too many details, making overly precise statements, and backing high profile commitment to technological functionality, rather than to business goals, restrict their options, lead to mechanical decisions, and so make managers predictable. They have to designate the battleground, both inside the organization and in the commercial world. They must recognize, and not oppose, the inevitable systemic realities, both environmental and organizational. The best that managers can do is to supervise the evolution, and to try and steer their company in some way so that it can 'go with the flow'. To do this they must see the whole environment; too much focus often means that they fail to 'see the wood for the trees'. Many decisions will make themselves, or more precisely will be constrained by organizational procedures. Good managers recognize the danger implicit in rigidly defined policies; for these restrict the necessary flexibility and variety of response, and then the manager has little or no influence over the decisions taken within the system.

We have seen that communication of information is crucial to the control mechanisms of the system, to its coherence and cohesion, and hence to its ability to generate variety. The replacement of an old information system with new technology or the integration of IT into the planning processes of an organization, is fraught with problems. But nowadays this cannot be avoided; intentionally or unintentionally, IT will permeate planning. Often the history of IT within a company will affect planning; 'the song is ended but the melody lingers on'. All too often it seems impossible to scrap obsolete systems. A displaced system will have evolved defences which could be antagonistic to the new. Even if it is possible to scrap the old procedures and technology, the disposition of the organization towards them, and of them to the organization, may still remain; a dispositional inertia which may prove very difficult to overcome. It is not uncommon that the disposition of monolithic computer centres, developed with enormous capital expenditure over the past twenty years, will impose their wishes on future computer policies. The proposal of writing off the cash invested to create the obsolescent structure, along with the power base that goes with spending such large sums, may place a block on any innovative idea. Of course new ideas, such as end user computing, will also require large sums of money, and this will cause even more political tension. Caution and evolutionary change is usually the most expedient way. Resistance to change is readily apparent in the reluctance of managers to use Management Information Systems (MIS), Executive Information Systems (EIS) and Expert Systems (ES). It may be that such systems are not necessarily beneficial, they could well be examples of technological myopia (misguided faith in, and too narrow a focus on, the functionality of technology). But all too often they are not even given an opportunity to prove themselves; an example of technology myopia (possibly missing the opportunities offered by the technology).

Consequently, we return to the need for strategic management and the preparation and disposition of information resources within an organization, enabling it to function and to contend in a preferred way with not only the commercial competition, but also the uncertainty and complexity inherent in an unknown future. The concept of disposition involves flexibility, balance, alertness, patience, tolerance, perseverance, innovation, quality, motivation, productivity, experience and many other strategic aspects. The methods described in this chapter are aimed essentially at the functional aspects of information systems. These methods, all presently in use by the IS community, can be seen to fall far short of our meaning of strategy.

The way forward

The myth of 'being in control', so readily demonstrated in many failed applications of information technology, illustrates the related folly of believing in rigidly proactive management. The only logical approach is to initiate plans, but to be flexible enough to react quickly to whatever risks or opportunities appear; and so maintain the initiative. A blinkered faith in planning, and using the past as a mirror to the future, is likely to lose the initiative by constraining the understanding, insight and lateral thinking of quality employees. Companies must come to grips with both the importance *and* the limitations of IT. They must recognize which technologies and systems are essential to their existence and make them secure. They should reject the indulgence of championing obviously irrelevant fashionable technologies but be prepared to evaluate the grey areas where the relevance is unclear – this can only be achieved by top quality IT staff, who place the good of the company before loyalty to their craft. Companies must resolve the position of the IT executive within their corporate hierarchy. Although there are trends towards making this a full board-level appointment, it does beg the question of the suitability and availability of candidates. Such positions require a much broader and more subtle strategic view of IT, and an understanding of the fundamental role that alert and free-thinking employees will play in this future.

We can see the relevance of Mintzberg's [1] recognition of the role of manager as figurehead, leader, liaison, monitor, disseminator, spokesman, entrepreneur, disturbance handler, resource allocator and negotiator. The present breed of technocrats, many of whom see machines replacing people, are, in general, totally unsuited for such responsibility. Good 'hybrid managers', with a mixture of business and technical skills, are scarce. So in the near future we can expect a number of initiatives, similar to that of the British Computer Society (BCS), to help develop the skills of the 'thinking manager'.

This balanced view of opportunity and risk means that, together with a continuous, but properly managed, investment in the technology, there must be an increased emphasis on developing policies for the effective management and utilization of personnel, *at all levels in the organization*. Not only must this policy ensure that misplaced optimism in the benefits of technology does not run roughshod over human aspirations, but also, it must release the potential fount of ideas and innovation in the workforce as a whole, and in particular with respect to the beneficial application of technology. To do this, we need to understand better how technological systems affect both business and individual performance. Equifinality in systems means there are many different routes to a solution, and the inherent ambiguity and variety means that lateral thinking is essential. Within the remit of seizing commercial opportunities, there should be an agreed policy of damage limitation, because damage there is likely to be from systemic risk factors. Success is more likely through a strategy of keeping systems small – "*small is beautiful*" – small is flexible, small is controllable. Flexibility means new tactics can be developed as and when needed to take advantage of the environment. Flexibility means a willingness to reverse any commitment to historically successful procedures. An understanding of systemic risk may in some instances, even lead to a considered rejection of integration and standardization, the cornerstones of current IT wisdom, where perhaps these are seen as a security danger or as a source of unnecessary complexity.

One important lesson of the previous two chapters is that the meaning of words such as 'control', 'strategy', 'tactic' and 'system', is highly problematic. We have shown how a computer system (in common parlance, the hardware and software) is not an information system from our perspective. Similarly we have concluded that any long term attempt to be 'in control' of an unknown future, is misguided and doomed. During the remainder of this book we will be discussing the work of the leading researchers in the field of information systems, and so we will be using their words in the way we believe they were intended. We would stress that this usage may not be in total accord with our own inter-pretation. It is not that we are being deliberately perverse; inconsistency of meaning is quite common among researchers, many of whom assume, for the best motives, the existence of a consensus meaning of these vague words in order to tackle the 'problems in the real world'. We advise the reader to stop and consider whenever words like 'control' are used in a throwaway manner, and to check that this 'real world' is not some idealized, preconceived and prejudiced intellectual contrivance.

Suggested reading

The works of Michael Porter and of Henry Mintzberg, especially the two books mentioned above, are essential reading for anyone remotely interested in business stategies. The following book comes highly recommended as containing many of the classic papers of the Information Systems literature.

> Wetherbe, J.C., Dock V.T. & Mandell S.L., *Readings in Information Systems*, West Publishing, St.Paul, 1988.

We also recommend two highly readable English translations of the works of Machiavelli and Sun Tzu.

> Bondanella, P. & Musa, M., *The Portable Machiavelli*, Penguin, New York, 1979.

> Sun Tzu, *The Art of War*, Oxford University Press, Oxford, 1963.

Discussion issues

1. Read the classic texts of military strategy, by Von Clausewitz and Sun Tzu. Then discuss whether the military metaphor of strategy is really valid in the business context? Perhaps there is a systemic reason why it is so readily accepted? 'Old soldiers never die, colonels and above retire and go into management'. Maybe 'old biologists' would be more appropriate management material? Perhaps a study of the behaviour of biological organisms would furnish a better metaphor for commercial competition? Also read the political strategy of Machiavelli.

2. We all sense personal indeterminate interpretations for words such as 'information' or 'system', and these go beyond any collective definition that has gained authority merely through a consensus. Our interpretations may even contradict such consensus meanings. That is why even though much of this chapter revolves around the concept of 'disposition', we deliberately left the meaning of that word vague. It is important that readers search for their interpretation of this word. The following was the result of a brainstorming session with a postgraduate student at LSE. *Disposition is the faculty of setting the system in order, or the condition of being set in order; the situation and position of the elements of the whole relative to itself and to the environment. It is the due arrangement of the several parts of a system in reference to its general systemic structure, and especially for the accomplishment of a purpose. This arrangement can be planned in preparation for a tactical action. Disposition can be the distribution of systemic components, their allocation, destination, preparations or measures taken, the arrangement of systemic duties, or the condition or complexion of affairs. It relates to the ordering, control, management, direction, appointment, administration and dispensation of the components. It is the way or manner in which a system has been disposed, or is situated or constituted, in that it determines the nature or the course of events. That nature, tendency, qualities or constitution of a system, is considered in relation to its apparent or observed influence. It is an inclination, intention, aptitude, capacity or purpose; the condition of the system being (favourably or unfavourably) disposed towards its environment. A disposition is a permanent, normal and natural condition.* Consider whether you agree (or disagree) with any of this interpretation, and discuss your own meaning for 'disposition', and for other words like 'system', 'strategy', 'tactic', 'information'.

References

1. Quinn J.B., Mintzberg H. & James R.M., *The Strategy Process*, Prentice-Hall International, London, 1988.
2. Parkinson, C. Northcote, *Parkinson's Law*, Penguin, London, 1986.
3. Porter M.E. & Millar V.E., 'How information gives you competitive advantage', Harvard Business Review, Vol.63, No.4, 149-160, July-August 1985.
4. Earl M. (ed.), *Information Management : The Strategic Dimension*, Oxford University Press, Oxford, 1988.
5. Porter M.E., *Competitive Strategy*, Free Press, New York, 1980.
6. Wiseman C., *Strategy and Computers*, Dow Jones-Irwin, Homewood, Illinois, 1985.
7. Ives B. & Learmonth G.P.,'The Information System as a Competitive Weapon', *Communications of the ACM*, 27(12), 1193-1201, 1984.
8. Nolan R.L., 'Managing the crises in data processing', *Harvard Business Review*, Vol.57, No.2, 115-126, Mar-Apr 1979.
9. McFarlan F.W. & McKenney J.L., *Corporate Information Systems Management: The Issues Facing Senior Management*, Dow Jones-Irwin, Homewood, Illinois, 1983.
10. McFarlan F.W., McKenney J.L.& Pyburn P.,'The information archipelago - plotting a course', *Harvard Business Review*, Vol.61, No.1, 145-156, Jan-Feb 1983.
11. Madnick, S.E. (ed.), *The Strategic Use of Information Technology*, Oxford University Press, New York, 1987.
12. Zachman, J.A.,'Business Systems Planning and Business Information Control Study: a Comparison', *IBM Systems Journal*, 21(1), 31-53, 1982.

4   The organization of the information systems function

- *The organizational environment*
- *End user computing*
- *The changing role of the IS department*
- *The changing structure of information systems*

The advances in technology and the increasing number and range of applications place considerable demands on IS management. The role and structure of IS departments have to adapt in order to realize the opportunities and control the risks discussed in this book. This chapter re-examines the organization of the IS function in the light of these changes. Our focus on the IS department means that we shall not consider the impact of the technology on the rest of the organization. There is conflicting evidence as to whether IT increases or decreases the influence and power of middle management relative to that of senior management. Whether IT favours more centralized or decentralized organizations depends upon the unique situation of the individual company. Such a discussion is outside the scope of this chapter; readers are referred to the growing body of literature [1,2].

Before discussing the principal organizational issues, we shall briefly outline the characteristics of the organizational environment. Understanding the nature of this environment is essential in order to appreciate the political arena within which technological change has to be managed. We shall then consider the key shift towards end user computing, a move that encompasses many of the technological and organizational pressures on the IS department. This leads finally to an examination of the changing role of the IS department and the implications for its structure.

The organizational environment

All organizations, except perhaps the very smallest, are arranged in terms of groups, rather than of individual members of staff. This is both functional for the organization, in terms of the division of work, and satisfies the individuals' needs for social support and interaction. Groups may be created in a highly formal manner; for example, through the appointment of individuals to a particular department or committee, or they may be informally created, for example, based on catching the same train to the office. They can vary greatly in a number of aspects, including size, homogeneity, and the tasks at hand. Different groups are interlinked together through common needs, and also because individuals are typically members of a number of overlapping groups. For example, a person may be in company middle management and the marketing department, as well as in a group of avid pipe-smokers. However, individuals normally only feel a strong sense of membership for one group, typically their immediate workgroup.

From our perspective, perhaps the most important aspect of the group is the development of group norms. These are implicit rules and values, that determine acceptable and expected behaviour from members. These extraordinarily powerful norms keep the group cohesive and govern how its goals are achieved. They also determine how relationships are carried on with other groups, as well as constituting a standard against which individuals can validate their opinions. In some cases, the norms include sanctions against members who break the norms; as when a group of machine shop workers may ostracize members who produce too much or too little output. This behaviour is not restricted to manual workers; a management group may reject a member who consistently lunches with their staff rather than with their group. All groups develop norms, some norms being more powerful and wide-ranging than others; however, a basic norm is usually the systemic desire for the group to expand its influence. Thus, groups tend towards an operational disposition that maintains or expands their share of organizational status, power and resources. Where a group is particularly cohesive, it may fight surprisingly hard when it feels threatened by another group, or when opportunities appear for increasing its influence.

The desire of individual groups for power and status, each possibly supported by ideological concerns that further project conflicting goals, transforms an organization into a political system based on conflict and coalition. Weaker groups form coalitions to defend themselves against incursions of the strong. Much organizational conflict, such a familiar part of the organizational landscape, originates from the political manoeuvres in the struggle for power and status. The introduction of IT has provided a significant catalyst for conflict; large chunks of territory come 'up for grabs', as organizational structures, roles, and tasks are re-evaluated. This is an excellent opportunity for both individuals and groups to profit from company reorganization and a redistribution of resources, in the shape of staff, equipment, duties and prestige, and thus influence and power. A valuable political resource that is inherently affected by the arrival of IT is the control of information, on which many groups base much of their power.

The IS department is a relatively recent specialist group that initially had to develop somewhat of a siege mentality in the face of opposition from more established groups. The IS department is in a curious position in terms of organizational power. Its relative youth and the absence of senior management representation has tended to keep it low in the 'pecking order', compared to the well established departments, such as finance or production. Until recently, this was further justified by its peripheral relationship to the main functions of the organization. However, over the last decade, it appears to have gained in power; its monopoly position regarding the supply of CBIS gives it considerable leverage in setting development priorities and the resultant redistribution of resources. Thus, more established departments have had to accommodate this new upstart whose increasing command of resources enhanced its organizational visibility.

It is very difficult to gauge the impact of recent developments upon the power balance between users and the IS department. Although the increasing importance of CBIS to organizations might tend to increase IS department power, users are increasingly gaining control of the development and operation of new systems (end user computing), and this is likely to reverse the power shift. IS department power has been seen as comprising technical, structural, conceptual and symbolic aspects [3]. The technical and structural exercise of power concerns the ability of the IS department to influence the design of individual systems and the constraints applied to users, for example, in the need to obtain IS department approval for end user developments such as hardware and software purchases. The conceptual and symbolic exercise of power is more subtle, referring to the ability of IS specialists to influence the goals and values of users regarding, for example, the association of IT with progress and advancement.

Information systems development can be viewed both in terms of a technical and a political process. Users and developers may have incompatible goals and opposing value systems; each side may aspire to increased status through the control of the development process. Thus, political conflict between different user groups and between users and developers can easily occur: "Political actions are not isolated episodes to be interpreted within the context of rational problem-solving. It is the other way around" [4]. This instability is increased as these activities are taking place in a volatile time of change when people's goals and assumptions are becoming more uncertain. Even after the launch of a new installation, its evolution is still very much subject to political pressures. Researchers have found that organizational politics were a better explanation of the course of further development of a computer system, than those based on technical aspects, cost-effectiveness or reactions to a changing environment [5].

Resistance to change

Organizational conflict between users and developers has traditionally been categorized as *resistance to change*. This is a much misunderstood area, partly due to the loaded nature of the somewhat emotive terminology. 'Resistance' conjures up images of something negative, unlawful and unwarranted, perhaps even hopeless, whereas, on the other hand, 'innovation' and 'implementation' are associated with positive, beneficial, legitimate processes.

A major misconception is that resistance is abnormal. Whereas organizations currently face major internal and external pressures for change, change itself is nothing new; change, resistance to change and inertia are normal organizational processes. People and human systems are highly adaptable, but new concepts take time to root, especially in times of uncertainty and major change. Resistance is not the preserve of lower-grade staff; managerial resistance is usually much more subtle and effective. The intentional neglect of IT plans is more likely to prevent their introduction than the ugly pitched battles that took place in both the USA and UK. Resistance is also unlikely to be confined to reluctant users with no experience of computers. It may be apparent in existing users, who prefer the current computerized system to a proposed one. Resistance may also be exhibited by IS specialists who do not wish to change their working practices, particularly the shift from a production role to that of user support or maintenance.

A second major misconception is that change is beneficial and legitimate - the assumption that developers have *'God on their side'*. Rather, resistance can play a healthy, homeostatic, defensive role, particularly if the proposed change has the potential to be detrimental to the organization. Resistance is perfectly rational where the people concerned face a loss of power, status, and even their jobs. A related misconception is that resistance is based on a lack of information. In the 1969/70 UK strike at the Ford Motor Company, management sought to end the dispute by explaining directly to the staff the 'beneficial' implications of the proposed changes. However, the workforce then realized even more clearly the drawbacks and the dispute intensified.

Another major misconception is that resistance is simply *Luddism*, a resistance to new technology in any form. But there is rarely anything simple about resistance, either in its manifestation or its causes. In this it resembles industrial disputes: "A strike is a social phenomenon of enormous complexity which, in its totality, is never susceptible to complete description, let alone complete explanation" [6].

This complexity can be seen in the many forms that resistance may take. Resistance may be highly active, with individuals and groups engaged in political *counter-implementation* tactics [7], such as trying to stall projects by endlessly forming committees, or through blatant sabotage, such as jamming equipment with honey or paperclips, or 'accidentally' pouring coffee into the machine. There is a long history to the use of apparently rational argument aimed at stifling change; figure 4.1 is an example which shows some 'principles' employed to do just that in academic institutions at the turn of the century.

Principle of the Dangerous Precedent:
If something has not been done before, it is either wrong or a dangerous precedent that it would not be fair to burden our successors with.

Principle of the Fair Trial:
Small adjustments to the old system should be given a fair trial before any major changes.

Principle of the Unripe Time:
The idea is a good one, but this is not the right time to carry it out.

Figure 4.1 Cornford's rational 'principles' [8]

Campaigns against change may be highly visible, with public meetings, or much more covert, relying on huddled conversations. Alternatively, resistance may be passive, where individuals merely opt out and fail to cooperate. Such users may blame the new system for all their problems or just ignore it, both during and after implementation. Another variant is the acceptance of the technology without making any changes in the traditional working procedures. In hospitals for example, the benefits realized from automatic analyzers were much less than expected because they continued to be sited in laboratories rather than in the wards. Resistance may remain pent-up, or latent, awaiting a chance to express itself in the form of low morale, low productivity, high labour turnover, absenteeism, industrial disputes and psychological withdrawal. Any of these manifestations of resistance may take place during the system's development or they may not occur until the system is operational. Resistance is complex and likely to be highly erratic, frequently changing in form and intensity.

Similarly, we find a multiplicity of 'causal' factors that can be combined in a myriad ways. In individuals there are various psychological factors such as a natural complacency, or fear and uncertainty regarding the future. Some may not feel a need for a new system, or the new system may not fit their cognitive style, requiring a significant effort for them to adjust their way of thinking. Social factors, such as transgressing the shared values and group norms, may provide the fuel for resistance. Changes to management style, such as an increase in formalization, may also add to the difficulties. Similarly, a history of failed initiatives, exaggerated into organizational myths, may weigh heavily on current changes. A mismatch between the new system and the existing structure places strains on both. Certain aspects of the implementation method, such as a lack of consultation with users, may also serve to increase resistance. The new system itself, if it is of poor quality or with excessive complexity, or has a high degree of innovation, is likely to provoke resistance. Users who are not particularly averse to new technology may simply prefer a different design of new system. Finally, resistance is naturally likely to increase where there are significant adverse 'objective' consequences, in terms of job losses and loss of status.

Resistance to IT should be seen as just another example of the general issue of resistance to any organizational change. Such complex political problems are not the natural preserve of IS technicians; the problems of resistance and conflict are not susceptible to technological solutions. Improved political tactics [7] may be needed as part of the 'toolbox' of information systems development. These include recruiting a high-level *fixer* to push the project through any political turbulence. However, both the availability of political opportunities and the risks attached to such tactics are highly dependent on the particular situation.

Policies to overcome resistance should be matched against the apparent source of the problem [9]. To facilitate the introduction of a system faced with people-determined resistance requires a concentration on the users, through: enhanced education; coercion and persuasion; and participation, in order to gain commitment. Where resistance is diagnosed as system-determined, the priorities become: educating the developers; improving the user-system interface; aiming for a better fit with the organization; and user participation. However, in view of the number of factors involved, most resistance is likely to stem from the interaction between users and the system. These emergent properties imply: solving organization problems before IS development starts; increasing user incentives; and improving user-developer communication.

We would emphasize the need to understand resistance, bearing in mind the particular situation in hand. This understanding is not facilitated by taking a highly 'rational' organizational model, where it is assumed that the goals are clear and shared by all groups, and where the organization is assumed to function according to the formal structure and formal lines of command, all dancing to the tune of a 'mission statement'. Rather, one should take a pluralist, political view, assuming that groups have conflicting objectives and that informal relationships are as important as the formal. Authority is negotiated rather than implicit in the organization's structure. Change is likely to be a political problem; an information system is a tool for coping with this change, but it is also a cause of further change. Management must not assume that these latter changes will be accepted across the organization merely because they lay questionable claim to a scientifically rational optimum. Clearly, in order to achieve their own objectives, IS management must become more adroit at both understanding and handling the mechanisms of organizational power and resistance to change, when promoting their optimistic view of IS on the organization.

End user computing

As if to demonstrate that resistance is often directed at the imposition of change, rather than at the technology itself, one of the most significant current trends in information systems is that of end user computing (EUC). This comprises the purchase, development and operation of CBIS by users, relatively independently of any IS department. EUC already represents the major proportion of IS budgets in many organizations. Rather than spending large sums on additional central mainframes, operated by an IS department, budgets are now beginning to be dominated by networks of user workstations. Users can now "*Leap to Freedom*"; freedom from an IS department widely perceived to be centralized, unresponsive and expensive. Such a move is typically motivated by the desire of users to gain control over their technological environment as well as to relieve the frustration occasioned by the ever-lengthening software development backlog. EUC has been facilitated by the availability of inexpensive microcomputers with powerful, task-based, user friendly software packages, and an increasing user knowledge and familiarity with IT. There are a host of opportunities and risks attached to EUC and organizations have the demanding task of navigating their way through some very complex issues. This task is too difficult for IS management to carry out alone; it requires an equal contribution from an enlightened user management in order to strike an appropriate balance. However, powerful pressures make such cooperation difficult to attain and maintain.

In many respects EUC is a cost-effective, immediate solution to the software backlog, reducing the demands on hard-pressed IS departments. User developed systems should have more relevance, matching more closely user requirements and providing a means of incorporating their knowledge and values into the CBIS. This eliminates the perennial problem of user–analyst communication that undermines traditional requirements analysis, and smooths the final, frequently stressful stages of replacing the old system with the new. It benefits users, increasing their control over both the development process and the shape of the new system, as well as providing an invaluable learning mechanism. The resulting system may be less costly to develop as users can avoid many of the more cumbersome and expensive IS department procedures. There may also be gains for the IS department, who can focus their expertise on key corporate systems, or systems that are technically complex, rather than spending their resources on small, less demanding, but nonetheless time-consuming projects. EUC may actually provide beneficial competition for IS departments, especially those that have grown inefficient through their previous monopoly.

However, the dangers of EUC are equally great, confronting both IS and user management with new challenges. Management problems stem from the prospect of large numbers of users independently developing systems throughout the organization. This highly dispersed activity is likely to run out of control as responsibilities cross boundaries between different user groups, and ensnare the IS department in a web of confusion. These pressures place a potential strain on the organization's structure, in terms of decision-making, budgeting and the provision of support. Without some form of coordination, this disorganized approach to a new and rapidly changing technology may result in continually 'reinventing the wheel'. There is also the worrying prospect of enthusiastic untrained amateurs developing unmaintainable, undocumented computer based systems, and then leaving the organization with no-one who understands them. Furthermore, users who spend excessive amounts of time on CBIS development are doing so at 'opportunity costs' to their own job. There is also the danger that users will develop private information systems that either duplicate or bypass authorized corporate systems.

Without specialist training in systems analysis and design, user-developed systems are likely to be poorly engineered in terms of testing, security, back-up, validation, documentation and audit. Software bugs may not just degrade the user's system but may risk the integrity of corporate data, where these systems link into central databases. As well as being unmaintainable, because of poor design, the user-developed system may well be incompatible with other systems. Users that run into difficulties are likely to approach the IS department, thus further adding to the software backlog. If the IS department is consulted too late to salvage the system, the end result is likely to be considerable resentment on both sides and a significant waste of development effort. On the other hand, the general-purpose nature of much hardware and software means that a large proportion may be recycled elsewhere in the organization.

It may appear that user-developed systems are cheap enough to be financed through the user department's existing budgets, but hidden costs are likely to make the total much greater. The cost of telecommunications, implementation, training, maintenance and general support can far exceed the cost of the hardware and software, that is without taking account of user time spent in developing the system. Overheads may push the initial $5,000 investment for the machine and software towards a total cost as high as $25,000. Furthermore, especially in its early stages, EUC rarely aims at high resource utilization or planned development, raising the prospect of under-utilized equipment and systems that become obsolete as a result of (sometimes predictable) changes in the organizational or technological environment.

The apparently simple notion of EUC actually comprises a wide range of different situations [10], reflecting the gradual evolution of user expertise. Initially, small simple applications are developed by a single user for their own use, but then 'power users' emerge, who are able to develop larger, more complex, mid-range applications. This stage may in turn be followed by 'delegated development', where users (or IS specialists employed within the user department) develop larger, multi-user systems for their colleagues. The final stage sees departments explicitly planning and managing CBIS development.

Non-programming end users   Naive users that only operate systems through menu-driven interfaces;
Command-level end users   More advanced users who can retrieve data and generate their own reports, typically using a fourth generation language or database package;
Programming-level end users   Users that write short programs for their own purposes, in a procedural or non-procedural language;
Functional support personnel   Skilled programmers that support other end users within the user department;
End user support personnel   Information centre staff;
Data processing programmers   Application programmers based within the IS department.

Figure 4.2 Categories of users and developers (from [11])

Each stage requires a different form of support. Thus, user support is not a simple relationship between a single consultant and a group of homogeneous clients; it is a much more complex network of interdependencies [11]. Those involved can be classified into a hierarchy of IT skills, as shown in figure 4.2. Users at each level require a different degree of support, obtaining it from those at lower levels, but they can also provide support to users at higher levels. Support may be provided formally, as part of a person's job description, or informally, perhaps through user groups. The learning process is a dynamic one, such that many users and user groups will pass through different stages of the learning cycle, requiring different support at each stage. Of course, not all individuals or groups will get beyond the early stages and may require a constant level of support for the foreseeable future.

Gerrity and Rockart [12] identify four approaches to EUC. The *monopolist* approach, often the first to be adopted by IS management, firmly retains full control in the hands of the IS department, by minimizing the risks but frustrating user initiatives and achieving fewer benefits. The opposite approach, *laissez-faire*, allows user management to employ their own budgets independently and thus potentially realize both the benefits *and* drawbacks detailed above.

The third approach, and the one used extensively in practice, is that of *information centres*. Originally developed by IBM (Canada) in the 1970s, these are separate units intended to promote, support and control EUC. The information centre becomes a *clearing house* for the development of end user systems, a *shop window* for standard items, and a centre for advice and education. Although the centre requires a relatively high level of resources in terms of modern equipment and attractive surroundings, the key factor on which success largely depends, is the development of new skills and attitudes from the IS staff involved. The change from being producers to becoming advisors and educators involves a fundamental reorientation that is beyond the capability of many IS specialists. Information centres have nevertheless proved popular, especially amongst large US corporations. In most cases, information centres *must* be consulted by users before development or procurement commences. Gradually, if development expertise shifts from the information centre to user departments, the centres, their task completed, can be closed and their remaining support functions returned to the main IS department.

Although preferable to the first two of Gerrity and Rockart's approaches, information centres have drawbacks. They are very much a centralized approach to a localized demand for support. As a general-purpose, largely reactive, support centre, they may not be able to provide the detailed expertise in a particular functional area or the proactive leadership necessary to direct EUC. Gerrity and Rockart advocate a fourth approach, *Managed Free Economy,* that envisages giving users freedom to act within certain guidelines. This requires an explicit end user strategy, a close working partnership with the IS department, and an integrated approach to end user support. Although it is hard to dispute these requirements, achieving them is no mean feat in a situation often characterized by distrust, and organizational manoeuvring for resources and power.

Effective EUC requires a subtle balance between the support and control of users by IS specialists. However, the IS literature is generally much more specific regarding aspects of control (such as project management, quality assurance) and much vaguer regarding support mechanisms. Control seems to fit more closely with the traditional values of IS specialists who, protective of *their* technology, may regard users with distrust and disdain. There is a lack of discussion of the host of non-technical human issues such as health dangers, job design, etc. [13].

The belief that end users should be controlled may rest on a misconception that users constitute enthusiastic amateur programmers, who threaten to swamp the organization with miles of unmaintainable 'spaghetti' code, just as professionals did in the 1970s. While this may be true in a few isolated cases, a more appropriate view is that users acquire sophisticated tools either to perform their jobs more effectively or to enhance their status. Users normally want to learn gradually how to use these tools before tailoring them to encompass more complex activities. Thus, EUC should be regarded as an evolutionary learning process, not as a traditional systems development cycle and not as part of programmer training. Although the concern felt by IS specialists may be based partly on genuine worries that users will develop unnecessary, poorly engineered systems, there may also be a distinct fear of losing organizational power, even their very jobs, as their monopoly fades into history.

The changing role of the IS department

The growth of end user computing and the growing centrality of CBIS to organizational functions has significant consequences for the role of the IS department. The traditional role of producing isolated computerized systems was peripheral to the main business of the organization. This role comprised the functions of application systems development, operations, technical services and administration [14]. The operations function consisted of providing a mainframe-based data processing service, supported by the technical services function that maintained the hardware and systems software. The administration function covered IS department planning and budgeting, staff management and training, and the development of standards. The new IS role is much broader and more complex, comprising three main functions: the provision and maintenance of the information systems infrastructure of the organization; the support of end user computing; and a long term research and planning function. This places the IS department much more within the mainstream of the organization.

The new *infrastructure* function centres around the development and operation of the network of corporate systems that cross departmental boundaries, and the involvement in interorganizational systems. This infrastructure links together departments and provides communication with suppliers, customers and external services. The aim is to provide reliable, secure and cost-effective services to user departments, through the use of networks, central databases and central main-frame computers. The growing demands mean that capacity planning is becoming more important, to ensure that the infrastructure can cope with fluctuating levels of traffic. Such fluctuations have to be catered for if service quality is not to deteriorate, at a point when the users themselves are under most pressure. Capacity planning implies monitoring the usage and performance of both whole systems and individual components (e.g. disk drives). The requirement for a secure infrastructure implies the provision of procedures for error detection and correction, back-up and recovery, as well as access control to all parts of the systems. This function also extends to the secure archiving of old files. Maintenance, including both enhancements and trouble-shooting, requires a short–medium term planning horizon if it is to cope with day-to-day problems and planned upgrades.

The management of this infrastructure requires a more sophisticated approach than traditional operations management. It has to incorporate the demands of both network management and database management within the notion of providing a range of services to users (e.g. electronic mail). This provision of services is becoming an increasingly important part of the IS role, implying that the complexities of the underlying technology should remain hidden and the service element emphasized. Thus, there is a need for IS departments to replace the previous technical culture with much more of a service culture.

In answer to the pressure towards end user computing, the *user support* function centres around the provision of advice and education. This is supported by the evaluation of new products by the information centre staff and the availability of demonstration systems and a full range of documentation. Typically, advice to users includes a strong element of persuasion to adopt organizational standards in terms of hardware, software, development methods, and data handling. Formal (or informal) consultancy services should help the user, firstly, to conceptualize the problem, secondly, to select an appropriate technology, thirdly, to design a solution and finally, to implement the solution. However, the effective delivery of such consultancy is highly dependent upon the availability of a sufficient number of well-trained IS staff. Where departments cannot, or will not, develop their own systems, the IS department will retain its traditional systems development function. The training of users may be provided internally through the information centre, which gives the opportunities to develop the training within the specific context of the organization's needs, as well as increasing user motivation by emphasizing the objectives of the organ-ization with regard to technology. However, it is often simpler and more cost-effective to utilize external courses.

Long term research and planning should be separated from day-to-day operation and short term development. This function includes IS strategy and policy formulation and long term planning, applied to the organization's infrastructure and applications portfolio, rather than the detailed planning of individual systems. Studies may include the investigation of the appropriateness and feasibility of large-scale technological changes at the level of the organization. This implies a concern with the broad problems of technology transfer rather than the narrow pragmatism associated with the implementation of an individual system. The concern should be the implications for the business in terms of profitability, structure and human resource development. This is an area where there is a dearth of IS expertise, that no increase in the number of technical computer scientists will alleviate.

Make or buy?

An increasing concern is the extent to which organizations should develop and operate information systems themselves (*in-house*) or buy in services. Externally produced software packages and information services have become increasingly more sophisticated and cost-effective, compared to in-house development. Buying in is usually considerably simpler and, for many requirements, there is a large range of products from which to choose. Buying in tends to reduce uncertainty, as the price and service level is usually guaranteed; it gives organizations access to specialized skills; and represents less commitment from internal staff. However, there are two serious drawbacks to buying in: the lack of control over the evolving system and the loss of internal technical expertise in the particular area. A combination of buying in and end user computing can lead the IS department to become largely composed of generalists, increasing the organization's dependence upon outsiders. This situation closes a well-trodden IS career path, which may exacerbate long-standing problems of IS staff recruitment and retention. Furthermore, bought-in packages or services are usually highly general; as they are not tailored to the individual organization, they may be not only less efficient, but also less effective than in-house products. For highly confidential applications, they represent increased vulnerability, with outsiders possessing an ominous understanding of the operation of the software and the way that sensitive data is stored.

Perhaps the most extreme example of buying in is the growing practice of *facilities management*, where the operation of some or all of an organization's routine information systems are contracted out to a third party. This partial return to the traditional bureau services of the 1960s is fast becoming a sizeable market; in the UK it is reported to be approaching £1 billion. The rationale for facilities management resembles that for other bought-in services, with the supplier offering expertise and a guaranteed price and service level. A proportion of the supplier's economies of scale can be passed onto the user organization in terms of savings of perhaps 15-20 per cent over in-house operating costs. In an environment characterized by a shortage of skilled staff and fluctuating demand, this becomes an attractive proposition. In theory, it also allows the user's IS department to concentrate on long term, strategic issues, rather than using its energies 'fire-fighting' day-to-day operating problems.

The risks to the user organization from facilities management centre on the resultant loss of control of its information systems, especially to a powerful single supplier. This loss of control may constrain the organization's freedom to direct its information systems to its own advantage, as well as increasing its vulnerability from a security viewpoint. Usually, some or all of the user organization's IS staff will be transferred to the facilities management supplier. The IS staff may favour this option from the perspective of career prospects, but it is hard to see it as other than a vote of no confidence in the IS department by user management. Even with certain services hived out, there is a continuing need to monitor the supplier's performance. In practice, there may be disputes about exactly which work is covered by the contract. While the move towards facilities management is often justifiable on cost-efficiency grounds, it hardly squares with the notion that information systems are a key corporate resource.

The role of the chief information officer

The changing role of the IS department is reflected in management changes at the top of the IS function. The technically oriented Data Processing Manager of the 1960s and 1970s was largely superseded by the more generalist Information Systems Manager of the 1980s. Both of these were relatively divorced from senior user management, often reporting to the Chief Finance Officer (CFO). However, in large, information-intensive organizations, such as airlines and banks, the head of the IS department is now being given the title of Chief Information Officer (CIO), or IT Director, with a corresponding rise in status.

In some organizations, the CIO has been raised to a level equal to the CFO, becoming an integral member of the senior management team. They may report directly to the Chief Executive Officer (or Managing Director) and have a seat on the board. The rationale for this rise in status comes from a growing recognition of the importance of information systems to the whole organization. A senior manager is now required to oversee IS planning and strategy formulation, and to maximize the organization's often considerable investment in information technology. Furthermore, a serious conflict of interest is likely if, on the one hand, the CIO is charged with providing a high level of service to the whole organization, and on the other he reports to the head of just one user department, the CFO. In such situations, there is a strong argument for placing the CIO at the same level as the heads of the main user departments.

The CIO has to straddle the divide between the technical arena of information systems and the rest of the organization, represented by the non-technical senior user managers. The major part of this role is in the field of long term strategy and planning. The CIO not only has the difficult task of integrating the IS plan with the business plan, but should also contribute to the formulation of the overall business plan, as part of the senior management team. The CIO is expected to be proactive, suggesting application areas for the introduction of particular technologies, and generally promoting the use of IT at senior levels. He also has the responsibility of overseeing the management of the organization's IS/IT resources, including coordination with important user departments that may possess considerable IT resources.

To fulfil this new role, CIOs require a complex balance of skills. Firstly, they must have a sound understanding of business management, in order to link IS with business needs and to advise on strategic opportunities and planning. Secondly, they must have a good knowledge of technology management and a grasp of the potential of information technology, in order to develop appropriate IT policies. Thirdly, they must have expertise in departmental management, in order to organize a growing function in such a way as to motivate specialist personnel, while at the same time controlling costs that threaten to explode out of control. Finally, in order to forge a working partnership with user departments, the CIO requires a high level of communication and political skills. Thus, compared to five or ten years ago, there is an increased need for business and organizational skills, and these skills are exceedingly difficult to 'teach' to technical managers.

This elevation of the CIO may not be accepted easily by the traditionally strong user departments. The CIO may be seen as an interloping technologist, who not only seeks to control an increasing proportion of the working arrangements of the other departments, through policies of standardization etc., but also to dilute their organizational power from this new status. However, in practice, many CIOs do not possess technical backgrounds; a 1986 UK survey reported that 30 per cent had general management backgrounds. This sizeable cross-over from general management to IS management is not apparent in the opposite direction. Very few technical IS managers seem to have either the skills or the desire to manage other departments. To meet the need for *hybrid* CIOs, it is increasingly common to train general managers in IT skills rather than the other way around. The technical component is thus considered less important, with technical advice obtainable from the second tier of IS management. With the exception of certain charismatic individuals, the chances of a person working their way up through the IS ranks to the post of CIO are not great. It is hard to predict the reactions of IS specialists to this loss of the organizational 'high ground'; a loss they have never really occupied in the majority of organizations.

The appointment of a high-level CIO is certainly not appropriate for all organizations. In terms of McFarlan & McKenney's strategic grid, organizations whose IS departments are in the 'factory' or 'support' situation probably require an IS manager with a fairly technical bias to manage the department. The post of CIO is relevant where information systems are already more central to organizations, or are becoming more central, i.e. in the 'strategic' and 'turnaround' situations respectively.

The changing structure of information systems

Centralization versus decentralization

The extent to which information systems should be centralized or decentralized has been a perennial debate, almost since computers first arrived in organizations. Traditionally, the discussion centred on technical functions, such as processing and data storage. Systems management and systems development was tagged on largely as an afterthought. Early CBIS were mostly highly centralized due to the constraints of the fledgling technology, and the fact that companies owned just one machine. Centralized systems were initially easier to control and could achieve cost-efficiencies through economies of scale. *Grosch's Law* exemplified this early thinking; it claimed that computing power was proportional to the square of the cost of the processor, favouring ever larger central mainframes. However, by the late 1970s, advances in both processor and network technology, and the associated development of distributed systems, had invalidated this 'law'.

An important benefit of distributed systems is that they can be designed to fit the organization's preferred operating and management structure, relatively free from technological constraints. Hence the centralization debate has shifted towards management and organizational issues. The changing role of the IS department and the proliferation of interdependent systems have complicated the demands placed on the IS management structure. The traditional debate treated information systems in isolation from the rest of the organization; this may have been appropriate in the 1960s, but it is clearly no longer the case. It is evidently foolhardy to discuss the structure of a system that permeates an entire organization without considering the underlying organizational structure.

Before discussing the relative merits of centralization and decentralization, it is essential to recognize that we are dealing with a rather complex, ambiguous concept. King [14] distinguishes three separate perspectives through which it is relevant to discuss centralization. The first, *location,* concerns the physical siting of the equipment, but as the price falls and the hardware multiplies, this becomes less of an issue. King's second perspective, *control,* refers to the organizational level at which decision-making takes place. Centralized control implies that decision-making is concentrated at senior levels of the organization while decentralized control means that decisions are taken at various levels. The third perspective, *structure,* refers to whether responsibility is 'centralized' within the IS department or 'decentralized' to user departments: this is the end user computing debate discussed above. Another complicating factor is that IS functions are extremely varied; Earl [15] distinguishes between *operations, development* and *direction,* arguing that certain functions should be centralized and others decentralized, depending upon the particular situation. Considering the interdependencies between these functions, a balance must be struck in every case. With today's complex, interconnecting, organizational information systems, centralization–decentralization should be treated very much as a continuum, exhibiting degrees of centralization, rather than a dichotomous choice.

Centralization has a number of advantages in terms of the coordination of the activities of separate functional units. Centralization improves the prospects for standardization and integration, reducing the problems of incompatibility, and facilitates the monitoring of costs and performance. It tends to promote continuity, albeit at the cost of excessive bureaucracy in an atmosphere of remoteness in decision-making. The improved coordination serves as a cost-efficient approach to resource utilization, aimed at reducing wastage, duplication and sub-optimization (optimizing an individual sub-system at the expense of the total organizational system). For IS department staff, a centralized operation probably offers greater career opportunities, allowing them to engage in a variety of projects, as well as to develop expertise in a particular technical area. Not only is it easier to recruit and retain IS staff, it is also easier to reallocate staff to cover vacancies and thus alleviate the problems of a high staff turnover. Central-ization also eases some security considerations; for example, it is often easier to protect the integrity of data through strict central access control. Experience suggests that centralization is an appropriate approach where resources are costly and usage is relatively limited.

There are various pressures currently pushing towards greater centralization, including increasing demands from senior management to control expanding IS budgets and a growing desire of IS staff for a professional career structure. The need to manage the increased complexity of applications and the growing security threat, also point towards strengthened central control and coordination. In addition, the increasing need to share data favours more standardization and integration. Finally, the growing complexity of the technology demands a greater level of technical specialization within organizations; a function that is usually maintained centrally.

On the other hand, decentralization has equally powerful advantages, especially the opportunity for increased motivation and involvement, through the distribution of autonomy and responsibility. A decentralized approach, with its bottom-up orientation, is much closer to the people on the ground (users and IS staff). Decentralization encourages usage by inspiring feelings of local ownership and control; the technology is situated close to its users and is, in many senses, *theirs*. Whilst concentrating less on the narrow cost-efficient utilization of the technology, decentralization potentially offers gains in user effectiveness and user productivity, through a greater exploitation of the technology. Where local sites are responsible for their own IT budgets, cost-efficient usage is strongly encouraged rather than imposed by *diktat*. Decentralization can mean simpler systems tailored to users' requirements. Decentralized systems are typically more flexible, being easier to extend, improve and change in the face of changing requirements. Local IS staff develop increased expertise in application areas and are more likely to build up better relationships with users, thus becoming more responsive and providing an improved level of service. In general, a decentralized approach is preferable where equipment is cheap and usage is heavy and varied.

The current pressures towards decentralization, in the shape of the explosion of end user computing and the proliferation of low cost technology renders excessive centralization untenable. Also, growing user knowledge and the existing software development backlog are pushing in the same direction. Decentralization is really the only justifiable approach towards an innovative and effective use of new technology, with creative individuals demanding a say in the management of their technological working environment. Excessive standardization fails to encourage creativity; creative, high pay-off, applications are rarely the norm. Open public standards perpetually seem to be arriving 'any day now' and the diverse needs of individuals cannot be dealt with satisfactorily by a bureaucratic IS department frightened to leave the safety of standardization. Across many industries, there is a growing movement towards a general decentralization of control and responsibility in the management of organizations. This can be seen in the breaking up of large bureaucratic organizations into smaller companies or individual profit centres: 'small is beautiful'.

The traditional debate mistakenly assumes, that a 'rational consensus' will emerge easily; that once the optimal structure is discovered, then all the various groups and departments within the organization will accept it. In this book, we emphasize a more realistic, pluralist approach that interprets organizations as a collection of groups, each with their own (often conflicting) goals in terms of power and the acquisition of resources and status. Thus, there is unlikely to be an overall consensus supporting an optimal solution. Information and information technology are *political* resources within the body politic that characterize most organizations. Thus, inter-group conflict is likely, in respect of setting priorities for systems development and in the control of the technology and systems. In many cases, the centralization–decentralization debate is more likely to be decided on the basis of political power, rather than efficiency and effectiveness, although the latter notions will appear frequently in the political arguments: "The rational elements are tools used by participants to gain new ground or to protect ground already won. They also serve as authoritative facades that mask political motives and legitimize self-interest" [4].

This issue of the location of control of information systems is one of the most important facing the IS profession. In most cases, the key factors affecting the degree of centralization are likely to be non-technological rather than technological. There is a pressing need to fit into the organizational structure favoured by the particular firm, which largely stems from the organizational culture (the traditions and values of the organization) and current business pressures. Some organizations have a history of decentralization, others have always been more bureaucratic and centralized. The actual and potential usage of the system, in terms of the size and homogeneity of user demands, is of prime importance, while factors such as the size of the firm and the characteristics of the industry may also be influential.

Excessive centralization or excessive decentralization conjure up nightmares of frightening proportions and an intermediate position seems inevitable. Organizations need to develop policies that produce a large measure of decentralization, but within a framework of central guidelines. This balance is very difficult to achieve in practice, and there are no easy answers; the issue comes down to a question of judgement in individual situations. In general, the overall direction, plans and priorities should be determined, or at least approved, centrally, but with the involvement of local sites (including user departments). Normally the centre should be responsible for major procurement and the development of organization-wide systems, as well as maintaining a strong monitoring role to oversee the activities of local sites. The highly specialized technical functions, such as systems programming and network management, should generally remain centralized, but as many as possible of the other functions should be decentralized. Thus wherever feasible, local sites should be responsible for the development and control of local systems, but within guidelines and standards set centrally. However, the rigour of these central guidelines will depend upon the particular organization. The degree of centralization adopted (or attempted) is a matter of negotiation. This should reflect both present and future organizational realities, existent in terms of structures that are managerially desirable, and that are also acceptable to both staff, customers and suppliers. The conflict between centralization and decentralization is just another manifestation of the age-old need to balance order against freedom. Functions and systems are interdependent and there will always remain a disputed middle ground.

Functional management versus product management

This is a further intrinsic tension. A functional structure, with staff grouped according to job title (e.g. applications programmers, systems analysts), does not suit the nature of teams involved in IS development. Rigid divisions between specialists working on the same project lead to poor coordination. The absence of a single strong individual, responsible for the management of an entire project, allows projects to run out of control, there being no obvious person for users to approach with queries or complaints. From this perspective, a project structure is preferable, with staff organized into project teams, each led by a project manager and consisting of a mixture of specialists.

Organization by project team benefits the individual project, improving effectiveness and leading to better relations with users. The main difficulties with this type of organization are skill utilization and team stability. Rigid project teams result in valuable specialists, such as network experts, being employed on general duties (e.g. writing COBOL routines for a payroll program) because of the demands of the particular project. Additionally, projects vary so much that the team membership is bound to be unstable, such that teams need to re-form with different skill mixes between each project. If teams develop separately, it is harder to maintain standardization of methods, and switching staff between teams becomes a non-trivial operation, and leads to difficulties in integrating systems developed by different teams. Project teams tend to encourage IS staff to develop either general skills or skills applicable to a single application area, rather than encouraging functional specialists. This may not be in the best interests of the organization. A functional structure, with each group of specialists relatively segregated, eases the development of standards and tends to produce specialists. This gives a clearer career structure for each function.

The solution to this tension between the two forms of organization proved to be a combination of both forms into a matrix structure. Project teams, led by project managers, are superimposed onto a functional structure, in order to gain the benefits of each approach. The main drawback, apart from adding complexity, is that IS staff have two supervisors, each with conflicting interests: the functional manager concerned with efficient staff utilization, and the project manager concerned with project completion.

The situation is exacerbated by the growing complexity of the technology, leading to more opportunities for specialization; for example, systems security and multi-media requirements were rarely treated separately in the past. On the other hand, the popularity of small systems has resulted in a merging of skills in the shape of analyst-programmers. The growing service role of the IS department has not ended the debate; the choice is now between a functional structure and a product structure, where teams develop and support individual products or services in particular areas. For example, teams may be formed for office systems or sales order processing, and may be based either within the IS department or within user departments. Once again, some form of matrix organization may be appropriate or else a mixture of functional and product management, depending upon the characteristics of the particular situation. Thus, another balance has to be struck, that can only be achieved by management on the spot weighing up the opportunities and risks of various alternatives. This 'messiness', or ambiguity, is an inherent feature of today's IS management.

Functional Unit	*Responsibility*
Operations	Corporate systems
Telecommunications	Network provision
Technical support	Hardware & systems software
Database administration	Corporate databases
Systems development	Corporate & critical systems software tools
Internal consultancy	Feasibility studies; external services; information centre; IS marketing
Training	End user & IS staff training
Strategy	Planning & monitoring technology diffusion
Research & development	New technologies; forecasting
Administration	Accounts; personnel management
EUC units (within user departments)	User support & development

Figure 4.3 A large IS department in the 1990s

IS departments through the 1990s

IS departments of this decade are likely to be very different from their predecessors. They are likely to be larger, more complex, and flatter than the previous narrow, hierarchical structures. Although IS departments are likely to vary considerably in structure, because of the requirements of particular organizations, it is still instructive to consider an example (figure 4.3).

The infrastructure function is provided by the operations, telecommunications, technical support, and database administration units, supporting the hardware, software, networks, and database aspects of the infrastructure. The systems development unit develops and maintains the corporate systems that make up the infrastructure and other critical systems. This unit also distributes software tools, such as development environments, for use throughout the organization. The user support function is catered for by the internal consultancy unit and the training unit. The former markets internal and external information services to user departments, and acts as the information centre. The long term planning and research function is provided by a separate strategy unit and a research and development unit. In addition, there is an administrative unit that supports the rest of the IS department in respect of budgets, personnel management etc. Finally, there are the various EUC units located within user departments.

In the 1990s, IS departments are likely to be subject to frequent change; temporary units may be established to support particular initiatives and IS staff will be ambiguously located within both IS and user departments. The overall direction will be service focused, and will encompass multiple technologies, rather than just computers. IS will be characterized by a combination of specialists and support units, organized in a complex blend of function, product and matrix styles. Control will be distributed both vertically, through the management levels, and horizontally, between the IS department and users. However, the exact mixture will depend upon the circumstances and demands of the individual organization.

Conclusion

The organization of the IS function must be adapted to reflect the changing role of information systems within the organization, and especially the growth of end user computing. This realignment and restructuring takes place within an organizational environment of political interests. Senior user management, together with IS management must negotiate a new order, a blend of centralization and decentralization, that meets the requirements of the organization in terms of providing an effective information infrastructure supporting computer-based applications that fit their organizational niches. The goal is fairly clear, but the detailed organizational design and the tactics required to reach the goal are highly dependent upon the awareness and skill of individual managers and the unique combination of factors prevailing at the time.

Discussion issues

1. Discuss the likely internal transitional problems as a traditional IS department begins to change its role and structure (as outlined in this chapter).
2. Discuss the changing role and structure of the IS department in the light of the political forces operating in the organizational environment.
3. Interpret the organizational forces described here in terms of systems thinking, in particular relating to our interpretation of disposition, variety, strategy and tactics.

Exercises

1. Using role play, as a group act out a meeting between the IS managers and user managers to discuss the extension of end user computing. Try to place yourself fully in the role that you are playing, and try to imagine what your character feels about the issues raised at the meeting. It may be worth video-taping the final version of the meeting.
2. By visiting users, perhaps starting with your company's or college's Computer Services Department, try to depict the existing IS organizational structure and compare it with the position five and ten years ago.

References

1. Attewell, P. & Rule, J.,'Computing and organizations: What we know and what we don't know', *Communications of the ACM*, 27(12), 1184-1192, 1984.
2. Bjorn-Andersen, N., Eason, K. & Robey, D., *Managing computer impact: an international study of management and organizations*, Ablex, NJ, 1986.
3. Markus, M.L. & Bjorn-Andersen, N.,'Power over users: Its exercise by system professionals', *Communications of the ACM*, 30(6), 498-504, 1987.
4. Franz, C. & Robey,D.,'An investigation of user-led system design: Rational and political perspectives', *Communications of the ACM*, 27(12), 1202-1209, 1984.
5. Kling, R. & Iacono, S.,'The control of information systems development after implementation', *Communications of the ACM*, 27(12), 1218-1226, 1984.
6. Gouldner, A.W., *Wildcat Strike*, Routledge & Kegan Paul, London, 1955.
7. Keen, P.G.W.,'Information systems and organizational change', *Communications of the ACM*, 24(1), 24-33, 1981.
8. F.M. Cornford, *Microscosmographia Academica*, Bowes & Bowes, London, 1908.
9. Markus, M.L.,'Power, politics and MIS implementation', *Communications of the ACM*, 26(6), 430-444, 1983.
10. Panko, R.R., *End user computing: management, applications, and technology*, Wiley, New York, 1988.
11. Rockart, J.F. & Flannery, L.S.,'The management of end user computing', *Communications of the ACM*, 26(10), 776-784, 1983.
12. Gerrity, T.P. & Rockart, J.F.,'End user computing: Are you a leader or a laggard?', *Sloan Management Review*, 25-34, Summer 1986.
13. Smithson, S.C. & Hirschheim, R.A.,'End-user computing and the user-system interface: a five-level framework', in: Kaiser, K.M. & Oppelland, H.J. (eds.), Desktop information technology, North Holland, Amsterdam, 1990.
14. King, J.L.,'Centralized versus decentralized computing: Organizational considerations and management options', *Computing Surveys*, Vol.15, No.4, 319-349, 1983.
15. Earl, M.J., *Management strategies for information technology*, Chapter 7, Prentice Hall, Hemel Hempstead, UK, 1989.

Suggested reading

The organizational environment

Crozier, M., *The Bureaucratic Phenomenon*, Tavistock Publications, 1964.

Handy, C.B., *Understanding Organizations*, 2nd ed., Chapter 6, Penguin, Harmondsworth, Middx., 1981.

Resistance to change

Hirschheim, R.A. & Newman, M.,'Information systems and user resistance: Theory and practice', *Computer Journal*, Vol. 31, No.5, 398-408, 1988.

Keen, P.G.W.,'Information systems and organizational change', *Communications of the ACM*, 24(1), 24-33, 1981.

Markus, M.L.,'Power, politics and MIS implementation', *Communications of the ACM*, 26(6), 430-444, 1983.

End user computing

Panko, R.R., *End User Computing: Management, Applications, and Technology*, Wiley, New York, 1988.

Role of the IS department

Zmud, R.W.,'Design alternatives for organizing information systems activities', *MIS Quarterly*, Vol.8, No.2, 79-93, 1984.

IS departmental structure

Earl, M.J., *Management Strategies for Information Technology*, Chapter 7, Prentice-Hall, Hemel Hempstead, UK, 1989.

King, J.L.,'Centralized versus decentralized computing: Organizational considerations and management options', *Computing Surveys*, Vol.15, No.4, 319-349, 1983.

5 Information technology and information systems

- *Trends in information technology*
- *Transaction processing systems*
- *From transaction processing to IS crisis*

In discussing computer-based information systems (CBIS), due regard must be paid to the underlying (information) technology. Much has been written about the 'IT Revolution', eulogizing the advances made in hardware, software and telecommunications. Managers, however, should beware the seductiveness of 'progress', as identified by technocrats, and should avoid becoming enmeshed in the intricacies of the technology. It is overly simplistic to claim that the development of CBIS has been solely technology driven, but it would be equally naive to neglect its key role in influencing the pace and direction of development. In this chapter, we shall briefly, but critically, highlight some of the main trends in information technology in order to provide a technological backdrop for the subsequent discussion of information systems.

Before discussing the more contemporary CBIS (database systems, network services and office information systems) in the following chapters, we shall briefly examine their forerunners, transaction processing systems, which still provide the foundation of modern CBIS. From this historical starting point, we shall demonstrate, through a number of real examples, many of the problems and pitfalls that have occurred in the introduction of information systems.

Trends in information technology

Various authors (e.g. Forester [1]) have documented the impressive technical advances in information technology, in terms of increasing performance and reliability with decreasing size and cost, together with the possible implications for organizations and society. It is not our intention to repeat their analysis; rather, this brief sketch serves as a reminder of the considerable achievements while bringing the discussion down to earth by reconsidering the claimed benefits in the light of information systems practice.

A frequently quoted analogy emphasizing the achievements of IT in cost–performance since 1950 is the comparison with developments in the motor car. Had they enjoyed the same technical advances, a Rolls-Royce would now only cost $2.00, and have a power rating equal to that of the QE2 cruise liner, whilst its fuel consumption would have dropped to three million miles per gallon, and its size reduced to 0.16 of a pin-head. Whilst such comparisons are not intended to be taken seriously, the following underlying trends are real enough.

Increase in raw computing power

The impressive advances made in microprocessor technology have become part of modern folklore, as increasing amounts of raw processing power have become available, increasingly cheaply. Whilst the power, in terms of MIPS (millions of instructions per second) or RAM (random access memory), of today's desktop microcomputers would have staggered commentators of twenty years ago, it should be remembered that it is the effective application of that power that is the true importance. In most organizations, examples can be found of such processing power being wasted; for example, the provision of high-performance workstations for simple word processing, or where processing power has been allocated to individuals on the basis of status rather than need. In December 1989 a UK government department scrapped a £300,000 ($500,000) minicomputer system, featuring word processing, spreadsheets, graphics and database management, in favour of a simple word processing package running on networked micro-computers – the users had no need for the other facilities.

There is a thin line between the provision of resources based on sensible estimates of future requirements and the circumstance where *Parkinson's Law* operates, with work expanding to consume all available resources. In considering the increased availability of computing power, it should be recognized that these resources can be consumed very easily by the demands of sophisticated graphics-based software or the response time required from large transaction processing systems. Operators of very large systems, such as airlines, can testify that computing power remains a scarce resource despite the gains of the past years.

Increase in storage capacity

Similarly, there has been a considerable increase in secondary storage capacity; mainframe magnetic disk drives (e.g. IBM 3380) can now hold 2.5 gigabytes of information, whilst mass storage systems, comprising a 'honeycomb' of tape cartridges, hold 440 gigabytes. For microcomputers, magnetic disks are available with capacities of hundreds of megabytes, as well as optical CD-ROM disks,

Compact Disk - Read Only Memory, with a capacity of 550 megabytes. All these capacities are large, and getting larger.

However, the techniques for managing both the vast quantities of information and the complexity of their interrelationships, have not kept pace with the physical possibilities. The problems of retrieval and of conceptual design will concern us in the following chapter, but even the apparently straightforward management of the physical file can cause problems. Users often fail to appreciate the cost of keeping data online (approximately $25,000 per gigabyte per annum), and as their files are 'out of sight, out of mind', the amount of data held on disks has been growing geometrically at up to 50 per cent per annum. The sheer volume of data held online provides food for thought; one large UK building society (S&L) has 600 gigabytes, and one of the major UK banks retains 2.1 terabytes requiring a staff of thirty people to manage it. Thus, despite the apparent availability of cheap online storage, the situation remains a serious, although a somewhat different, problem.

Increasing diversity

There is a considerable diversity of computers, ranging from liquid-cooled supercomputers, costing several million dollars, through mainframes, mini-computers, workstations and microcomputers, down to relatively inexpensive pocket-sized machines. Corresponding diversity is to be found in other components, both hardware and software. In addition to the traditional keyboard, input devices include various pointing devices, such as the mouse, light-pen, data-glove, and finger-ring, as well as various optical scanners and voice input. Output devices encompass printers, screens of varying resolution, and voice output. There is a larger choice in systems software, and an ever increasing range of programming languages and software development tools. The attractions of ready-packaged software have resulted in its being made available in large numbers across countless applications. There are few trades or professions that do not support a majority of their functions with a wide range of alternative computerized systems. Although such diversity has increased the opportunities for tailoring a system to a particular business situation, it has also increased the risk of complexity, by extending the number of alternatives beyond what could, or should be handled, and by connecting together incompatible hardware and software. Purists will argue that the scope of this diversity is limited; most processors still follow the basic Von Neumann architecture, and the data structures used by programs are necessarily limited. However, the structures, even built upon such simple foundations, enable numerous links between a system and its environment and clearly increase combinatorial complexity.

There has also been a considerable diversity and specialization amongst the users, developers and suppliers of information technology and services. Many end users have become highly expert in particular applications or systems. New jobs have emerged within IS departments, such as database administrators and network specialists. Although the need for ever greater investment in research and development favours larger corporations, considerable scope remains for innovative ideas from small companies and for specialist expertise from medium-sized niche suppliers. Thus the price of diversity is that the market, products and actors have become more complex, and the effort needed to keep abreast of technical and commercial developments correspondingly greater.

Falling prices

As the price per instruction executed or per byte of data stored has tumbled impressively, the move towards one computer per desk has led to a dramatic increase in the number of computers in organizations. Together with continuing demands for more powerful machines, this has produced a considerable overall increase in organizations' IT budgets. But the falls in unit costs of hardware and packaged software have not been accompanied by corresponding falls in unit costs of training, implementation, and maintenance, demand for which has increased considerably. The tools and techniques for in-house software development may well have improved the productivity of programming tasks, but again total budgets are increasing in the face of increased demand.

Increasing functionality and flexibility

Developments have led to a tremendous extension of tasks and applications that can be attempted using CBIS, creating a well-publicized impression that, no matter what the problem, the solution is IT. This is dangerously misleading as IT can be irrelevant or even positively harmful to the complex amalgam of commercial, social and organizational problems constantly faced by management.

IT tools are becoming increasingly flexible in their manner of use. This is a mixed blessing; for instance, the increasing number of text fonts available for word processing has resulted in greater choice, but also in *fontitis*, where the use of many different fonts in a single document renders it virtually unreadable. Similarly a large range of colours are often used thoughtlessly in screen displays, and readers infer meaning into the choice of colours, where none exists.

The opportunities offered by the increased functionality and flexibility have to be set against the drawbacks of increased complexity. This is especially true of software, where the larger, more complex and sophisticated packages have become increasingly difficult to develop and test, which in turn has led to development delays and yet more program 'bugs' in delivered software. Despite the general improvements in user-friendliness, the added scale and complexity means that software is now much more difficult to learn and use.

Increasing user-friendliness

To achieve widespread acceptance, CBIS have had to be both useful and usable from the perspective of inexperienced end users. The growing sophistication and power of hardware and software provide speed and functionality, but without some form of intervention, they can form unmanageably complex systems, usable only by a few highly skilled individuals. The appearance of 'user-friendly' systems, partly or wholly based on WIMP (Windows, Icons, Mice and Pull-down menus) technology offers one resolution to this complexity. There is a growing trend towards *direct manipulation* [3]. Instead of memorizing arcane command languages, a graphical desktop interface enable users to point at screen icons with a mouse, thereby selecting commands from the menus provided.

The price of increased user-friendliness is the extra hardware resources required to support sophisticated interfaces, and certain design trade-offs. Designers have emphasized the virtues of consistency, simplicity, visibility, familiarity, and adaptability. However, all these apparently worthy aims have their darker sides. A consistent interface, where similar actions are carried out in similar ways, reduces learning but can lead to dull uniformity. Simplicity is rarely obtainable with complex, multi-functional systems. The visibility of objects of interest may merely deteriorate into screen clutter, in the same way that a mouse adds to the clutter of the 'real' desktop. Familiarity can lead to misleading metaphors; for example, users may not be able to retrieve documents from the 'desktop' wastebasket in the same way they can from the real one. Finally, adaptability too often results in a larger command set and yet more complexity.

At times, such interfaces act as a barrier between the user and the stored data and programs, giving a misplaced illusion of control. For example, the fact of an icon appearing on a screen may not signify that the file, or the program it represents, is complete or the most up-to-date version – an earlier user error may not have been detected. Although user-friendly interfaces are becoming commonplace, users should not be seduced into thinking that merely moving a mouse around somehow transforms a difficult problem into a simple one.

Shift of control to the users

Whereas, in the early days of computing, the hardware was located in special air-conditioned rooms, the technology is now more often located within the users' offices. As discussed in Chapter 4, this movement of machinery out of the IS department has been accompanied by a shift in control away from IS specialists to the user departments. End user computing has transformed the agenda for the management of information systems.

Improved connectivity

Communication is an essential part of so much information processing. The electronic manipulation of information on a single stand-alone machine offers certain benefits, but the ability to link machines and packages electronically greatly amplifies both the opportunities and risks. However, although connectivity has the potential to improve communication, it may also be irrelevant, as when communication is not required, and it can be damaging if the communication tasks divert staff away from more directly productive work, or if it serves to inflame conflict within the organization. In addition, improved connectivity can lower the organization's defence, exposing it to significant security risks.

The focus of this book is not information technology, and so we shall now turn our attention to information systems, starting with the oldest type of computer based information systems (CBIS), transaction processing systems.

Transaction processing systems

This type of system traces its origins back to the earliest commercial applications of computers. In the 1950s and early 1960s this comprised batch processing of punched cards and magnetic tape; disk-based, online real-time processing only appeared in the late 1960s. Transaction processing systems are characterized by the simple processing of highly structured data; payroll, accounts receivable, order entry, stock control and airline reservations. The processing algorithms are routine, deterministic and well understood, and there is no ambiguity in the goals of the system; for example, clear rules are laid down in terms of contracts of work for payroll decisions. Apart from some early 'glitches', when domestic water bills of $200,000 made newspaper headlines and when corporations became embarrassed when their systems threatened customers with legal action when the amount owed was $0.00, in general, transaction processing systems have been particularly successful. They enable the inherent benefits of computer-based systems to be achieved: speed and accuracy applied to large quantities of data. They can be programmed to produce simple reports to support the day-to-day operational control of organizations. Significant changes in organizational structure have resulted, with many clerical workers displaced by the automation of repetitive tasks. Many organizations rely totally on these systems for their routine 'bread and butter' processing. However, it may be the case that the benefits of such systems have been subsumed in an excess of less useful but much more high profile and technically prestigious (and expensive) IT projects. Because of the problem of evaluation, it is very difficult to demonstrate the benefits of information systems conclusively. Some managers feel that the '80-20 rule' applies: 80 per cent of the benefit results from 20 per cent of the investment in IT. Whilst not as technologically exciting as, say, artificial intelligence, transaction processing systems have provided many years of invaluable service.

Considerable expertise has been developed in the tasks associated with this simple data processing. The inherent problem of *'garbage in, garbage out'*, whereby inaccurate results are produced from errors in data input, has been addressed by data collection controls and verification procedures. Some, but by no means all, worries about efficiency that result from the sheer amount of data, have been partly resolved through advances in file processing techniques. A good instance of the objectives and operation of a modern transaction processing system is that of the Trans World Airlines reservation system [4]. This particular system has successfully grown to accommodate electronic mail, baggage control and hotel reservations, in addition to simple seat reservations. However, other systems, each initially with a single function, have proved too difficult to be integrated. Where such integration is necessary, IS management is faced with difficult questions – should a totally new multi-functional system be developed from scratch, risking considerable upheaval as well as introducing fresh system 'bugs'? Alternatively, should one of the present systems be extended? And if so, which one? There are no easy answers; managers must decide according to the prevailing circumstances, considering the available resources and the estimated costs, benefits, risks and opportunities of the various alternatives.

Whilst many transaction processing systems have been very successful, often becoming essential to an organization's survival, clearly their applicability is limited to only a part of an organization's information processing requirements, that is routine, high volume, conceptually simple tasks. In most organizations the obvious candidates for these simple traditional transaction processing systems have already been implemented. However, advances in database and network technology have created a demand for more complex systems. Therefore, the opportunities created by extending the range of transaction processing must be balanced against the considerably increased demands (in such terms as processing power) taken together with the inherent difficulties of databases and networks.

From transaction processing to IS crisis

Over the last thirty years, organizations have been faced with a bewildering array of different types of computer-based information systems. Every few years a new, supposedly revolutionary type of system emerges, usually accompanied by exaggerated claims as to its ability to solve real (or imaginary) problems. The new type of system remains 'flavour of the month' until the next 'breakthrough' appears. Such developments often contain considerable growth potential, but whilst some take root and flourish, others remain weak and straggly, despite much attention and encouragement from their supporters and investment from their sponsors. They start strongly, but become unmanageable after a few years.

The evident success of the early transaction processing systems led many commentators to subscribe to the *First Step Fallacy*. In the same way that successfully climbing a tree is hardly the first step towards space travel, many early writers were overly optimistic regarding the benefits of large-scale computerization: "Information technology promises better answers. It promises to eliminate the risk of less than adequate decisions arising from garbled communications, from misconceptions of goals, and from unsatisfactory measurement of partial contributions on the part of dozens of line and staff specialists" [5]. Thirty years later, evidence abounds of poor decision-making, faulty communications and goal conflict despite the vast sums poured into information technology. However, at the time, further encouraged by the advent of powerful general-purpose mainframes (e.g. IBM 360), over-ambitious proposals emerged to extend the narrowly-based, single-function transaction processing into real-time management information systems to support general management processes. Using cybernetics for intellectual support, this led to the notion of *total* organizational information systems, where all the organization's information processing requirements would be integrated into a single computer system. This proved to be a 'will-o'-the-wisp'; the faint hope that such systems would increase control and provide a 'scientific' basis for management collapsed in the face of the problems of capturing and integrating all management information from the diverse parts of a constantly changing organization. Large monolithic information systems just cannot produce flexible organizations. Ackoff [6] demolishes five key assumptions of early MIS thinking:

- Rather than lacking relevant information, many managers are struggling to emerge from an excess of irrelevant information; information overload.
- Because of the vagaries of decision-making, managers are likely to ask for more information than they actually need and designers are likely to supply more than is asked for, leading to yet more irrelevant information.
- Decision-making does not necessarily improve with extra information; much depends on the skills of the individual decision-maker.
- Increased communication between departments, especially between departments in conflict, does not necessarily improve performance.
- In order to control their information systems, managers must not only understand how to use them, but also they must understand how they work.

The failure of the grandiose MIS did not prevent the emergence of two important developments that have formed key dimensions of today's IS infrastructure. Advances in file processing led to database systems (Chapter 7), whilst research work on the US Department of Defense's ARPANET network pioneered data communications (Chapter 8). Combined with word-processing technology, they produced the office information systems (OIS) discussed in Chapter 9.

The success in developing the technology has not always been matched by the employment of that technology. An extensive catalogue can be compiled of information systems failures: systems that were seriously delayed, considerably over budget, or finally fail to satisfy user requirements. Progress has been made, but at considerable cost in terms of a huge waste of precious financial and human resources, as well as the more intangible losses of customer goodwill. A 1984 study estimated that 20 per cent of UK IT expenditure was wasted, a total of £800 million. We would argue that this is mostly because developers failed to treat information systems as social systems, with the technology as but one component. It is primarily the failure to appreciate this simple fact that has led to today's crisis in organizational information systems. The 'hard systems' thinking of computer science, has proved to be, at best, inappropriate, and often highly destructive when applied to information systems. This can be seen in the following themes that run throughout the short history of information systems. The cases quoted are mostly recent, demonstrating that the problems are far from solved. Unless otherwise indicated, the cases refer to the UK, although similar catalogues can be produced for most countries.

Performance fails to live up to the promise

A frequent problem is that a system, especially a large system, that works in a laboratory or on paper is unable to deliver the required performance in an operational situation. A £4 million export refunds system for the Ministry of Agriculture produced holdups stretching to six months, instead of the anticipated 28-day turnaround, delaying the payment of £130 million to exporters. Similarly, a £7 million system for the Passport Office proved to be slower than the existing manual system, with turnaround increasing from fifteen days to two months. The situation was only eased by the Government offering a free two-year extension to passport holders. The failure alienated staff who responded with industrial action. In another example, system developers underestimated the processing power needed for British Telecom's huge Customer Services System and an additional £50 million had to be spent on upgrading the hardware. In the latter case, software faults resulted in serious billing problems – overdue bills were not pursued and overcharges remained undetected. In total, this project was delayed by three years and costs soared £150 million over the original budget. A UK newspaper experienced severe problems with its ambitious colour printing system and started legal proceedings against the supplier of a supposedly portable optical scanner that took more than three people to lift. The Irish *Garda* (police) command and control system crashed when the uninterruptible *(sic)* power unit was struck by lightning; the system was down for three days for repairs.

Other examples include a system for a publisher, abandoned after three years development and a six-fold increase in hardware capacity; it was so slow that users mistakenly assumed it had stopped working altogether. A large air cargo system was shut down after only two weeks' operation; it could not cope with the throughput, leading to a cargo backlog that overflowed the available warehouse space. The failure to cater for peak traffic loadings has caused problems in a number of financial systems. The Brussels Stock Exchange system crashed in October 1989 due to an excess volume of transactions; it was out of action for two days. During the 1987 Black Monday stock market crash, nine of the twelve New York Stock Exchange systems collapsed at some point during the panic. Some displayed patently incorrect information while others just jammed, adding to the general chaos. Some commentators have argued that the programmed selling of stock by computer-based systems exacerbated the price falls, leading to an unnecessary crash. This has apparently failed to dent the optimism of many dealers who are reportedly still planning to extend programmed buying and selling through the use of decision support systems and expert systems.

The consequences of poor performance can be dwarfed by those of software errors. A bank erroneously transferred £2 billion because the software chose the wrong date for payments and duplicated payment instructions; such payments are guaranteed and technically the mistake was irrecoverable, although informal trust between banks meant the money was recovered. Another bank blamed its system for the loss of 120,000 share certificates. The system garbled the addresses of shareholders as it could only cope with five-line addresses, not six lines, and the bank became liable for hundreds of thousands of dollars compensation.

The bigger they are, the harder they fall

The temptation of achieving major successes with large, integrated systems, combined with the traditional 'mainframe' mind-set and traditional systems development methods, has resulted in the production of large, complex systems. These have proved particularly prone to problems and, in some cases, have led to total failure. The development process, involving large teams of programmers, runs inevitably into coordination and communication difficulties, so that it may eventually run out of control [7].

When these large developments run into difficulties, they become headline news. One spectacular cost over-run concerns the Department of Social Security's

Operational Strategy. This was reportedly the largest civil computerization project in Europe; the expected cost in 1982 was £700 million but the actual cost (in 1989) was nearly £2000 million. It had been cost-justified on the basis of staff savings of 20,000 clerks but, at the time of writing, it is not clear whether anything like these savings can be achieved. The project was severely criticized by the House of Commons Public Accounts Committee and the Audit Office for a serious lack of financial control. Unfortunately, the world does not stand still during the several years' development needed by such large projects and changes in social security legislation added to the delays and cost over-runs. In operation, staff complained of the system's inefficiency and reportedly often reverted to the manual system. Hundreds of terminals had to be returned because of a hardware fault and bugs in the software led to payment books being sent to post offices for collection by claimants without the claimants being informed, and vice versa. In total, more than 20,000 faults were logged in a year and staff became so frustrated that industrial action resulted. This debacle occurred after a previous attempt, the Camelot system, had been killed off in 1982 after three years' development and £6 million written off.

Another large UK project to run into difficulties concerned the national control system for electricity generation, which was reported to be nine years late with the cost escalating from £10.52 million to £95.1 million. An Inland Revenue integrated tax system was abandoned after 200 man-years' work; it was estimated that 100 man-years were needed to complete the project although the original total estimate was only 36.5 man-years. The developers had not learnt from a similar project that succumbed to the same fate in 1983. In the USA, the Patent and Trademark Office had to stop development of a $448 million project due to mismanagement. The project was one year late, 55 per cent over budget and, while the benefits had been overstated by $444 million, the costs had been understated by $60 million. The public sector does not have a monopoly of large failures; a large bank recently wrote off £21 million on two large-scale projects, one of which was producing 2,500 faults per month.

Military systems can usually be relied upon for spectacular failures. A message system commissioned in 1980 for SHAPE (Supreme Headquarters Allied Powers in Europe) was sent back to the drawing board for the third time in 1989. An RAF command and control system was recently reported to be five years late. A battlefield artillery system, commissioned in 1976 for delivery in 1985, experienced 'software problems' and is not expected to appear until the early 1990s. A command and control system for frigates was completely abandoned. Database design problems were blamed for the limitations of one naval command and control system, while the Ministry of Defence's Export Services Organization's database system suffered a delay of more than two years. The US

WWMCCS command and control system remains unfinished after seven years' development and the expenditure of nearly $400 million. This system experienced two changes of name as the responsibility shifted between the USAF and the Pentagon and the project experienced the familiar problems of complexity, poor communication with users, changing specifications and budget cuts.

Excessive complexity

The old adage *Keep It Simple Stupid (KISS)* is especially relevant to the introduction of CBIS. Most users prefer systems that are conceptually and procedurally easy to both learn and use. Unnecessary complexity merely leads to glazed eyes and a return to the manual system. A handful of enthusiasts may delight in the complexity but such members of staff should be encouraged to restrict these hobbies to their leisure time. Simplicity should be seen as a virtue in organizational information systems. This can be seen in *Mooers' Law* that states: "An information retrieval system will tend not to be used whenever it is more painful and troublesome for a customer to have information than for him not to have it" [8].

In 1986, a 'total' reservations and finance system for a UK hovercraft operator was written off at cost of £800,000 in favour of a simpler system. Ironically, a tailor-made financial monitoring system for the Government's Alvey Directorate, whose remit was to increase the use of IT in industry, had to be replaced by a much simpler spreadsheet.

Promotion of inappropriate systems: solutions seeking problems

Periodically there emerge from research laboratories new types of information system that seem technically attractive but for which there may not be an obvious immediate demand. Whilst one can argue that many important developments, such as word processing and spreadsheets, emerged in this fashion, other solutions, such as video-conferencing and videotex, have found few successful 'problems' after many fruitless years of trying. The more recent examples of expert systems and hypertext remain unproven and, in the cold light of day, their prospects are not particularly encouraging.

Manufacturing industry has experienced problems with CIM (computer integrated manufacturing) systems. One large UK manufacturer was brought to the edge of bankruptcy, and even General Motors was reported to be still not getting the required performance after spending hundreds of millions of dollars. Many manufacturers found that the greatest gains were achieved from pre-automation reorganization, followed by limited or no CIM systems.

No type of information system is universally applicable; each is appropriate in certain cases only. The scope of each system is limited to particular problems and it is up to managers to match systems to problems. For example, word processing systems, considered generically, are appropriate to a very wide range of situations whereas desktop publishing systems, say, are applicable to a much smaller range. Neither is universally applicable despite the marketing propaganda. Systems can be shown to be appropriate, according to the criteria of their vendors, but these criteria may be wildly inappropriate. Many businesses pursue organizational effectiveness in terms of the quality of their product, staff or management systems. However, quality is an elusive goal that can be either enhanced or reduced through the employment of IT.

Centralization of a naturally distributed activity

The need to simplify the control processes of complex technical systems has led to a tendency to centralize both the activity itself and its control. And yet, information and information processing are naturally distributed throughout the organization. Centralized word processing 'pools' separated the operators from the rest of the organization and their remoteness proved to be both inefficient and ineffective. Where the function remains distributed, but control of that function is being centralized, often threats to a work group's territory from the new power structure will result in power struggles. After control is finally centralized, there are grave dangers of an excessively bureaucratic organization, peopled by a demoralized workforce. Given sufficient autonomy, most members of staff are likely to be more productive and enjoy greater job satisfaction.

The vulnerability of centralized computer systems was amply demonstrated during the 1984 pay dispute within the Department of Health and Social Security. The trade union caused considerable disruption (reportedly costing £150 million), at little cost to itself, by calling out on strike a relatively small number of data processing staff at a handful of computer centres.

Formalization of the unformalizable

Certain simple structured information and information processing procedures (e.g. invoice production) can be easily formalized and programmed into an automated system. However, much of the information which managers use to take decisions, is informal and unstructured. Much of this information cannot be formalized – attempts to do so are doomed to failure. Research has shown that organizations where the informal system has been abolished have been unsuccessful.

While much has been made of the increasing flexibility of information technology, this has often not been translated into flexible information systems.

In the Hillsborough football stadium disaster of 1989, when 95 people died, the fire brigade emergency system was too inflexible. Precious time was wasted because the system could not proceed without the full postal address of the ground, even though all concerned knew where this major landmark was sited. Further flexibility problems were seen in a health insurer's system; after a development delay of two years, the newly introduced system was found to be too inflexible in validating claims, leading to excessive rejections and a large backlog to be processed manually.

The consequences of IS failures are usually a considerable financial loss, often to users. The contract between the supplier and the London Fire Brigade for a command and control system was a fixed-price contract. However, the £3.2 million system was finally delivered four years late at a cost of £8 million. The supplier blamed the fire brigade for frequent changes in the specification, requiring upgraded hardware and twice as many lines of code. Legal proceedings commenced in November 1989. However, surprisingly few cases have actually resulted in court proceedings despite severe losses; it seems that both parties prefer to reduce the embarrassment by settling out of court.

The cost of the resulting inconvenience from IS failures is incalculable. The failure of a UK computer manufacturer's factory distribution system caused their new centre to close for two weeks, resulting in delivery delays of eight weeks to customers. When another manufacturer's distribution centre failed, due to a faulty cable, the system erroneously allowed back-ups of files to be corrupted in addition to destroying current data. The warehouse operations degenerated into chaos. Other consequences include staff unrest resulting directly from botched information systems development.

Rather more serious consequences have been documented by Peter Neumann in *ACM Software Engineering Notes,* including five Japanese workers who died in incidents involving robots. Following one incident where a radiation machine may have caused two deaths, the manufacturer's short term solution was rather novel. Although the machine had originally cost $1 million and had been encased in concrete seven feet thick, the fault was to be rectified by removing the top of the 'up' cursor arrow key and covering the key with sticky tape.

It has also been suggested that inadequacies in *HMS Sheffield's* radar may have been responsible for her loss in the Falklands campaign – it apparently did not work because the radio telephone was using the same frequency to call London. The loss of an Air New Zealand airliner with 257 deaths may have been due to data error in the in-flight computer. Similarly, the crash of a Boeing 737 airliner onto a UK motorway in 1989 caused concern regarding possible faults in the aircraft's computerized warning systems. It has been suggested that a Canadian train crash with 26 deaths should have been prevented by the computer-based signalling system. In some cases, tragic results occur indirectly: a woman, who was mistakenly told she had an incurable disease, killed her daughter and tried to kill herself and her son.

The performance of CBIS in 'safety-critical' systems is causing increasing concern. Problems with the UK Air Traffic Control Systems have been linked to a number of near-misses, and bugs are still being found in the sixteen-year-old Heathrow system. This system, proven *(sic)* in practice, may be reaching the end of its useful life but the prospects of fresh bugs resulting from rewriting 1600 man-years of code are frightening. The newer Prestwick Oceanic system, installed in March 1987, had ten major failures during the first summer and minor failures every other day. On one occasion all information on the whereabouts of aircraft was lost. In addition to the safety worries, these problems have led to considerable cost and delays to airlines. The US National Airspace System first proposed in 1981 with a delivery date of 1992 and a cost of $10 billion had, by 1987, slipped to delivery in 1995 at a cost of $16 billion.

Software errors and poor man–machine interfaces, have also been linked to accidents at various oil and chemical installations. The accident at Three Mile Island nuclear plant exemplifies the complexity of CBIS. As soon as water started to leak from the ailing reactor, 500 alarms were activated in the control room and 800 other indicators were triggered along the 900 feet of dials and gauges that comprised the control panel. The operators were overwhelmed by the ensuing information overload.

Considerable concern has been expressed over the reliability of computer-based systems within air defence early warning systems and their associated missile launch systems. Over the years, there have been many false alarms caused by, for example, flocks of birds being mistaken for enemy missiles. Serious worries regarding the number of software errors in the Strategic Defense Initiative (SDI) project provoked the resignation of David Parnas, one of its leading experts. Parnas [9] argued that it was impossible to verify that the software worked properly, without testing the system in use. As this is impossible, we can have little confidence in the system, and thus SDI ceases to be an effective deterrent.

However, the ingenuity and sheer doggedness of organizations in overcoming IS failures and scraping together a happy ending has to be respected. The London Stock Exchange 'Big Bang' in October 1986 heralded a totally new electronic stocks and shares market. Before switchover, firms were desperately head-hunting staff. On the first day, most systems were patched-up or stop-gap solutions – many had to be replaced within 12 months. However, the initial problems were mostly due to overloading of facilities and they settled down relatively quickly as additional hardware was brought in. This should not disguise the failures: the

.AEF share transaction processing system was delivered two years late and at least one major securities firm wrote off a system after three years' development.

Lack of IT or insufficient computing power has been implicated in various 'disasters'. The UK Meteorological Office partly blamed its failure to predict the 1987 hurricane on inadequate computing facilities. Also, computer-linked sensors might have detected the fault that caused the space shuttle *Challenger* to explode in 1986, killing seven astronauts. Finally, it is worth noting that, although many CBIS have been less than successful in achieving their aims, they have been particularly popular as a scapegoat for organizational or human failures.

Conclusion

The introduction of any new CBIS into an organization brings with it both opportunities and risks; i.e. positive benefits and negative drawbacks. Whilst some of the opportunities may be identified relatively easily from the vendors' claims, the risks are usually much less obvious. However, there will be risks – *there is no such thing as a free lunch* – and management must be aware of this and attempt to identify and minimize the risks. In some cases the opportunities clearly outweigh the risks, in a very few cases the risks are so great that no manager would take that particular gamble, but in many cases (perhaps even the majority) the balance is hard to determine. This situation should be seen within the prevailing climate of technological optimism, where managers, with limited understanding of the technology can be intimidated into introducing inappropriate systems by the fear of exposing their ignorance or being labelled an *old fogey* with few promotion prospects.

Exercise

Consider, in some depth, an individual transaction processing system. If possible, arrange a visit to a local installation to study the system at first hand. Talk to both the IS management and user management about how the system works and how well it works. Take a historical perspective, by finding out when it was first developed and by whom (in-house, external developers), and try to compile its subsequent history. What were the main factors in its success (or lack of success)?

Where visits are infeasible, invite speakers from industry who can provide similar information of an individual system from their own experience. If this is also not practicable, as a last resort, use a published case study such as [4].

Discussion issues

Compare a social system (e.g. your college or company) with a technical system (e.g. a computer system) and a socio-technical system (a class of students or a project team using a computer system). In each case, list the key criteria for success and compare the three lists.

References

1. Forester, T. (ed.), *The information technology revolution*, Blackwell, Oxford, 1985.
2. Parkinson, C. Northcote, *Parkinson's Law*, Penguin, London, 1986.
3. Shneiderman, B., *Designing the user interface: strategies for effective human–computer interaction*, Addison-Wesley, Reading, Mass., 1987.
4. Gifford, D. and Spector, A., 'The TWA reservation system', *Communications of the ACM*, 27(7), 650-665, 1984.
5. Leavitt, H. & Whisler, T., 'Management in the 1980's', *Harvard Business Review*, Vol.36, No.6, 41-48, 1958.
6. Ackoff, R., 'Management misinformation systems', *Management Science*, Vol.14, No.4, 147-156, 1967.
7. Brooks, F.P., *The mythical man-month*, Addison-Wesley, Reading, Mass., 1975.
8. Mooers, C.N.,'Mooers' Law or why some retrieval systems are used and others are not', *American Doc.*, Vol.11, No.3, 1960.
9. Parnas, D.L.,'Software aspects of strategic defense systems', *Communications of the ACM*, 28(12), 1326-1335, 1985.

Suggested reading

Trends in information technology
  Forester, T. (ed.), *The information technology revolution*, Blackwell, Oxford, 1985.
  Wilkinson, G.G. & Winterflood, A.R. (eds.), *Fundamentals of information technology*, Wiley, Chichester, 1987.
History of information systems
  Somogyi, E.K. & Galliers, R.D.,'From data processing to strategic information systems - a historical perspective'. In: Somogyi, E.K. & Galliers, R.D. (eds.), *Towards strategic information systems*, Abacus Press, Tunbridge Wells, Kent, 1987.

6 The integrity of information systems

- *System integrity*
- *Controls*
- *Possible actions*
- *Developing a security policy and making it work*

System integrity

Accidents, mismanagement or negligence, design flaws, deliberate theft, fraud, sabotage, labour strikes, abuse of facilities, disaster, disruption are everywhere [1]. The security hazards implicit in information systems have received enormous publicity in recent years, and far too often they are rationalized away as individual (and correctable?) programming bugs or misunderstanding on the part of management and users. The development, implementation and introduction of more sophisticated IT applications has introduced further, even more complex structure into organizations [2], a structure not of their own making. It has culminated in the old checks and balances being no longer valid or disappearing altogether. When stored in a computer, programs and data can be altered quickly and easily, but they lack any permanent physical existence, so there is a tendency to print out frequent hard copy. There ensues an explosion of traditional paper files reflecting more the transitional nature of the programs and data, rather than referring to their current state on the computer. Computer networks have complicated matters even further, by promoting quick and easy communication, which all too often 'punches a hole' through layers of defence. Computers themselves have been used as part of that defence, but data-entry and processing has been concentrated in the hands of people who often deny the need for programmed supervision, and who have the technological means at their disposal to circumvent such regulation anyway. Unwittingly, these people have been given power within companies, but they are often without position or responsibility, and have no sense of accountability.

Customers can make the problem worse, expecting the delivery of products and services within the much shorter time-scales made possible by technology, while at the same time demanding greater guarantees. All of this tends to undermine the integrity of the processes that maintain the identity and stability of an organization. Now more than ever before, information is highly concentrated, and the very existence of an organization can depend on the integrity, that is the material wholeness, of either itself or its information system. Defending the integrity of both the organization and its supporting information systems should not be left to chance. However, understanding the full implication and complexity of the necessary security measures takes considerable time and effort. Often the standard response of systems managers, who have probably been 'lumbered' with the responsibility, is simply to institute the standard series of protection measures described in their computer system administration manuals. If implemented properly, these should catch the majority of threats. The problem is that once such measures are implemented, or *thought* to have been implemented, the system manager may well sit back thinking his work complete.

Formal attempts at analyzing the security situation are often confused and confusing, and can degenerate into searches for rigid classifications of hazards to integrity. Such attempts are often based on a belief in mechanisms and procedures that deny the true systemic nature of the risk. The impotence of technology to date, in dealing with its growing self-inflicted vulnerability and insecurity, could easily lead us to the conclusion that the technology itself is seriously flawed. However, because of the fundamental position that technology now plays within organizations, it is not good enough to be fobbed off with the bland platitude that 'no security is foolproof'. Therefore, from the basis of our understanding of systems behaviour, we will explain what is happening, what we can do about it, and how.

We start by recognizing that effective communication is crucial to maintain the cohesion and coherence, that is the wholeness, the integrity of any organization. Proper management has its basis in communication, and every effort should be made to ensure that the communication is relevant and reliable. This has been achieved over the centuries by Western commerce, which has evolved various stable communication procedures, both formal and informal; but these procedures are now being swept away by the new technologies. Some, like telephone or fax, although revolutionary and possibly disruptive forms of communication, can be handled by normal company practice. They are mere channels that conform with the standard command lines of an organization, notwithstanding some security implications (such as phone-tapping, or the nuisance of cold-calling and junk fax). However, IT, by the convergence of communication and computer technologies, has also entered into the domain of decision-taking, and has thus cut across old organizational boundaries. With its very existence based on new technology, a computerized information system will introduce a fundamental change into any organization, and thus any compromise of the integrity of such a system may cause various forms of disruption. The fact that information systems are integrated into organizations, to a greater or lesser extent, means that maintaining the integrity of information systems cannot be isolated from general security issues. Furthermore, because of the reliance modern organizations place on their information systems, security must inevitably represent a corporate priority for the future. Thankfully all is not bad news, for IT can also be a powerful weapon in the unending battle of protecting the integrity of both information systems and the organizations they serve.

Controls

An information system enables the internal management of an organization's sub-systems, and helps it cope with the external environment. Any disruption to an information system, and thus to the management of its responses, will affect the effectiveness of an organization. Similarly, any disruption to the organization can affect the information system also. Thus integrity issues are concerned with the well-being of the IS itself, and of its relationship with both the surrounding organization and the external environment. Replacing or renovating an old information system by using new technology is an opportunity for enhancing the integrity of the organization that is often totally ignored. However, information technology has not been in existence, nor has it been stable, for long enough to be well understood; the price of this opportunity is the introduction of new hazards, implicit in untried systems.

It is common to classify security risks as being internal and external to the system (or the organization) [3]; however, given the intrinsic ambiguity in any choice of system boundary, we choose to avoid this particular classification. Similarly we avoid identifying risks as being accidental or deliberate, as this distinction can be vague and also overly concentrate on preconceived causes. Instead, we prefer to focus our classification on the behaviour of the control mechanisms that serve the system. However, we stress here that the word 'control' is used to imply actions intended by the system to cause effects that are predicted on expectations based on prior experience, and therefore the control mechanisms will evolve along with the information system and the organization. Risk, particularly systemic risk, is implicit in the uncertainty of the environment and in the ambiguity of these ever-changing internal sub-systems. And there is risk, even in the endeavour to be in control. Therefore, we attempt to identify how control mechanisms evolve within a system in its dealings with the environment, and see how they can be disrupted and compromised, but at the same time balance this against the potential of these mechanisms to enhance security, be it of an organization or its information system. However, this classification is by no means complete and makes no claims to any inherent virtue, it is just a useful starting point for discussion. We would stress that the groupings we identify here are not necessarily mutually exclusive. They are a choice of convenience and a result of the intellectual shortcomings of the authors. At no time do we mean to imply a 'tidy' structure to these controls. The examples within each classification are those which come immediately to mind, and it is left to the reader to expand on the catalogue. Ultimately a mixture of technical know-how, individual commonsense, but predominantly a perpetual vigilance built on lateral thinking, is needed to overcome or to mitigate these problems.

Environmental control: As with most traditional security applications, the physical environment is always of major concern. Of course, there are a wide range of interpretations of what is meant by environmental control. Adverse weather conditions can affect the functioning of computer systems: a lightning strike can reduce micro-chips into small mounds of brown ash. Storms, floods or earthquakes are likewise catastrophic: it makes sense to place expensive computer facilities above ground level if there is the slightest risk of flooding – although there is the apocryphal system inversion of an airtight (and hence watertight) computer room on the top floor of a high-rise building being flooded when the sprinkler system was set off by a cigarette smoker. The tangled spaghetti of cables from microcomputers have caused many accidents. Construction materials are critical to security – it is only commonsense not to use combustible materials. Glass can cause increased solar gain and heat damage, even fire, and broken glass can seriously injure staff. Transparent partitions increase visibility and help prevent accidents, yet if badly laid out they will enable unauthorized individuals to spy on possibly sensitive information. An efficient layout, set for ease of operation and for a safe, speedy evacuation in an emergency, can be a security risk too, as it gives an easy thoroughfare for unwanted visitors. The choice of location is another obvious source of trouble: a glamorous location diverts major funding from other projects, it may be costly and politically destabilizing for the company, and it identifies and advertises the centre as a target. On the other hand, camouflaging a computer centre in a drab run-down area near social unrest increases the likelihood that staff will be attacked on the way to work.

Equipment control: This will involve many traditional methods of preventing damage to, or theft of, equipment and storage media. Universities across the world have paid the price for informal and trusting attitudes, with the loss of numerous microcomputers and disks; thieves even open up computers to steal micro-chips. The ready portability of lap-top computers means that they are often carried outside secure environments, where they can be left on trains or stolen from cars. Although the machine is easily replaced, the loss of possibly sensitive information stored on it can cause great embarrassment to the owner. Unsecured communication cables can be intercepted, outside the building as well as inside, enabling illegal access to sensitive material. The breakdown of maintenance and housekeeping equipment can mean the closedown of all computing; there have been examples of fires caused by paper entering heating ducts. The requirement of a 'clean' power supply is critical – apart from the continuity of supply being essential for all processing and the prevention of loss of data, power surges can cause physical damage to the machines and logical damage to disk-file stores.

Logistical control: This is probably the most important aspect of traditional security. Checks should be made to ensure that the awareness of staff in respect of security is consistent at all times and over long periods, with no lapses of concentration, not only in the day but also at night, and during 'comfort-breaks' or shift breaks. The checks themselves should be checked to prevent predictability, enabling them to be bypassed due to perceived regularity. Third parties, such as visitors, customers, suppliers or maintenance engineers, should all have clearance and be identified, controlled and monitored at all times during their visit. Even in low-security computer centres, the layout of the entrance and reception areas should be properly designed as the first level of a layered security. Each layer should have its own alarms, surveillance methods and procedures for checking credentials. New technology has delivered many new sophisticated procedures for checking entry, although even the best methods can be easily circumvented if 'tailgating' is not strictly prohibited both on entry and leaving each secure area. Delivery doors should not be placed simply for ease of entry for delivered goods, if that entry bypasses all security levels. Humidifiers, ventilation shafts and air conditioning vents may allow unwanted entry from outside, bypassing security. It is not paranoid delusion to take urban terrorism, social unrest and criminal attack very seriously.

Suitable housekeeping procedures are extremely important: waste materials should be properly disposed of, paper can easily cause fires; all commercially sensitive documents should be shredded; all unguarded doors and windows should be closed (or preferably be self-closing); the position of panic buttons ought not to be at elbow height; cigarette smoking should be restricted; and food and drink should be kept well away from electronic hardware. Such self-evident precautions are all too often ignored.

Legal control: The attitude of legal systems to information technology is highly ambivalent. For example under current English law, stored data is not property, and so cannot be stolen. Provided that he owns the flexible disk used to steal the data, then the thief cannot even be charged with the theft of the medium. And it is only recently that software has gained copyright protection in countries like Australia and Saudi Arabia. Of course, even where copyright exists, piracy of programs is rife. All over the world, the attitude of microcomputer users towards copyright, and to intellectual property rights in general, is dubious to say the least.

A number of countries have introduced forms of data privacy legislation which enable individuals, for a minor charge, to check that their personal entries on commercial (but not political, military, police or medical!) databases are correct, to have redress if they are not, and to insist on confidentiality and privacy. But, if the data is stored in text form rather than in cross-referenced tables, these laws can create major headaches for organizations holding the files. In order to conform with the law and satisfy every enquiry, the company will have to scour their huge file-base for the smallest reference to the applicant's name, but ignore any data on different persons with the same name. When found, all information that is not of direct relevance, or which may be of a confidential nature to others, should then be withheld from the applicant. This will introduce a major cost overhead for any computer centre, since such processes are highly judgement-laden and very labour intensive. However, such legislation can be avoided, simply by storing the data in a country where legislation is less strictly enforced. The use of international communication links makes this a viable proposition, especially if the remote site is used as a cheap storage facility, much as Taiwan is used as a cheap construction facility.

There is also the question of liability for this new technology. The failure of particular programs to conform to specification, or a negligent service, has implications for the commercial viability of the supplier company. It could be a time-bomb, especially if the particular promised product or technology, that has tied-in customers and suppliers, does not materialize. Other so-called 'competitive advantages' could ultimately cause legal problems, as American Airlines found in the threat of being sued under antitrust laws over their SABRE system. Until the legal situation stabilizes, it is wise for both suppliers and customers to check the 'small print', and be extremely careful about personal and corporate liability.

There may be legal restraints on the use of particular pieces of software and hardware, as happened with the US embargo on the transfer of high technology to Eastern Bloc countries, with all the extra-territorial implications for Europe and Japan. Given the global supply of technical components, the introduction of local restrictions could cause real financial difficulties for companies building even small numbers of embargoed components into large-scale commercial systems, not to mention the enormous increase of bureaucracy that such restrictions entail.

Software control: Computer 'worms', initially seen as beneficial to computer systems by autonomously optimizing the use of storage resources, are evolving into viruses that precipitate deliberate acts of industrial/political sabotage. According to the 'hacker subculture', the Friday the 13th computer virus, also known as Jerusalem B, was developed by the PLO to disrupt microcomputers at certain targeted Israeli organizations. It spread through much of America, Western Europe and Japan in a very short time, often causing the total destruction of data on hard disks, with the loss of months of work. In response, the computer industry has produced programs which 'scan' file-bases for known viruses and then give methods of 'disinfection'. Such defence may prove to be an illusion. With the present number of known viruses at over three hundred, and growing fast, they may not be able to cope with the sheer scale of the problem. But more problematical is a new generation of self-mutating 'stealth viruses', which use AI methods to identify what the user is doing, and will either disappear, relocate, or stop the machine (taking some disks with it) if any attempt is made to use a debugger or scan program. And it is not only microcomputers that are at risk, worms and viruses can also infect mainframe computers: in November 1988 the Internet worm caused such great consternation all over the USA, that much of the June 1989 edition of the prestigious journal, *Communications of the ACM*, was dedicated to a discussion of the problem [4]. A famous set of experiments by Fred Cohen (see [5]) in 1983 showed that, in an attack on a VAX computer running UNIX, a program could start with basic user privileges and reach full system privileges in between 5 and 30 minutes. Experiments on a much larger IBM mainframe had similar success in times ranging between 6 and 20 hours. No computer system is immune to *Homo sapiens*, the ultimate computer virus! Even apparently innocuous procedures, such as electronic mail, can be a threat. PC-DOS 'control codes' can be placed within an 'innocent' mail message (not a virus) which, if read by a personal computer using the ANSI.SYS device driver, can reprogram keys, which when pressed can perform unwanted operations such as totally wiping clean the hard disk.

Data control: Loss of data can be very costly, whether by theft of a storage medium, or by disclosure or even browsing, or by accidental or deliberate modification of that data. The problem is exacerbated by the fact that, except in the case where the medium is stolen, there is normally no indication of the theft until the inherent value of the data is used competitively against the rightful owner. The guardian of the data has to be alert to attack from all quarters; screens give off electromagnetic radiation, which can be intercepted by industrial spies up to half a mile away, and then reconstructed. Equipment, which costs less than $200, can make a nonsense of security for much screen-based information. Equipment to prevent this sort of problem is designed under the Transient Electromagnetic Pulse Emanation Standard (TEMPEST). Unfortunately, in some countries it is perfectly legal to eavesdrop in this way, but it is illegal for businesses to take countermeasures against such surveillance. In the UK, the Law Commission document [6] states *"There are forms of eavesdropping which the [Interception of Communications] Act [1985] does not cover. For example, eavesdropping on a VDU screen by monitoring the radiation field which surrounds it in order to display whatever appears on the legitimate user's screen on the eavesdropper's screen. This activity would seem not to constitute any criminal offence"*.

Telephone operators are often given access to sensitive files so that they can answer innocent enquiries. These operators, not knowing the sensitivity of the material, may then thoughtlessly answer further, but now highly sensitive questions, without asking the enquirer for the correct access permissions. This all-too-common fault of manual systems, becomes far worse with sloppy computer systems. The very speed of a computer's response, and the fact that data files are often not divided into levels, each with different access permissions, means that internal checks have not been organized to cope with spontaneous requests. No one can blame the telephone operators for being unaware of security structures that exist only in the minds of those that understand the context of the data.

Missing, incomplete and inconsistent data can be a problem too. Questions of accuracy, relevance, being up-to-date are also very important and can affect the integrity of the company. Misrepresentation of a customer's status, or incorrect accounting data all can cause great offence, and possibly leave the company liable for compensation under data privacy legislation.

Communications control: The spread of computer networks and their use in distributed systems, now makes uncontrolled access into communication channels one of the major headaches facing the managers who have to maintain integrity of the system. This means that the capture, input, output and dissemination of data have all become points of weakness. Failure to keep them secure does not only concern data theft; incorrect data leading to customer dissatisfaction can be equally devastating.

Despite experience to the contrary, designers still believe that their systems will only be used according to their specifications and intentions. But there is more than one way to use any technology, and alternative anti-social perspectives can have profound implications for stakeholders in a system. Consider how banks view automatic teller machines (ATMs) as a major competitive advantage, even though every year hundreds of million dollars are stolen from ATMs [7], and customers are attacked, even murdered when withdrawing money.

Document/Documentation control: The paper medium is often considered a poor relation in this new technology, yet it too should be treated with the highest priority. Writing the documentation for a computer system is often seen as demeaning, or just plain boring, by systems developers, and so is done hurriedly, and badly, causing hugely increased costs of maintenance when the system is operating. Complexity in dealing with the sheer volume of library material and system documentation can cause a great waste of time and effort. The uncontrolled distribution of multiple paper copies can lead to confusion about the state of the system and whether copies are up-to-date and consistent.

Care should be taken with the paperwork relating to physical products. Such documentation is much more than just a record of whether or not they have been paid for. The computerization of the delivery process is a situation ripe for fraud. If the only physical receipts and bills of lading are sent with a consignment, then theft is made even easier; steal both the goods and the documents, delete the computer record and then the perfect crime has been committed. So a careful audit trail, with numerous checks and balances, is needed to combat such crime, but paradoxically this very information, or the fact of a flow of information between sites, can inform the criminal what to steal, where and when.

Control of requirements: It may not be unreasonable to assume that systems will be delivered according to specification. Realists may well secretly assume that an innovative project may not be delivered exactly on time, nor totally within the original budget, and that the final performance may not precisely match the original specification. Thus, small margins and contingencies may be built into projects. However, IT projects seem almost to be in a class of their own, regarding their ability to outstrip other innovations in terms of delays, cost over-runs and the failure to meet user requirements, as with example the UK Department of Social Security's (DSS) Operational Strategy described in the previous chapter.

Even systems that are delivered according to the specifications may still become failures. It is notoriously difficult to specify accurately user requirements, which in many cases change considerably during the development of a system. For example, the DSS's Operational Strategy experienced constantly changing social security legislation after the system specification had been frozen. This confusion is exemplified by new jargon words appearing in the IT community: *vapourware* – software, often paid for, but never delivered or even written; and *shelfware* – software ordered but never used. The US Department of Defense have recently published some startling figures for systems they have specified: 1.5% used as delivered, 3% used after modification, 29% used then abandoned, 29% vapourware and 47.5% shelfware (source: B.Bewley, National Centre for Information Technology, 1990 Members Conference).

Financial control: Naturally, control of *the bottom line*, careful auditing of expenditure on computer systems, is essential, including the financial justification and evaluation of the systems, since they may involve such enormous capital expenditure. Computer fraud depletes the finances of the organization. But exactly what *is* computer fraud? Fraud by operating a computer? Fraud planned using a computer? Fraud of a computer? The ambiguity of the concept is one of the major reasons why legislation concerning IT is so difficult to define and introduce. Theft of equipment will, at the very least, restrict access to a capital asset, increase insurance premiums and be a drain on resources, apart from causing disruption to operations. The theft of information or services could actually result in direct (and unfair) competition for the organization and may make its marketing position untenable, since the rogue organization need not include research and development costs in their price calculations. One aspect that is not often considered under this heading is the runaway costs of projects and project over-runs. These should be included since they will affect the integrity of the organization and its standing in the business community. The expected cost of the DSS system in 1982 was £700m but the actual cost (in 1989) was approaching £2000m. It had been justified on the basis of staff savings, but it is still not clear whether any savings were actually made.

Large sums of money have been stolen via computers from the host company or its customers and suppliers. The computer security literature is full of examples, from the simple 'salami fraud' (of diverting small fractions of bills to other accounts over a long period of time) and the instant 'hit and run' on company assets, to some highly elaborate 'stings' conceived after poring over core-dumps or using statistical analysis of communication records.

Personnel control: Ultimately security cannot be divorced from good personnel policy, and this applies as much, if not more, to management as to the workforce. It is essential that they implement strict policies on 'hiring and firing'. Staff who are dismissed should be told to clear their desk (under close scrutiny) and escorted immediately from the building. They should not be given any opportunity to cause damage, although there can be no guarantee that a malcontent has not placed a 'time-bomb' in the computer system ahead of dismissal. Companies should face the reality that some computer personnel, even though lowly placed in their organizations, have the power to cause enormous damage, either deliberately or accidentally.

Recruitment procedures, therefore, should recognize the sensitive position of computer personnel. Interviewers should have a good knowledge of professional standards in this field, and they should also understand the capabilities and limitations of the technology, as well as being able to discern the abilities or inabilities, attitude and ethics of a particular technologist. But enquiries into a potential, or actual employee's ethics can become a privacy issue. Problems of consistency and accuracy can open the door to discrimination. Some states in the USA have legislation that prohibits questions about politics, religion and trade union affiliation.

Many technologists may believe in sophisticated technology for its own sake, and ignore the business needs of their employer. Every company needs to engender disciplined and ethical behaviour among its staff. Condoning the use of illegal copies of software, apart from the legal implications, has a knock-on negative effect, and projects the wrong attitude to the work force. Similarly, the playing of computer games can be a major drain on company resources, precipitating a cavalier approach towards other company assets. Such behaviour should be recognized as symptomatic of sloppy work practices, which can lead ultimately to safety dangers for personnel, or to financial risks for the company. However, this is not easy to stop, because many games have a 'gold-key' exit to a spreadsheet to mislead management.

People are the main cause of breaches of security, but they are also the first line of defence. They are the means of minimizing the damage, raising the alarm and 'keeping the show on the road'. First aid for a damaged system can only be achieved by the best people, who really know what they are doing, and who are committed, motivated and loyal. Trained individuals are in short supply, and staff turnover can have serious implications; it is not uncommon for companies to have to cope with a destabilizing 30% annual turnover in computer staff. But good people only work in an environment that they find acceptable. Companies are often totally dependent on key personnel, and so staff motivation, via training and retraining schemes, is fundamental to any sensible personnel strategy.

Control of control: Even the methods of risk prevention can cause risk! The 1989 Clapham rail disaster in England was caused by faulty repairs to trackside signals. Fighting fires, whether it is with water, carbon dioxide or halon gas, can cause damage. Similarly, all security measures carry the price of extra cost, time and equipment, inconvenience, interference with normal activities, annoyance, slowing down of production, and the limiting of legitimate access. When does the monitoring of work become monitoring of workers? Although it is crucial that security procedures are not by-passed just because they may cause irritation and resentment. Simply paying lip-service to security procedures can give a false sense of security and can precipitate failure, as in the case when the sloppy management of personal identification allows free access to outsiders with counterfeit passes. Via awareness training, all staff should be made to recognize the importance of security and the need to test the performance of security procedures. However, this should not be at the expense of a mindless acceptance, because it is the staff alone that can recognize and cope with the systemic risks that can and will emerge outside the prior experience of any security system.

Possible actions

As part of homeostasis and of growth, every system will evolve control mechanisms to protect its integrity. But every change involves risk. Computers give a major opportunity to enhance organizational security, but they also introduce the possibility of far greater security headaches. Recognizing the above aspects of control as a risk to the integrity of a organization can only be a start. It should be followed up with an understanding of what to do, how to do it, and what happens beyond or even despite the intentions of management. This requires a mix of approaches.

Taking an introverted view of computer security is a mistake; it is essential to recognize that an information system is fundamental to the integrity of an organizational system. Therefore, security should be fashioned into every computer system, as part of an overall security policy looking to safeguard the integrity of the whole organization. There must be continuous observation and experimentation, to identify the systemic opportunities and risks. Security procedures should not be added as an afterthought, as this invariably only adds a superficial layer of defence, yet of a complexity far outweighing its benefits, and which, if penetrated, leaves the company wide open to attack.

In a successful system, the security control mechanisms does not overly disrupt the other tactical and strategic procedures that factor into the success. In a successful organization there should be a balance between profitability and security, and between organizational control and individual freedoms. Therefore, and most importantly, there should be a balance between, on the one hand a rigid acceptance of formal security procedures, and on the other a freedom to question situations, where certain suspicious circumstances may be accepted by the security system, but may provoke valuable defensive responses by the motivated employee. Employees are the most flexible form of defence for any organization.

Formal systems may identify many of the predictable hazards, but only vigilance by the staff can recognize and deal with the unusual risks. This vigilance can only come from understanding the control mechanisms, and the risks and opportunities, and from a positive attitude to the way that the company detects, deters, corrects, prevents, tolerates, mitigates dangers, and recovers from damage.

Detect: It is essential to follow up on unusual phenomena in the performance of the system, both the organization and the information system. Reports by customers or employees could be the first signs that the integrity of the system has been compromised. Some larger companies form so-called *tiger teams* to undertake *penetration studies* in order to search out weak links in security, and then correct them before any competitor can take advantage. Mistakes and design flaws can be an opportunity for fraud or the potential cause of physical damage. It is best to be aware of these defects so they can be corrected, or at the very least alarms be set in place. Fire, heat and smoke detectors should be placed sensibly as part of proper control procedures, including automatically calling the police and fire brigade.

Audit trails, checks and balances should be used to trigger an alarm at the occurrence of any unusual transaction. Here the use of computers can prove highly productive. But risks vary with time, new risks emerge continuously, so security needs an attitude of permanent vigilance and reassessment of hazards on the part of staff. However, tiger teams can prove counterproductive, inducing stress in employees feeling threatened by the team, and exacerbating inter-departmental antagonisms.

Deter: The literature is full of anticipated problems, such as fraud, theft and malicious damage. Implementing certain 'good practices' can deter attacks. For example, the segregation of duties among staff, and the insistence that staff take vacations while their work is covered by a totally different team, means that complicated collusion is needed to propagate a fraud, and this increases the probability of discovery. Determination to prosecute, vigilant surveillance (video and sound) and auditing of staff, systems and the environment, and random checks all add to deterrence. However, if these deterrents become too oppressive to personnel, they are counterproductive; they may even prove a challenge for otherwise reliable staff to 'beat the system'.

Correct: Should the detected errors turn out to be flaws in the design of the system, then every effort should be made to see that they are corrected. Such corrections and modifications should be validated all the way back to basic system requirements, and this is a very time-consuming and expensive process. Problems such as inadequate checks on access, program bugs, the regular late supply or delivery of goods, a badly designed office layout or the dangerous state of, or placement of, equipment and cabling, should all be corrected before they can cause permanent damage.

Prevent: Structures and policies should be put in place that make it difficult for accidental or deliberate lapses of security to occur. However, believing that this can be achieved through the development of a theory of fraud [8] is misconceived. Pigeonholing individuals in terms of factors related to their dishonesty, opportunity and motive, each on a scale of zero to ten, multiplying them together before dividing by a thousand to get the probability that they will be dishonest, is crass and meaningless. It shows an inflexible mentality that will misconstrue the intrinsically singular nature and spontaneity of the opportunity and motives behind many breaches of security. Similarly, defining the profile of a computer criminal, and statements such as '15% of people are not strictly honest', are meaningless measurements that give no insight to specific cases, especially in an industry with a critical shortage of skilled practitioners. But there are many valid and sensible preventative methods: the use of cryptography to make documents unreadable to anyone without a key; the use of biometric devices or smart-cards for permitting access to computer facilities; the regular changing of passwords and user IDs; checking the identity and location of each external network user by calling-back and using profile data; not allowing smoking or drinking near computer equipment; protecting key personnel from threats of violence. We leave it to the reader to expand on this list by observing their particular system and organization in action.

Tolerate and mitigate: If it is at all possible, damage limitation should be a property of systemic defences. Evaluating 'net risk' is evident folly, but developing an understanding of potential hazards will give an idea of the kinds of hazard that can be tolerated without too much damage to the system. Perhaps they can be condoned because, although some risks may prevent the achievement of a required goal, that goal may be of low priority, or flexibility within the system may circumvent these risks with alternative ways for achieving that goal. The demands of maintaining security will themselves cause problems, yet they should be tolerated, as security ought not to be rejected just because of inconvenience. The causes of a hazard could actually be intrinsic to the system itself. It may be simpler to ignore the damage by, for example, rejecting faulty products via a quality assurance program, than to overhaul the complete system.

If the cost of making changes to the system is so great as to outweigh their value, then it is more cost-effective to mitigate these risks in some way. Probably, the most common ways are to take out insurance, or to accept the losses and build them into the price structure of company products and risk losing customers.

Recover: Naturally, backup systems are necessary to recover from the whole spectrum of failure, from minor faults to disasters. Recovery from most minor faults can be covered by contingency plans or by the quick action of individuals, although rash and misguided actions, even if well intentioned, can cause worse problems. Ad hoc recovery from minor problems may be a company's strategic disposition, but in the long term it could be facing a 'death of a thousand cuts'.

A casual day-to-day disposition towards fault tolerance and recovery is not enough to deal with disasters. These require quick and appropriate recovery procedures, to prevent serious damage to the organization. There should be a division of responsibility, in order to identify who should react. Recovery from disaster requires major preparation and planning, in particular, recovery from a major computer disaster is not just a matter of rebooting a machine and reloading programs. Within a disaster recovery scenario there must be the identification of the critical links in the information flow, and procedures for dealing with a breakdown. Backups and standby systems are essential. Critical links can include buildings that are susceptible to fire, flood or earthquake: the total loss of a computer room could mean the commercial disaster of no computing. Particular equipment may be critical: a network failure could mean no communication with markets and ensuing credibility or cash-flow problems.

Key computer personnel are a potentially weak link: if the only individual who knows an idiosyncratic installation is no longer available, through injury, retirement or dismissal, then there is no system support. Software can become a critical defect in the functioning of the computer system when it is flawed, or when legal rights to its use are withdrawn. Recovery is hindered when a technical installation is dependent on operating standards that are no longer supported. Of course standards are needed for efficient working, but a company should not lose the flexibility of keeping abreast of alternative standard, and even non-standard approaches; as a matter of policy it is best to avoid being tied-in, *à la* Michael Porter, to a dependence of any kind.

Equifinality is fundamental to the well being of any system - there should always be alternatives for achieving the same functionality, and the failure of a single component should not bring the total system to a halt. From the earliest development stages, the systems design should accommodate a means for a company to extricate itself, with a 'parachute', ready for the time when any part of, or even the whole installation becomes obsolete.

Developing a security policy and making it work

Far too often in the past, security was treated in an amateur fashion by both large and small companies, and, except for specific highly sensitive issues, was given only minor importance. Now that information technology has invaded every facet of business, every aspect of security has become sensitive. It is no longer feasible to deal with security in a cavalier way. Every company, whatever the size, should have a clear policy towards security, and be predisposed to a flexible response to threats in its environment. Paradoxically, although a cause of danger, IT can also be an effective defensive weapon. However, by their very nature, the full extent of threats to the integrity of a system can never be known in advance; the only defence is the development of the necessary technical skills and a perpetual vigilance within the organization - qualities dependent on a well-trained workforce with a highly refined sense of ethics. These virtues will not come about by accident. In large organizations they should be carefully planned and nurtured by a specialist security team, that supervises all aspects of security policy and has the backing of the whole organization. Naturally the size of the organization will affect the size of the team, although even in small companies at least one individual should accept this responsibility. Much of what follows is a synthesis of the approaches taken by the better large organizations, which place more emphasis on security issues, however, these general principles are valid for most companies, no matter what their size.

Organizations should start by defining the scope of security within their particular context, with the preparation of general guidelines. They should consider the creation of a permanent high profile security team, which will include members from senior management to give it teeth and credibility. Active participation by senior management is essential, nominal support is not enough. This security team should be conceived to act in an advisory role and not as a permanent secret police. IS security should not be allocated (and thus demoted) to a single department - such as to ordinary security staff or to computer personnel, all of whom have vested interests and limited perspectives. However, there can be very real dangers in the creation of such a team, for it may become a major force in the organization. Therefore it should be seen to be impartial and should not cross organizational boundaries unnecessarily. The team's members can become unpopular and isolated because of its (justifiable) high expectation that ordinary staff will be motivated, honest and alert.

Security does not come cheap, and the allocation of proper funding for training, hardware, software and people should be guaranteed. Data processing and technical staff will be needed in the team for technological expertise, as will representatives of the security guards. Legal and accounting expertise is critical, if the team is to deal with questions of liability and finance. The team should be led by someone who is totally committed to security, and does not treat it as a sideline. The team will be dealing with substantial documentation, much of it computerized, so a security librarian will be required to deal with it all. For most medium-to-large organizations, both these latter two posts should be full-time. These can be onerous and specialized tasks, so it is easy to see why security is left to 'one man and his dog' in smaller organizations.

Before the team can start work, it is standard procedure for them to confirm the organizational view of security. Then the roles and responsibilities of personnel in the team may be defined, along with a coordinating framework for its operations. At this stage they can state the team objectives, organize the logistics of rooms, meetings, schedules, documents, and then declare their modes of operation (policy statements, reports, monitoring, recovery plans). Senior management should restate its total commitment to, support for, and involvement with the team, before it starts work on policy. The team are then in a position to review current practices and to study the effectiveness of present company security policies, always assuming there are any. They can then develop an understanding of the organization, and document its procedures; check on all aspects of the control mentioned above; and survey current insurance policies and practices relating to backup systems. They should identify key personnel and pinpoint potential problems and bottlenecks. Part of this work will be to create audits and prioritize critical factors, but we would recommend that they not place too much emphasis on the mechanistic use of quantifiable measures.

The team can then start preparing the ground for the new security measures that they will be recommending. Part of this preparation will be the setting up of structures for the management of security. Only then can they develop and justify a budget for their work. To succeed they will need the commitment of personnel at all levels of the company, and not just with senior management. In order to achieve this commitment they will need to involve all departments and interests concerned, and this should be ALL departments, since they are all stakeholders in the organization's future. Training courses in security awareness will be a major part of this process. Also, staff should have easy access to all security material and documentation, including a clear, coherent and concise policy document, and an organizational chart showing responsibility and accountability for security. Reporting mechanisms should be developed, which will explain to the whole company just what the team is doing and why it is so important. The team are then in a position to prepare an action plan, which can identify the operations needed to detect, deter, correct, prevent, tolerate and recover from lapses in security. To be credible this really should be seen to come from the highest level.

Within an organization that has effective security planning, there are clear divisions of responsibility and accountability for all aspects of the plan. The team will place relative priorities on the elements of the plan, and set time scales for achieving each goal. They will spell out inspection mechanisms, schedule clear timetables for compliance, and indicate flexible measures to combat non-compliance. Continuous monitoring and testing will be essential, but this is more than just testing fire alarms! The team will precipitate and supervise frequent and irregular security drills, initiate training schemes, and be the focus for the introduction and fostering of positive attitudes towards security. A high profile manager will be designated to oversee all local security issues. At all times the team will give clear explanations of their reasons, so that their actions can be justified to the whole company. This is especially the case when implementing mechanisms for internal control, internal and external audits, and any other checks and balances deemed necessary.

Disaster plans will also be prepared; potentially catastrophic failures are too important to be simply lumped in with an action plan. Such major risks will be identified, and countermeasures formulated well in advance, ready to deal with the worst. Part of this planning process will be having in place backup systems, archives of programs and data, and procedures to reinstate them. This will need the setting up of tests on a regular but unpredictable basis, that check on the company's ability to respond to, and recover from, disaster.

The team has a permanent innovative role of regularly updating the security system, and every so often initiating a complete overhaul. It should not be disbanded once their plans are in place, but should be viewed as a company asset. Continuity of the team is crucial; turnover in membership is essential in order to invigorate it with new ideas, but this change should be managed to cause as little disruption as possible to the smooth working of the team.

Conclusion

Such teams have proved highly successful in defending larger organizations against threats to their integrity, but at a price. The message that runs throughout this book is 'understand and then balance opportunities against risks' – the question of security teams is no exception. Security should not be seen as solely the prerogative of the team. Ideally every single staff member will be alert to the inevitability of unexpected behaviour within the system, will recognize exposure to risk, and be unwilling to accept the inertia of conventional wisdom and thereby analyze anything they perceive as unusual. Patience, perseverance, motivation, commitment, loyalty, hard graft, flexibility of response, and most importantly a painstaking belief in quality work, will be the virtues required from all staff. But even these virtues will be to no avail if designers continue to make their systems so complex as to be incomprehensible – 'keep it simple, stupid'.

Exercise

Readers should be aware of, and discuss the evaluation criteria for security in computer systems. The US Department of Defense Trusted Computer System Evaluation Criteria (TCSEC) [9], known universally as the 'Orange Book' due to the colour of its cover, is a most important standard intended to describe the efficiency of security features in computer systems. The TCSEC criteria are intended to support three objectives:

1. To provide guidance to developers as to the requirements that products should fulfil in order to satisfy trust requirements.
2. To provide users with a means of comparing different systems according to degree of trust.
3. To provide a basis for specifying security requirements in product acquisition specifications.

The criteria are divided into four divisions: A, B, C and D. A is the highest division and is reserved for systems with the most comprehensive security, while the D division is for systems with minimal protection.

Other countries, in particular those in Europe, have experience in security evaluation and have developed their own guidelines. France, Germany, the Netherlands and the UK [10] have agreed to work towards a common, harmonized Information Technology Security Evaluation Criteria (ITSEC). It focuses on two major issues:

1. The security functionality, which is the definition and description of security objectives, functions and mechanisms.
2. The assurance of correctness and effectiveness in the evaluation target.

There are seven levels of evaluation, labelled E0, which represents inadequate confidence, up to E6 which represents the highest level of confidence. Correctness is deemed to refer to both the construction and operation of the system. Effectiveness is deemed to refer to suitability of functionality, binding of functionality, vulnerabilities and ease of use.

Discussion issues

1. A predisposition to security is a state of mind. As individual members of an organization, readers should be aware of the implications of security, and use that most scarce of commodities – commonsense. You should discuss and expand on the control issues and concomitant actions given in this chapter, after all it was only meant as a brief introduction to the subject. For example under the heading of personnel control, you could have included dealing with 'loose talk'; discussing company business or criticizing the company in public. Customers (past, present or potential) may be present, or possibly more damaging, journalists who may write articles detrimental to the company. You should discuss the pros and cons of joining societies and special interest groups, where experiences can be shared. Consider whether or not to employ external security experts, whether to trust them, why teams should be guided but not led by them. And so on.

2. Concentrate on the control of data and software, and 'brainstorm' about procedures that could enhance security. Consider simple ideas, such as the screen 'signing off' if it has not been used for a given period of time. This will prevent intruders gaining entry to a system that has been left unattended, and stop data left on the screen being stolen. What is more, the screen format could give hints on system structure, and worse, it could also enable miscreants to run a program which displays a valid screen image, while requesting passwords and other security information from users. Discuss ways of dealing with the ever-present threat of hackers, and various software problems such as *back-doors*, *logic bombs* and *Trojan horses*. You will find a great deal of material on the hacker sub-culture by gaining access to computer notice boards, and, by reading the numerous books and magazines available, such as the Hacker's Handbook [11].

3. When dealing with security issues, the boy scout motto, 'Be Prepared', is very apposite. An in depth knowledge of the wide range of security problems facing a modern computerized organization is essential. It is a good idea to collect press cuttings of security lapses, and in discussion, generalize and use them to speculate on further problems, and thereby propose defences.

References

1. Hamilton, P., *The Administration of Corporate Security*, ICSA, Cambridge, 1987.
2. Pfleeger, C.P., *Security in Computing*, Prentice-Hall, London, 1989.
3. Baskerville, R., *Designing Information Systems Security*, Wiley, New York, 1988.
4. Spafford, E.H.,'The Worm Story: Crisis and Aftermath', *Communications of the ACM*, 32(6), 678-688, June 1989.
5. Hoffman L. (ed.), *Rogue Programs: Viruses, Worms and Trojan Horses*, Van Nostrand Reinhold, New York, 1990.
6. Law Commission, *Working Paper 110 on Computer Misuse*, HMSO, London, 1988.
7. Norton, M., 'Crime on the Cards', *Banking Technology*, 25-27, December 1990.
8. Fine L.H., *Computer Security*, Heinemann, London, 1986.
9. U.S. Department of Defense, *Trusted Computer System Evaluation Criteria*, DOD 5200.28-STD, Washington, December 1985.
10. Bundesminister des Innern, *Information Technology Security Evaluation Criteria*, draft release, Bonn, May 1990.
11. Cornwall, H., *Hacker's Handbook III*, Century Hutchinson, London, 1988.

Suggested reading

An excellent analysis of combating computer fraud is to be found in:

Krauss L.I. & MacGahan A., *Computer Fraud and Countermeasures*, Prentice-Hall International, London, 1979.

7 Databases and the management of information

- *Structured database systems*
- *Text retrieval systems*
- *Hypertext*
- *Is information a resource?*
- *Information resource management*

Propelled by the increasing development and use of databases, there have been calls to treat information as a corporate resource, which should be managed in the same way as other organizational resources. However, in many cases despite significant technological advances, the supposedly simple storage and retrieval of information is riddled with problems. And furthermore, there are considerable theoretical and practical difficulties with the notion of information resource management. This chapter briefly discusses database technology, including structured databases, text retrieval systems, and hypertext, with particular attention being paid to their opportunities and risks. Then we critically evaluate the claim that information is a resource, before examining the practical aspects of information resource management.

Structured database systems

Here the database consists of records made up of discrete fields (e.g. employee number, employee name). It emerged as a solution to the difficulties experienced in managing the ever-increasing number and complexity of computer files. Instead of each program (or suite of programs) accessing and manipulating its own files, a large number of programs can share the same database, controlled by database management systems (DBMS) software. This reduces the redundancy of data, where the same information is duplicated across the files of different applications (e.g. employee address in the payroll and personnel files). Redundancy holds the danger of serious inconsistency – data might be updated in one file but not in the others. The centralization of data handling (within the DBMS) simplifies and shortens application programs, resulting in reduced development costs. Furthermore, user access is no longer constrained to the paths provided by the application programs. Database systems have become widely accepted, both in their own right as stand-alone information reporting systems and as sub-systems in support of transaction processing, office information, and decision support systems (DSS).

DBMS software originated in the file management software of the 1960s, with IBM's hierarchical IMS (Information Management System), emerging from the Apollo space project and Charles Bachman's IDS (Integrated Data Store) developed at General Electric about the same time. IMS, despite its often awkward structure, is still widely used today, especially in high performance online systems, such as the networks of bank cash machines. Bachman's ideas formed the basis of the 'network model' DBMS, which was presented as an ANSI (American National Standards Institute) standard in 1971. Attention then shifted away from these earlier models towards relational databases, that offer users and designers a straightforward tabular structure that facilitates both the development and use of databases. The solid mathematical base of the relational model simplifies the database concept, provides certain integrity controls that protect the database from accidental corruption, and reduces the likelihood of spurious output. But recently there has been a growing disenchantment with relational databases, because of serious doubts about their performance and their ability to 'model' the real world. The relational approach is currently under threat from the object-oriented and semantic data model approaches.

In terms of opportunities and risks for database systems in general, managers must come to terms with the following key issues.

Increased control of data: The centralization of the control of data through the DBMS can certainly greatly reduce redundancy and improve the consistency of stored data. Economies of scale can be achieved in integrity and security controls, that protect data from unauthorized access, and accidental or non-accidental corruption. Similarly, it is much easier to enforce standards regarding the format of data, and the operations permitted on that data. However, such centralization may cause both organizational and performance problems.

Improved data access and data sharing: DBMS offer a relatively straightforward interface, via a query language that allows inexperienced end-users to search the database in the course of *ad hoc* enquiries. DBMS provide commands that can be embedded in application programs or stand alone as a report writer, for the production of regular, formatted reports that make stored data much more accessible to end users. The allocation of file handling to the DBMS has led to a reduction in development and maintenance effort, and hence has improved programming productivity as well as data access. The sharing of data by different users should reduce duplication in data collection and data entry, and should further improve access to data.

However, these benefits crucially require that users, perhaps from different departments, are prepared to share data. Individuals and groups may derive much of their organizational power and influence from their ability to control how, when and to whom certain information is released. They may not be prepared to relinquish that control and share *their* data, and thus conflict may arise. Disputes may occur over the responsibility for maintaining the accuracy and 'up-to-dateness' of shared data items, or through proposals to change the database structure or formats. Data sharing is more likely to lead to people problems rather than technical ones, and may not be an unqualified opportunity.

Data independence: DBMS permit the separation of logical (conceptual) and physical (file organization) aspects of data storage. Thus, the physical storage arrangements can be changed without affecting the overall design and vice versa. Similarly, considerable changes can be made to the database without affecting the application programs that access it, and vice versa. Thus, the dangers of adverse 'knock-on' effects from changes in just one part of a computerized information system are reduced. In addition, different views of the data (*sub-schemas*) can be provided to different users – for example, particular fields can be omitted, re-ordered or displayed in a different format. However, although the end result is usually a more flexible system, complete data independence is not currently achievable and some changes can still cause unforeseen consequences.

Performance of centralized databases: Usually DBMS (especially relational), with their various controls and integrity checks, and large numbers of file indices, are somewhat demanding in terms of processor power, primary memory and secondary storage. Where speed is particularly important, perhaps due to the large number of transactions and customer expectations (e.g. airline reservations), or for safety critical applications (e.g. emergency services), traditional file-based systems still have a performance edge. In the summer of 1989 a number of large UK users publicly rejected relational databases for their high volume systems because of performance worries. The cost of DBMS, in terms of performance, complexity and the price of software, may not be justifiable for small systems, where there are few economies of scale.

Whilst centralization has clear advantages in controlling access to the data, it is likely to increase operational costs when large numbers of users need to share the same database. High telecommunications overheads and poor response times may result in overloading of the central database processor. Advances in networks have encouraged the development of distributed databases, where the data is divided (or reproduced) among a number of sites. However, these face significant design problems as well as the extra integrity overheads needed to ensure that updates are broadcast to every site (and received and acted upon), in order to prevent inconsistencies. While progress has been made in performance efficiency, the problems are far from solved.

Vulnerability: While failures are almost bound to occur in any system, a failure in a database that is supporting numerous applications, can be especially costly. A few years ago, problems with bugs in a new release of a supposedly well-proven DBMS caused one bank's ATM network to crash twice in four days. The complexity of the software means that the cause of failure may not be readily apparent and, consequently, recovery becomes that much more difficult. The creation of large easily-accessible databases, containing sensitive or confidential data, has considerable implications in terms of security and privacy.

Organizational conflict: Centralization may improve control, at least from the perspective of the IS department, but there are severe organizational implications. Resenting the need to share their data, users may object to losing control over this key resource to the IS department, and to the intrusion of the IS department's monitoring activities. User departments are unlikely to welcome such interference unless they can recognize significant benefits to their own position. Organizations should beware the long term reduction in the motivation of 'knowledge workers' caused by distancing them from their data. Even within the IS department, applications programmers may resent the security controls applied to databases that are accessed by their programs.

Database design: The *logical* design of a database is often the most problematic area of database development. The *First Step Fallacy* strikes again: the ease of slotting values into fields does not mean that the complexities of the 'real world' can easily be modelled to form a robust schema for the database. Data modelling [1] entails identifying: relevant *entities*, where these are objects of interest to the system; appropriate *attributes* of those entities, where these are characteristics of interest; and *relationships*, where these are links between entities. For example, a personnel database might contain the following items:

Entities	employees
Attributes	employee number, name, address, skills
Relationships	'works for' [a particular supervisor]

However, problems often arise in applying this simplistic classification to the real world [2]. It is frequently a somewhat arbitrary choice as to which entities are deigned to belong to the model, and which should be omitted. In addition, it is by no means obvious, whether, for example, a 'contract' should be categorized as a relationship between individual entities, or as an entity in its own right, with its own attributes, such as term length and penalties for breaking the contract. Similarly, the fact that an employee works for a particular department could be recorded as a relationship between the employee and the department, or the department name could be an attribute of the employee entity. Thus, the final design often results from a number of rather arbitrary decisions.

The semantic limitations of relational databases have been recognized, and much research effort is going into the improvement of tools for modelling the 'real world'. However, this is fraught with difficulty. Although different views of the database can be offered to different users, these views are limited because the database depends upon a single underlying model of the real world. It is extremely difficult to derive a single robust conceptual model, especially when the modelling is being carried out by an external analyst who does not possess the necessary familiarity with the problem situation. Much depends upon the meanings attached by users to the concepts of interest. This can be a very difficult operation in a complex and rapidly changing organizational setting. It is all too easy to impose an alien structure on a situation, and then try to force users to adopt this strange conceptualization of their workspace. Even if users are encouraged to participate fully, it is unlikely that a complete consensus will be achieved when large groups share the same database. Different individuals may have irreconcilable views, due to their personal beliefs or to the norms and values resulting from their membership of a particular work group. Perceptions of reality may be extremely subjective [3] and this variance is much easier to accommodate in an informal system, than in a formally structured database. However, without this shared view of the problem situation, data sharing becomes much more tricky and the database concept loses much of its value.

Text retrieval systems

DBMS support the handling of highly structured, record-based data, however, much of an organization's data comprises relatively unstructured documents, in the form of reports, letters and memoranda. This textual information, with its richness of interconnected ideas, does not lend itself to the rigid structuring inherent in the data models that underlie DBMS. Developments in library and information sciences led to the production of text retrieval software, initially for the handling of bibliographic data and library catalogues. Documents are represented in such databases by *keywords,* and the retrieval software matches keywords from queries with those of the documents within the database. Keywords can be automatically extracted from the text or added manually. In order to avoid some of the problems of synonyms, and the ambiguity inherent in 'natural' language, keywords can be drawn from a controlled list of classificatory terms relevant to an organization's business. As such, this is an electronic form of filing and, like most filing schemes, if a document is filed incorrectly (given the wrong keywords), or if the searcher does not understand the filing scheme, then it is unlikely that the required documents will be found. Thus, if the searcher is also the 'filing clerk', or perhaps comes from the same department, then these systems can be fairly successful. However, where the searcher is unfamiliar with the database and filing conventions, success is much less likely.

Unlike structured database systems, where the exact matching of field values (e.g. employee number) is the normal mode of operation, text retrieval is much less deterministic. In these searches, the user usually requires documents relevant to their query. Richness of language and complexity of the interconnecting relationships between topics leads to different ways of describing the same or similar topics. Thus, much depends on the user's skill in selecting keywords and formulating queries, and on the accuracy and completeness with which keywords have been applied to the stored documents. This difficult process is further complicated by the subjectivity of relevance: different users, even with the same underlying problem and making the same formal query, may judge a particular document as having different relevance.

In addition to internal databases, external online databases have been accessible for many years via communication networks. Although such databases, when linked to the terminals of many users, can be offered as central organizational information stores, they are constrained by the necessity of users to know where and how to look for information. Unlike traditional filing cabinets, it is difficult to get an overall impression of electronic files, and impossible to 'open all the drawers looking for a pink folder'.

Considerable doubts surround the effectiveness of text retrieval systems: in one study [4], most of the documents retrieved were relevant, but the number retrieved amounted to only twenty per cent of the potentially relevant documents in the database. The overlooked relevant documents were missed because their keywords were slightly different to those of the query; the efforts of the searchers were thwarted by the diversity of natural language. Many researchers have approached the problem by using statistical and mathematical models, but such models are completely unable to deal with the human and behavioural aspects of searching for information. Advances in natural language processing have made a linguistic approach feasible in certain restricted domains [5]. A more promising general approach is perhaps the use of behavioural or psychological models that seek to support the user's information seeking activities, although our lack of understanding of the cognitive mechanisms involved has limited its progress. This is an area where there are no easy solutions, and managers should recognize the limitations of current systems.

In addition to traditional text retrieval systems, many large organizations have approached the document storage problem by introducing document image processing systems. Documents are stored as graphic images, rather than as textual characters; however, from the perspective of retrieval, they still suffer from the problem of indexing images in such a way that they can be retrieved.

Personal information management systems (e.g. Lotus Agenda) have recently appeared that try to address the problem of automatically categorizing information. They rely on the user designing a classification scheme, applicable to their work, and categorizing their data accordingly. On this basis, the software is able to file documents automatically. This may be feasible for an individual user, although the user may well reject the initial investment of time in laboriously designing the classification scheme. The different views of individual users are likely to constrain the use of this approach for shared databases.

Hypertext

Another way of structuring information can be seen in hypertext systems. Their conceptual origins can be traced back to the earliest speculations about mechanized information stores: for example, Vannevar Bush's proposed Memex of 1945. Experimental systems appeared during the 1970s (e.g. Englebart's NLS/Augment and Nelson's Xanadu system), but commercial implementations did not become available until the late 1980s with Hypercard for the Apple Macintosh, Notecards for Unix workstations, and Guide for IBM PCs.

Hypertext systems consist of *objects* from some form of central database, connected together by *links*. The objects (or nodes) can be chunks of text, structured data, graphics images, voice, or sub-systems (other programs called by the hypertext system). In use, each object is usually allocated its own screen window, providing an attractive means to view related information. Links between objects are easy to both create and traverse. Hypertext potentially provides important benefits: firstly, it encourages browsing, which may be a more natural way of searching for information than is the construction of formal queries to DBMS and text retrieval systems. Secondly, it supports multiple media; an important consideration with the improved graphics handling capability of computer hardware. Furthermore, it allows users to structure their information fairly easily and with few constraints.

Considered from another perspective, hypertext is an interesting concept because it creates *non-linear* documents. Readers can take different paths through a document, depending upon the links chosen. Thus 'chapters' can be read in different orders, depending upon the wishes of the reader. This alternative to the traditional linearity of books (and computer files) may be particularly useful for teaching material and reference books.

Whilst hypertext systems mostly meet their claims in respect of structuring multi-media information and providing good browsing facilities, there are a number of problems. Perhaps the worst problem is that of the complexity that results from myriad links between large numbers of nodes. In traversing large systems, it is very easy for users to become disoriented and 'lost in hyperspace', although this can be partially alleviated through providing system-wide maps and backtracking facilities. However, the problem of maintaining a large number of links in a fast-changing database can be a nightmare; the frequent addition and deletion of both links and nodes can result in a complex tangle of pointers leading nowhere. Users faced with such complexity are likely to simply opt out altogether. Structuring information may be relatively easy but significant restructuring may be much more difficult. Thus, although hypertext may be of considerable benefit for certain, relatively well-bounded and stable applications, it is unlikely to be appropriate for the more central dynamic storage role.

Is information a resource?

Before discussing the practice of information resource management, it is instructive to examine briefly the central assumption that information is in fact a resource. It is widely accepted that we are entering a post-industrial, *Information Age* where information becomes the key tradeable resource. It would seem almost unnecessary to question its status as a resource. However, it turns out that this question is rather difficult to resolve, partly due to the nature of information and partly due to our lack of conceptual tools.

Information is rather different to the traditional economic resources of land, labour and capital. On the one hand, information is clearly an essential part of decision-making, management and control. Conceptually, it seems to make sense that certain information be included in production functions, and it could be hypothesized that information obeys the law of diminishing returns to scale, where successive increments of information add less value. Also, in practical terms, certain information is regularly bought and sold, and some information may provide the organization with a (temporary) competitive advantage. This accounts for the popularity of external online databases for financial and business information, even though they are relatively expensive to access.

On the other hand, information behaves very differently to traditional resources in several key respects. Firstly, information is an intangible, human notion that resists any convenient form of quantification, and so prevents the application of most ideas from the field of economics. Secondly, information is a non-exclusive public good, which can be passed from supplier to recipient, while still retained by the supplier – 'more for you does not mean less for me'. Thirdly, information does not necessarily deteriorate with usage, but more with age. Furthermore, information is very heterogeneous, including facts, beliefs, judgements, opinions, advice, misinformation and propaganda. This variety, and the subjective and social importance given to the various types of information, is very difficult to explain in rigorously theoretical terms.

In terms of decision making, some information is obviously essential but research suggests that managers normally try to simplify the process by shedding information. Information overload is very common, in which case, certain informal information (e.g. opinions of peers) may be very highly valued, but much routine information may be deliberately ignored. Determining the value of information is an extremely difficult problem; it is highly context-dependent, so that often it is meaningless to fix monetary values on particular information items. In truth, most information used by organizations is of little commercial value to others; the hefty bills for accessing business databases are an exception. The relative failure of the UK Prestel national videotex system, discussed in the following chapter, was partly due to the problems of *selling* leisure information; the price acceptable to the market turned out to be pitifully low. In the context of the free exchange of information within, and often between organizations, and the traditional strong support for free public libraries, most managers have little experience in paying directly for information. Researchers have found that managers experience considerable difficulty in placing a monetary value on information that they regularly use for decision-taking.

It could be argued that this dilemma could be resolved by rephrasing the question slightly. For instance, it might be more correct to discuss *data* as a resource, rather than information, where the latter is interpreted data. Similarly, in the parlance of economics, the term *commodity* may be preferable to resource, as goods that are commercially traded, and thus classified as commodities, are socially determined. However, it is debatable whether such adjustments help very much in explaining the economic behaviour of information. Some commentators attribute our difficulties to a poverty of (economics) theory: "One should hardly have to tell academicians that information is a valuable resource: knowledge is power. And yet it occupies a slum dwelling in the town of economics" [6].

Information resource management

In the late 1970s, a distinctive approach to information management emerged in the shape of *information resource management*. Its central tenet is that organizations should manage their information in the same way as they manage other resources. It originated in three relatively distinct areas. The first, in the information systems management literature, where anticipation of the *Information Society,* peopled by *knowledge workers,* called for a theoretical exposition. This was found in theories such as Nolan's Stage Model that characterizes an organization as having reached maturity in information technology maturity when it manages its information as a resource.

Secondly, many early writings originated in the field of administrative and records management. In the 1970s, there was considerable concern over the amount of paperwork produced by the various levels of the US government, culminating in the US Paperwork Reduction Act of 1980, which called for paper records to be more actively managed.

The third source was the increasing evidence of the management and organizational problems found during database implementation. The expertise and effort required to develop, maintain and control databases, had prompted the appearance of a new role in the IS department: that of the database administrator (DBA). They are responsible for all aspects of the design, implementation and operation of the database systems, including security and integrity. This entailed controlling access to the databases and monitoring their usage and performance. The role is a technical one, yet many of the problems are organizational. With the DBA preoccupied with the short term technical problems of individual databases, many commentators saw a need for a longer term, planning function. This emerged in the strategic role of the *data administrator,* who is responsible for planning, coordinating and integrating databases. However, in the face of organizational difficulties, this strategic function often proved futile without some form of senior management support.

The growing budgets, ambition and power of the IS department, as IT services became more central to the organization's activities, had already heightened demands for representation at senior management level. Thus, high-level Chief Information Officer (CIO) posts were created in many organizations. The notion of information resource management became an acceptable *raison d'être* for this post, as well as being an easily memorizable slogan, even if it was not always a deeply held philosophy. Thus, the CIO became responsible for the management of the information asset and the articulation of the information resource management philosophy amongst senior managers.

While the management of information as a resource is hard to justify in theoretical economic terms, the 'pure' form is equally hard to justify as a pragmatic management policy. There is a tremendous amount of information flowing around most organizations, much of which is either useless, harmless or both. Such information does not need to be managed unless it interferes with useful information, but this does not necessarily imply treating it as a *resource.*

In the majority of cases, information management should be treated more like good housekeeping that prevents excessive duplication of acquisition and storage, and reduces information overload. It should include policies to link data stored in different forms (electronic text, graphics images, paper files) and to provide appropriate levels of security and back-up. This should include policies towards the compatibility of (electronic) file formats. But, integration is more than format specifications. Many departments store marginally relevant data, that they have difficulty in interpreting. A more effective policy would often be to store the names of experts within the organization to whom that data is central; such experts can then provide the required interpretation.

The construction of complex administrative procedures to control the collection, storage and distribution of all an organization's information is akin to counting grains of sand; it can be done but at the cost of creating a bureaucratic edifice of frightening proportions. Certain data does require careful validation, but this does not justify tying up key personnel in preparing and implementing irrelevant policies for information planning and for the valuation of information. Furthermore, information resource management, if 'swallowed whole', implies that an organization is merely a system for processing information. This positivistic model depicts the input of information into organizations and decision models, which in turn produce certain required outputs. It disregards the important social, political and cultural aspects of organizations. However, certain information does need special treatment. Apart from the information that is critical for the operation of the organization, other information of a sensitive nature requires specific management policies to protect it from outside interference. This information may be sensitive in business terms; for example, information that would be detrimental in the hands of a competitor, or of relevance to data protection legislation.

We have already noted that the control of certain information may provide groups with considerable organizational power and influence. Considering information as a political resource, rather than an economic resource, the move towards information resource management may be seen in a new, perhaps more sinister, light. The political beneficiaries of such a policy turn out to be none other than the IS department. Cynics might have some grounds for regarding the popularity of this approach as little more than self-interest, where organizational power, based on the control of information, accrues to the IS department.

These objections leave information resource management severely lacking as a general approach to information systems management [7]. It cannot be satisfactorily justified in theoretical terms and, as a pragmatic approach to the day-to-day management of an organization's information systems, it is inappropriate in respect of most information. However, for particularly important information, or where specific problems arise, the approach may provide managers with a useful perspective as a first step towards determining a solution. Even in these cases, it is seldom likely to be efficient or acceptable to remove the control of the information from the individual decision-maker, who should be assisted and not robbed. Senior management should be aware of the thin dividing line between broad company policies (regarding, say, the standardization of data formats) and excessive bureaucracy or distorted power structures. Information needs to be managed pragmatically, not mystified or deified.

Conclusion

The progress made in various types of database technology has been impressive, but there remain significant problems in storing information in such a way that it can be retrieved effortlessly. In skilled hands, the technology can become an extremely useful tool. However, managers should be aware of its limitations. Difficulties regarding the richness and ambiguity of language, and the different ways that people view the world are further compounded by the political aspects surrounding the control of organizational information. There are no easy answers that can be applied across the board. Management policies should be governed by particular problem situations, and include a consideration of both the people involved and the nature of the information, its usefulness and sensitivity. In many circumstances, *a little black book in the bottom drawer* can still outperform sophisticated database systems.

Discussion issues

1. Discuss ways of formally integrating different types of information; for example, word processing files, database files, paper files, calendars and diaries. Do you think that the overheads are worthwhile or should we rely on more informal, human methods?
2. Is information resource management meaningful or useful? Should it be an article of faith for IS professionals?

Exercises

1. Take a relatively short piece of text (perhaps something that you have written) and try to represent it in the form of an entity-relationship model.
2. For a small organization (perhaps an office in your department or college), try to determine the importance of the various information sets that are used/stored there. Create your own scale of importance.

References

1. Chen, P.,'The entity-relationship model: toward a unified view of data', *ACM Transactions on Database Systems*, 1(1), 9-36, 1976.
2. Kent, W., *Data and reality*, North Holland, Amsterdam, 1978.
3. Klein, H. & Hirschheim, R.A.,'A comparative framework of data modelling paradigms and approaches', *Computer Journal*, Vol.30, No.1, 8-15, 1987.
4. Blair, D.C. & Maron, M.E.,'An evaluation of retrieval effectiveness for a full-text document-retrieval system', *Communications of the ACM*, 28(3), 289-299, 1985.
5. Jacobs, P.S. & Rau, L.F.,'SCISOR: extracting information from online news', *Communications of the ACM*, 33(11), 88-97, 1990.
6. Stigler, G.J.,'The economics of information', *Journal of Political Economy*, Vol.89, 213-225, 1961.
7. King, J.L. & Kraemer, K.L.,'Information resource management: is it sensible and can it work?', *Information and Management*, Vol.15, 7-14, 1988.

Suggested reading

Structured database systems

Date, C.J., *Introduction to database systems*, Vol.1., 5th edition, Addison-Wesley, Reading, Mass.,1990.

McFadden, F.R. & Hoffer, J.A., *Data base management*, Benjamin Cummings, Menlo Park, Calif., 1985.

Text retrieval systems

Salton, G. & McGill, M.J., *Introduction to modern information retrieval*, McGraw-Hill, New York, 1983.

Belkin, N.J. & Vickery, A., *Interaction in information systems*, British Library, London, 1985.

Hypertext

Conklin, J.,'Hypertext: an introduction and survey', *Computer*, Vol.20, No.9, 17-41, 1987.

Information resource management

Trauth, E.,'The evolution of information resource management', *Information and Management*, Vol.16, 257-268, 1989.

King, J.L. & Kraemer, K.L.,'Information resource management: is it sensible and can it work?', *Information and Management*, Vol.15, 7-14, 1988.

8 Data communication and network services

- *Communication networks: the third wave*
- *Technological infrastructure*
- *Network management*
- *Network services*
- *Communications services*
- *Information services*
- *Risks*

It is difficult to overstate the importance of fast, cheap and reliable telecommunication networks for the growth of computer-based information systems. However, it is equally hard to overstate the problems of developing successful networks. They affect most aspects of information systems management, from issues of policy and strategy, to the much narrower technical details of implementation. In this chapter we shall first discuss the opportunities offered by networks, before briefly summarizing some of the recent technological trends. This sets the scene for an examination of the issues involved in network management and the alternative network services currently available. Networking is a high security area, and we discuss the risks involved, before concluding with a recognition of the need for a network strategy.

Communication networks: the third wave

Data communication networks have been termed the 'third wave' of information technology [1]. The first wave, aimed at cost efficiency, comprised the use of mainframe-based transaction processing systems, while the second wave, characterized by personal computers and online systems, aimed at improving organizational effectiveness. The third and final wave, based on computer networks, actually impacts the structure and work processes of organizations through the introduction of new work methods, such as telecommuting, and new products, services and marketplaces. The convergence of computing and telecommunications has already transformed many parochial data processing departments into suppliers of information services, and forced developers to relax their 'closed world' assumptions. Many commentators foresee considerable growth in the network market, as shown in the example of figure 8.1.

	European market ($m)	
	1988	1993
Electronic mail	150	720
Electronic funds transfer	140	530
Videotex	130	440
Electronic data interchange	40	260

Figure 8.1 The expected growth of the network market [2]

Networks offer considerable opportunities in two broad areas. Firstly, a fast, reliable communications infrastructure should increase the effectiveness and efficiency of an organization, through improved coordination and control. Information is naturally distributed around organizations and the development of successively faster computers counts for little if communication is dependent upon traditional telephone lines and couriers. Networks permit fast multi-media communication between widely dispersed sites, allowing the controlled sharing of hardware, software and data within an organization. Improved coordination promises significant cost savings through reduced inventories, improved treasury management, and a reduction in administrative costs and delays. These benefits could be passed on to the customer in terms of a faster and better quality service at more competitive prices. While improving central control, through the enforcement of network standards, networks also give the opportunity to decentralize. They can allow greater overall autonomy to local sites, through the provision of information and communication services. Furthermore, networks are already becoming an essential part of an organization's information systems infrastructure, providing the arteries for the communication that is the lifeblood of office information systems, factory systems, etc. Secondly, networks allow the development of new services; for example, automatic teller machines (ATMs) have radically changed the face of banking. Inter-organizational information systems are likely to change networking from simple machine interconnection to a technology that redefines the interface between businesses and their customers. The huge demand for a fast, reliable mechanism for the exchange of information between organizations, linked with the growing 'maturity' of both users and the technology, may mean that inter-organizational systems will become commonplace during the 1990s. They are likely to include both shared facilities, such as the SWIFT international banking network and electronic data interchange (EDI) networks, as well as systems claimed by a single firm to gain a competitive advantage over its competitors, such as the American Airlines seat reservation system and the American Hospital Supply Company's ordering system.

Technological infrastructure

Considerable progress has been made in channel technology with the advent of high speed, high capacity, fibre optic cables, satellite links and microwave radio. Fibre optic cables offer data speeds of up to 150 megabits per second, as well as being more difficult to tap into. The cost of satellite transmission has tumbled from $23,000 per circuit per annum in 1965 to approximately $50 in the late 1980s. Satellites are used by certain newspapers (e.g. *USA Today*) to link a central editorial site with printing plants all around the world. Similarly, microwave radio signals can be effective for relatively short-distance, line-of-sight communication. Radio transmission also promises much in the way of portable data transmission through radio links to base stations located on the public telephone network. This is likely to become a reality as personal communication networks become commonplace in the mid-1990s.

Traditional analogue signalling is being replaced gradually by digital signalling, which offers increased speed and reliability (less noise) as well as the ability to handle multi-media communication. ISDNs (Integrated Service Digital Networks), that combine voice and data traffic (and possibly video images) on the same high-speed channel, are being promoted as the future highways for telecommunications. Their supporters see ISDNs as the essential communications infrastructure for an *Information Society*, just as the development of a railway network fuelled the Industrial Revolution. However, despite much publicity, customer acceptance has been slow in most countries, with the possible exception of the French NUMERIS service, which has been able to offer a high level of financial inducements. This international reluctance of users to invest seems to arise from doubts about the benefits of integrated communication, the high costs (including specialized terminal equipment) and uncertainty regarding standards. Existing telecommunications networks may be adequate in the short term, leaving ISDNs as a long term solution looking for a problem.

Considerable progress has been made in the development of international communications standards that ensure that hardware and software from different suppliers can communicate. These complex network protocols, enshrined in the ISO/OSI (International Standards Organization/Open Systems Interconnection) seven-layer framework, have been widely accepted. The framework allows simultaneous control and error-checking at various levels, ranging from single bits to files, and from hardware interconnections to application software linkages, and deals with aspects of routing and failure recovery. These standards have been fairly successful in bringing order to the lower-level aspects of transmission, but a number of the higher-level standards remain to be set. Whilst standard protocols are essential, the process of setting standards is very slow, especially where this involves the deliberation of large international committees and where the results can have considerable commercial implications. The delay in setting standards inevitably results in a 'wait and see' policy by many organizations, and once standards are set, they may act as a disincentive to further technical innovation. The alternative for user organizations is to subscribe to a proprietary network, such as IBM's Systems Network Architecture (SNA), with the attendant risks of being locked-in to a single, commercially powerful, supplier.

Networks are usually classified according to the distance they cover. The first to appear were wide area networks (WANs), which originated with ARPANET, a research network set up in 1969 and funded by the US Department of Defense. ARPANET expanded from 20 nodes in 1971 to over 100 nodes by the late 1980s, stretching from Hawaii, across the USA to Europe. WANs are usually operated by third-party suppliers and, over time, many have become widely accepted by the communities they serve, such as the university BITNET network. These complex networks allow simultaneous interconnection of a large number of different machine types, through multiple paths over long distances.

However, much of the communication needs of an organization are restricted to the same site; it has been estimated that 90 per cent of all organizational information travels less than 0.5 miles, and 75 per cent less than 600 feet. Here local area networks (LANs) offer reliable, high capacity, high speed (up to 10 Megabits per second) links between microcomputers and peripheral devices (e.g. printers), as well as *gateways* to mainframes and external networks. As such, they have been termed the *glue* that holds office information systems together.

Compared to a centralized system, LANs give users improved performance, flexibility and extendability, as well as considerable independence of operation, and reduced vulnerability to central failures. Although LANs offer clear benefits, in terms of shared data, software and peripherals, they still represent a sizeable investment (several hundred dollars per machine). Where there is a clear need for large volumes of electronic communication, a fully-fledged LAN may be fairly easy to justify. After some years, a number of standards have emerged, including Ethernet and the IBM Token Ring, reducing earlier compatibility problems. But there is increased risk. LANs may be less secure than mainframes and less easy to reconstitute after failures. The cost and disruption associated with installing the necessary cabling should not be underestimated; most offices were not built with such needs in mind, and the routing/ducting of cables can be a mammoth task. Metropolitan area networks (MANs), covering a city or distinct urban conurbation, have been proposed as an effective way of linking WANs and LANs.

The PABX (Private Automatic Branch Exchange) is basically a sophisticated telephone exchange that has been proposed as both an alternative and a complement to LANs. A PABX offers a range of impressive voice facilities (e.g. rerouting and stacking calls, abbreviated dialling, conference calls) as well as acting as a central data switch that can use existing telephone lines. However, this advantage may be offset by the vulnerability inherent in any centralized system, so that a failure of the PABX may result in the loss of all data and voice communication. In addition, few organizations wish to clog up their low-speed telephone lines with data traffic. To date, most organizations have chosen PABXs for voice traffic and LANs for data. Expensive broadband LANs offer another alternative for integrating internal voice and data traffic but, as with ISDNs, there seems to be little interest amongst most users.

Network management

Private corporate networks, representing a large investment, provide the spinal cord for an organization's communications, rendering network management a key area in IS management. Network management has elements of all three management levels: operational control, diagnosis and remedy of faults; tactical management, medium term implementation and maintenance; and strategic management, a long term view of the future shape of the corporate network. Network management has to balance the conflicting pressures for centralization and decentralization of the organization's information systems. As such, both the setting of network standards and the provision of flexibility are politically sensitive areas.

The prime aim of network management is to optimize the performance of the network, ensuring an uninterrupted communications service to all destinations at a sufficient level of security. In functional terms, network management comprises all aspects of the planning, development, installation and maintenance of the networks. Networks represent an expensive finite resource, and so capacity planning and traffic monitoring are essential to avoid either bottlenecks or surplus capacity. There is a growing awareness that such problems are not susceptible to a 'quick fix' and can involve considerable expense and delay. The introduction of new, prestigious information systems, without regard to their impact on the network infrastructure or a sudden, unplanned increase in traffic can bring the entire network grinding to a halt. In addition to utilization, monitoring should include keeping track of costs, availability, response time, and security aspects.

Network management can be supported by various software packages (e.g. IBM's Netview), aimed primarily at the monitoring function. However, it is severely constrained by the complexities of multi-vendor systems, or even components, and the shortage of skilled personnel. Problems and uncertainties have led many organizations to contract out all or part of the function to a third-party supplier at a fixed price, or, where traffic levels are particularly low, to subscribe to a public network.

Network services

During the 1980s, changes in the regulatory infrastructure transformed the international telecommunications market. In virtually all countries, the telephone system has traditionally been a public monopoly of the Postal, Telephone and Telegraph authority (PTT), a policy that has prevented the costly duplication of facilities, eased international interconnections, and allowed uneconomic services to be provided on the basis of social need. However, this policy, extended to data communications, prevented new companies from offering services that were judged to be the prerogative of the PTT. A growing dissatisfaction with the performance of PTTs, together with an awareness of the opportunities for new communications services, led to varying degrees of deregulation, starting in the USA during the late 1970s with the break-up of AT&T's monopoly. It was hoped that competition would improve efficiency, reduce prices and encourage innovation through new services. In the UK, managed deregulation based on licences, commenced in the early 1980s. Only one competitor (Mercury) was initially allowed to compete with the privatized British Telecom for basic transmission.

Licences were fairly freely issued for value added networks (VANs), networks that offer services over and above basic transmission. These network services form a hierarchy, with those near the top providing the most added value. The hierarchy is shown below in figure 8.2.

Information services
    Services that actually provide information
        e.g. information retrieval systems;

Communications services
    Services that entail significant amounts of network processing
        e.g. electronic data interchange and electronic mail;

Managed data networks
    Networks that only provide low-level services
        e.g. protocol conversion and packet switching;

Basic transmission   In the UK this is only offered by British Telecom and Mercury.

Figure 8.2 The network services hierarchy

Basic transmission requires no further elaboration, and managed data networks provide the network management functions discussed above. The following sections discuss communication and information services. It should be noted that we are mostly concerned with network services for business. Network services for the home, including telemedical applications, debates on local issues, and the remote control of household appliances have found little acceptance to date. The major exception is the case of home workers (*telecommuters*), who use network services to stay in continuous contact with their organizations.

Communications services

Electronic data interchange (EDI)

EDI services provide an electronic interchange for the large amounts of structured transaction data (e.g. orders, invoices and statements) that flow continuously between organizations, including manufacturers, wholesalers and retailers. This inter-organizational service promises to speed-up transactions, allowing the opportunity of offering an improved service to customers. Also, the reduction in rekeying of data should reduce administrative costs and errors. This should be especially valuable for foreign trade, where there may be hundreds of different forms (bills of lading etc.); it has been suggested that such paperwork amounts to 7 per cent of the value of goods shipped in international trade. Significant cost savings are possible; General Motors estimated that $250 per car could be saved by cutting out traditional documentation, and IBM expects to save $60 million over five years. Some companies have reported considerable savings in stock levels and expenditure on delivery couriers. The speed and reliability of EDI fits neatly into the *Just in Time* philosophy of modern manufacturing, and is consistent with the support requirements of a global market.

The UK's INS service carries approximately 800,000 documents monthly for 900 subscribers and offers a gateway to the Geisco international EDI network. However, relatively few UK organizations have integrated EDI into their business. Further acceptance depends on the achievement of a critical mass of users and this seems to rely largely on major organizations exerting pressure on their partners to adopt EDI. For example, the UK National Health Service is reported to have decided that, by 1992, 80 per cent of its orders should be handled electronically. In the USA there are more than 5000 users, with General Foods reportedly using EDI for 25 per cent of their shipments. The US market is expected to grow to $1.3 billion per annum by 1991. Some of the early compatibility problems in document formats are gradually being resolved with the growth of international standards, although some doubts remain about the legal validity of electronic documents. There are also serious worries over the lack of control and audit of electronic orders and payments [3], without traditional manual checks and balances. A high level of automation and integration may result in the system authorizing an automatic payment as soon as an invoice is (electronically) received, with little or no human intervention. There may be considerable scope for electronic malfunctioning and fraud in these complex, highly autonomous systems; the potential impact of this is hard to imagine.

Electronic funds transfer (EFT)

EFT refers to the electronic transmission of credits and debits between banks, organizations and individuals, heralding a more *cashless* society. EFT includes both inter-bank transfers of vast sums of electronic money (e.g. through the SWIFT international network), and the ATM (Automatic Teller Machine) service of individual depositors. These services are, to a greater or lesser extent, in place and have been widely accepted by all parties. However, despite impressive levels of reliability, large sums of money are still occasionally misdirected.

The critical extension to EFTPOS (Electronic Funds Transfer – Point of Sale), would link banks to existing EPOS systems in shops. EPOS capture sales data (from bar-coded price tags), total the sales, and provide accounting and stock reordering information. EFTPOS enables immediate dispatch of debit instructions to the customer's bank, and the appropriate amount is automatically transferred to the shop's account at the time of the sale, without any cash changing hands. In principle, the process is the same as a cheque, but it is much faster and more cost-efficient. There are few obvious technical problems, but despite progress in certain countries (e.g. Norway), a national service in the UK has been stalled on the question of who pays for the network: the banks, the shops or the customer. Meanwhile, individual banks have been developing their own systems. Banks stand to make the greatest savings, through a reduction in handling costs; shops too should see some improvement in their cash flow. There are few obvious benefits for the customer, to offset against the need to ensure that their bank balances are sufficient to meet the greater speed of debits, and the effort needed to recover erroneous debits that have been paid automatically.

Electronic mail (E-mail)

Electronic mail, the transmission of electronic messages between individuals through a system of electronic mailboxes, originated in the 1970s with the ARPANET network. There are numerous varieties of electronic mail system, ranging from single site systems to industry-wide or public networks, but they are all based on the *store-and-forward* mode of message passing. As well as the obvious facilities for creating, sending and receiving messages, the more sophisticated systems permit multiple addressing, abbreviated addressing, the use of mailing lists and automatic status information (e.g. whether the message has arrived or the recipient has accessed the message).

E-mail is a potentially important service to the many knowledge workers who spend large amounts of time communicating, either by telephone or letter. It offers fast, desynchronized communication (the recipient does not have to be present). This is particularly useful for international messages between different time zones, where the real-time communication window may be only a few hours daily. E-mail claims to eliminate *'telephone tag'*, the time wasted in unsuccessful calls, where the person required is not available (and fails to return the call) or is constantly engaged. One estimate is that only 28 per cent of telephone calls are completed successfully at the first attempt. Unlike the telephone, E-mail does not interrupt recipients and it allows them time to think before answering. Compared to the telephone, significant time economies can be achieved when multiple copies of a message have to be distributed. In addition, it provides a record that can be useful for clarification, and for 'fixing the blame' for particular disasters.

However, the recording of messages tends to annul the advantages of openness and community feeling often claimed by supporters of electronic mail. Compared to telephone calls, E-mail cannot incorporate intonation and emphasis, and it may actually reduce social interaction; messages lack the verbal 'padding' used to maintain a working relationship. Interpersonal communication is more than the mere exchange of specific messages; it provides participants with the opportunity to discuss future activities and to exchange opinions on currently peripheral issues that may become crucial in the future. Rather, electronic mail encourages terseness, sometimes leading to the problem of *flaming*, where carelessly phrased messages precipitate aggressive responses, and a feedback of antagonism that can cause major social problems within an organization. In some cases (see [4]), social interaction actually increased; although there were fewer information-giving personal interactions, face-to-face meetings became longer, with increased discussion and participation.

However, E-mail cannot provide the immediate confirmation or request for clarification that is possible by telephone. Also, unwanted *junk mail*, that can consume valuable time, is difficult to filter out, except on the rather dubious basis of the sender's name. Although E-mail is very flexible, in that users can log-in to their mailboxes from anywhere in the world, it is crucially dependent upon the recipient opening their mailbox. The desynchronous nature of E-mail may not be an advantage if used as a ploy to avoid personal interaction or official control procedures, while still giving the impression of urgency. Finally, the recording of messages, including notes of senders and recipients, can be used as a subtle form of monitoring that is unlikely to encourage openness and loyalty.

The success of E-mail crucially depends upon the formation of a critical mass, a large enough community to encourage the *non-enthusiasts* to invest the time required to learn the (often rather cumbersome) procedures. In practice, electronic mail tends to replace internal memoranda rather than telephone calls. There is little evidence that electronic mail creates new communication links, although in many cases, the frequency of existing links has increased.

Whilst internal E-mail has been fairly successful in some organizations, there is much less inter-organizational or public use; in 1988 the *Financial Times* described it as an *unfulfilled promise*. By then, rather than the predicted one million public mailboxes in Europe, there were less than 200,000 (mostly within the UK). Even these figures can be deceptive: British Telecom claimed 112,000 mailboxes for its public Telecom Gold service, but of these, 43,000 belonged to its own employees. Other statistics suggest that only 50,000 UK mailboxes are really active. Although usage might increase with the recent introduction of international standards (X.400), the popularity of facsimile transmission may have stolen much of electronic mail's thunder.

The same mailbox principle can also be used for store-and-forward voice messages. These inexpensive systems eliminate the need for keyboard skills and may be appropriate for simple messages. However, they suffer from the same artificiality as telephone answering machines; voice communication needs feedback. Of course, success again depends upon the recipient opening their mailbox regularly.

E-mail should be seen as an additional option, appropriate in certain circumstances, but not a wholesale replacement for conventional communication.

Teleconferencing

Teleconferencing supports meetings where the participants are not in the same physical location. The most sophisticated variant, video-conferencing includes the real-time exchange of video images between sites, so that participants can both see and hear each other. Conferences can be set up quickly, without the delays involved in waiting for busy participants to travel long distances. However, the social interaction is likely to be synthetic. For better or worse, there may be less opportunity for the informal, agenda-fixing 'meetings' in the corridor or bar that normally precede the official meeting. Similarly, video-conferencing cannot replicate the political impact of a personal visit. Furthermore, the role of the chairman becomes more important, for example in deciding whose turn it is to speak, and thus who appears on camera. The dangers of a chairman *stacking* a meeting, for the benefit of one party, implies that video-conferences may be more suitable for non-contentious meetings.

The Ford Motor Company (Europe) has held regular video-conferences between Dagenham (UK) and Ford's German plants. Although expensive, video-conferences potentially save travel time and money, it is probably short-sighted to aim solely at travel savings as this may be unpopular where travel is seen as a 'perk' of the job. Due to their high installation and operating costs, and little enthusiasm from potential users, relatively few video-conference systems have been permanently installed within organizations. In some cases, video-conferences have produced benefits reflected in increased total communication and more personal visits. Experiments have taken place in various UK government departments with a view to using video-conferencing to facilitate the relocation of offices away from crowded central London to more 'attractive' sites elsewhere in the UK. Video-conferences have also been used for training purposes, although the economies achieved (in travel etc.) must be weighed against the costs in terms of cheapening, or diluting, the learning environment.

Other types of teleconference include the less expensive audio (telephone) conferences and computer conferences. The latter have been used mostly for non-urgent collaboration or leisure pursuits. They comprise the asynchronous exchange of messages on a specific topic, through a central computer, over a period of several days or weeks. While this seems a relatively simple and inexpensive way of ensuring that an organization's experts keep abreast of their specific field, the loss of face-to-face contact with their peers is usually an unwelcome economy. Furthermore, popular 'conferences' can result in a deluge of repetitive, circuitous information. Like most of the new network services, the various types of teleconference should be seen as additional communications options, only appropriate in particular cases.

Facsimile transmission (FAX)

FAX has achieved considerable growth in a relatively short time; the UK market has doubled every year from 1985 to 1988. In 1988 there were 659,000 terminals in Europe, and this is expected to rise to 6.3 million by 1994. FAX systems transmit document images across a network, simply but effectively, providing a fast reliable service for urgent documents, which can incorporate 'original' signatures and graphics images. Although FAX achieved success as a stand-alone service, add-in FAX boards are available for microcomputers, and provide some level of integration with other communications options.

Much of the success of FAX may be attributed to its conceptual simplicity, with its similarity to the familiar photocopier, as well as its overall ease of use. It is a very general solution, operating nationally and internationally, and usable in a wide range of applications from transmitting memoranda to news photos to fingerprints. This should be seen as a lesson to those who promote complexity for its own sake. The falling transmission costs of FAX have meant that junk FAX has become viable. This effectively transfers much of the costs (paper, machine utilization) to the recipient. In addition to provoking litigation, this practice has encouraged at least one irate organization to take revenge by transmitting back ten blank sheets of paper back for each page it receives.

Information services

Information retrieval systems (IRSs)

During the 1970s, IRSs began to appear in the shape of external online databases, utilizing text retrieval software, and were accessed by users through networks. The number of databases grew from six in 1973, to more than 3000 today. Originally they were mostly large mainframe-based bibliographic databases of scientific information, aimed at providing researchers with convenient access to vast stores of scientific literature. Whilst IRSs potentially offer fast, flexible access to a huge amount of information, they suffer from the problems of text retrieval discussed in Chapter 7, as well as being expensive and difficult to use. Even though most searches are carried out by trained intermediaries, they often result in an excess of non-relevant documents for all but the most specific queries.

However, an increasing demand for business information and the growing familiarity with IT within organizations, coupled with the development · of electronic markets, has led to the development of a new generation of such systems for financial and business information. These are more structured and easier to use, and have found some success with specialist users. Such systems provide stock market prices (e.g. Reuters), econometric data (PREDICASTS) and general business intelligence, including information on companies (Dun and Bradstreet), credit worthiness (UAPT Infolink), marketing information (MAGIC), law (LEXIS), patents (PATSEARCH), and news (NEXIS). They still require a certain amount of expertise, so that many inexperienced users prefer their searches to be carried out by information brokers.

The economics of such services are a particularly difficult aspect, from both the supply and demand sides of the equation. On the supply side, considerable investment in data collection and the mounting of databases has resulted in excessive prices in certain embryo markets. Many users are reluctant to pay high prices for information, except where this can easily be justified in commercial terms, or where there is no alternative. This has led to complex tariff structures with services becoming popular in particular industries (e.g. pharmaceuticals). The economic picture is further obscured by the strategic acquisition of information providers by multinational publishers, who wish to gain a foothold in the market and who are prepared to subsidize these services. In addition, the ease with which users can download information into local microcomputer databases, for further manipulation without further payment, affects the economics of both users and database operators. Databases are beginning to appear on CD-ROM disks that can be distributed on a subscription basis to users, who then access them locally without incurring hefty communications and usage charges. It is far from clear how to price such emergent technologies, which clearly cannot adopt the pricing structures of their predecessors.

Videotex

Videotex (known in the UK as *viewdata*) is an interesting example of a solution that arguably has still not found an appropriate problem. As such, it should be a warning to both innovators and technocrats. Developed by British Telecom (then the Post Office) during the mid-1970s, with the aim of increasing off-peak telephone usage, the pioneering Prestel service was introduced in 1980. Like other videotex systems, Prestel is an interactive information service, based on relatively cheap and familiar hardware: an adapted television set and conventional telephone line. Using straightforward, user-friendly menus, the user navigates through attractive colour frames of information. Prestel was initially aimed at the domestic market, offering news and weather, marketing and sales, and various items of leisure information. Currently it also offers home banking, electronic mail, gateways to other networks, a software delivery service for microcomputer enthusiasts, and tele-shopping (mail order).

Prestel was a technical success, but in terms of acceptance and profitability, it was a major marketing failure [5]; rather than the forecast one million users by 1985, the actual take-up was 52,000. There were a number of fundamental reasons for Prestel's failure:

- The architecture of a single central Prestel database restricted the amount of information to the largely superficial; gateways to information providers' own databases would probably have been more successful.
- Inability to compete with the very low market price of domestic information and the consumer loyalty to traditional information sources, such as newspapers and television. This was exacerbated by Prestel's complex pricing scheme and the competition from free teletext services (see below).
- The 'chicken and egg' problem of persuading information suppliers to invest in providing large amounts of information without a guaranteed audience, who could only be attracted by large amounts of information.
- Poor coordination between Prestel, the information providers and the television set manufacturers.

While a failure in the home market, Prestel achieved some success with services for closed user groups and its Micronet network for microcomputer enthusiasts.

A number of private business systems were successful: for example, the London Stock Exchange's TOPIC system for share prices, and Thomson Travel's holiday reservation system for travel agents. TOPIC boasts 10,000 terminals, and 7.5 million frame accesses per day against Prestel's 200,000, and Thomson's system is reportedly used for up to 28,000 bookings per day. With hindsight, it is not surprising that the business market proved to be less price sensitive than the domestic market. With the exception of France, where terminals were made available for free, most national videotex services have met a similar fate to Prestel. There are now Teletel terminals in about 3 million French homes, and the system is regularly used for telephone directory enquiries. Curiously, it has also been much used for pornographic activities – reportedly one-third of total usage. Another television-based information service, broadcast *teletext*, was introduced in the UK in 1976 as CEEFAX (BBC) and ORACLE (ITV). Unlike videotex, teletext offers just one-way communication with pages of information broadcast in the spare capacity offered by television signals. To maintain a reasonable response time, the number of pages is strictly limited. The service is offered free; the information being mostly public service (e.g. weather, news, travel bulletins) or marketing (e.g. television schedules, mail order announcements). While it may have some value for small frequently-changing news items, the market is clearly limited. However, based on existing market data, it seems that this is all most householders currently require in terms of electronic information services.

Risks

If, as outlined above, the opportunities are potentially huge, so too, unfortunately, are the risks. Although many of the technical problems have been overcome, networking remains a potential quicksand where companies gamble increasingly large amounts of investment capital; the investments of some American banks have already reached hundreds of millions of dollars. Few organizations can confidently take such risks in a fast-changing technological environment, where it may be difficult to distinguish future technological standards from the merely unproven, or worse, those fast approaching obsolescence. Furthermore, the financial justification for increased infrastructural investment is never that straightforward, suffering from the perennial evaluation problems, discussed in Chapter 11. Operating costs for voice and data communications can be substantial, exceeding 2 per cent of revenue; American Express is reported to spend $200 million per annum on communications. Despite the predicted market growth, the field of networking is littered with the carcasses of failed initiatives.

Networking usually entails increasing the complexity of information systems and their development process. Organizations must choose between numerous alternatives regarding the provision of network services. Private networks or individual links (channels), using leased communication lines, normally imply a significant initial investment, followed by operating costs that are relatively independent of traffic levels. The attractiveness of this option for large organizations, or for heavily-used channels, may be offset by the complexities of network management. The main alternative, the use of third-party network services, may be both expensive and involve the organization losing control of its communication network. The development of standards to instil confidence in the expected life of the technology, inevitably lags behind the changing technology and many incompatibilities remain. There is also a temptation, while planning networks, to interconnect all parts of the organization, whether this is appropriate or not. These choices, with their considerable financial implications, require organizations to have some form of network strategy in order to tailor the options available to the organization's needs. The achievement of a stable network, essential for any communication system, is fraught with problems.

The reliability of the technology has improved; but still *"networks obey the laws of gravity; they tend to go down"*. Slow, noisy and poorly utilized analogue telephone lines, have still not completely disappeared. A 1988 survey suggested that 25 per cent of packet-switched calls failed, mostly due to congestion or noise. Organizations can become over-dependent on networks; in 1985, the French Transpac packet-switching network collapsed due to overloading, leading to commercial chaos for the 25,000 business subscribers. The network failed because each node, when it became overloaded, automatically redirected its traffic to the next node, in turn overloading that node. The network collapsed in a domino effect. The complexity of networks, exacerbated by a chronic shortage of skilled technicians, can result in serious problems in tracking faults, minimizing the damage, and recovering from failures. Organizations may invest heavily, but still have limited control over their communication networks.

Furthermore, increasing worries over computer security largely hinge on the ability of intruders to take advantage of networks to breach an organization's defences. While remote logging-in and electronic mail may seem fairly innocuous, they do provide opportunities for intruders to break into the host system with potentially devastating results. Despite the allure of sophisticated command and control systems, certain highly sensitive military units have explicitly rejected any form of networking because of its vulnerability.

A prime source of business uncertainty is the unpredictable impact of new information systems, especially inter-organizational ones, on the structure and processes of the organization. These systems change organizational boundaries:

for example, electronic funds transfer threatens to change, or at least 'muddy', the boundary between retailing and banking, while that between airlines and hotels is being probed by joint reservation systems. A reduction in transaction costs from the use of network-based electronic markets may result in considerable changes in the institutional structures of organizations and whole industries. The emergent consequences for business practice and for commercial confidentiality, of a more widespread and tighter coupling between the information systems of different organizations, are impossible to forecast. Thus, these new systems raise far-reaching questions; many of which have not yet been fully thought through.

Conclusion

Network services have become a key area in the management of information systems, fraught with opportunity and risk. Organizations should carefully develop network strategies to stand a better chance of seizing the available opportunities, whilst avoiding the more obvious pitfalls. Plainly, these network strategies and plans should be closely coordinated to the overall business strategy to ensure that the communications facilities match the possible demands.

In order to prepare a strategy, an organization has to be in a position to make fairly firm choices from a wide range of options, based on predictions of traffic levels, future standards and the viability of suppliers. It is very easy to get these predictions wildly wrong. Network technology and services are changing rapidly and yet, almost by definition, organizations need a stable, integrated, compatible communications infrastructure. In addition, networks raise difficult social and legal issues; for example, it is impossible to predict the future social norms regarding the acceptability of widespread telecommuting. Many commentators consider that networks, together with air travel, are leading to a 'smaller world'. This is further demonstrated by the lowering of European national boundaries through the Single Market in 1992. However, national boundaries cannot be disregarded as, despite pressures for global competition and deregulation of trade, many countries will take divergent trading policies, including policies for trans-border data flow. Predictions in this area may be highly unreliable and subject to sudden change as a consequence of national and international politics.

This uncertainty implies that any strategy should emphasize flexibility and exercise extreme caution in the face of technological determinism. At the same time, organizations should attempt to develop sufficient expertise to be able to take advantage of favourable market opportunities and utilize networks in a competitive fashion, where appropriate. Thus, the strategy should contain relatively little concerning the purely technological aspects but should concentrate more upon the communications function and the human, organizational and business environment.

Discussion issues

1. Of the various network technologies discussed in this chapter, which ones could, or should, be used to support informal communication? Discuss the practical difficulties involved.
2. Discuss the potential impact on organizations of the wholesale extension of inter-organizational information systems.

Exercises

1. Regarding your own needs for leisure information, try to identify and use electronic information services that offer similar information. Compare these with traditional sources, using criteria such as ease of use and price.
2. Find out the costs and performance details (speed, capacity etc.) of using the various communication services (such as electronic mail and FAX) in terms of both investment and running costs. From this, draw up a communications policy for a small organization.

References

1. Cash, J.I., McFarlan, F.W., McKenney, J.L. & Vitale, M.R., *Corporate Information Systems Management*, 2nd edn., Irwin, Homewood, Illinois, 1988.
2. Purton, P.,'Europe's electronic trading bloc', *Datamation*, 76.13-76.14, Mar.1, 1989.
3. Hansen, J.V. & Hill, N.C.,'Control and audit of electronic data interchange', *MIS Quarterly*, Vol.13, No.4, 403-413, 1989.
4. Kaye, A.R. & Byrne, K.E.,'Implementing a computer-based message system', *Information and Management*, Vol.10, No.5, 277-284, 1986.
5. Arnold, E.,'Information technology in the home: The failure of Prestel', in: Bjorn-Andersen, N. et al (eds.), *The Information Society: For Richer For Poorer*, North Holland, Amsterdam, 1982.

Suggested reading

Impact on organizations
> Malone, T.W., Yates, J. & Benjamin, R.I.,'Electronic markets and electronic hierarchies', *Communications of the ACM*, 30(6), 484-497, 1987.

Technological infrastructure
> Halsall, F., Introduction to Data Communications and Computer Networks, Addison-Wesley, Wokingham, 1985.
>
> Tanenbaum, A.S., *Computer Networks*, 2nd edn., Prentice-Hall, Englewood Cliffs, NJ, 1989.
>
> Cheong, V. & Hirschheim, R.A., *Local Area Networks: Issues, Products, and Developments*, Wiley, Chichester, 1983.
>
> Tolhurst, M.R. et al., *Open Systems Interconnection*, Macmillan, London, 1988.

Network management
> Hall, W.A. & McCauley, R.E.,'Planning and managing a corporate network utility', *MIS Quarterly*, Vol.11, No.4, 437-449, 1987.

Electronic data interchange
> Sokol, P.K., *EDI: the competitive edge*, McGraw-Hill, New York, 1989.

Information services
> Cruise O'Brien, R. & Channing, M.,'The global structure of the electronic information services industry', *Oxford Surveys in IT*, Vol.3, 175-210, 1986.
>
> Winsbury, R. (ed.), *Viewdata in Action*, McGraw-Hill, London, 1981.

9   Office information systems

- *From word processing to desktop publishing*
- *From document production to knowledge work*
- *From integrated office systems*
    to computer-supported cooperative work
- *Opportunities*
- *Risks*
- *Conclusion: understanding the office*

Within organizations, the 'office' is clearly the central pivot for information handling. If we are moving towards a post-industrial society, where information is the key resource, and if information systems are beginning to be used for competitive advantage, it should be within the office that the major changes will manifest themselves. Almost from the beginning of commercial data processing, offices were seen as a prime application area; LEO (Lyons Electronic Office), developed in the early 1950s, was one of the first commercially used computers in the UK. Advances during the 1980s in computer hardware, software and networks have provided sufficient tools for office information systems (OIS) to become a reality. Particular technologies have now been mapped onto most individual office activities; for example voice messaging for telephone calls, word processing for document preparation and electronic mail for document distribution. Furthermore, users, hardware and software can be interlinked via local area networks. However, in most organizations, office information systems currently comprise little more than word processing systems. This chapter offers a brief discussion of why office 'automation' has so often stalled at this point.

This failure to proceed further is certainly not for the want of trying. There is considerable interest in using IT as a means of improving both the efficiency and effectiveness of the growing body of office workers. IT suppliers have not been able to resist the prospect of capturing the huge office market, flooding the market with numerous products. The size of the OIS market depends greatly on how it is measured, but estimates are uniformly large; for example, the UK market was put at $7 billion in 1987, while the US white-collar wage bill approaches $1 trillion. We shall argue that the success of word processing is a

146

fine example of the *First Step Fallacy,* and that many of the difficulties surrounding the application of more sophisticated tools stem from a general failure to understand the subtleties and complexities of office work.

From word processing to desktop publishing

Word processing must be one of the greatest of all IT successes in terms of acceptance and usage. Originating in 1964 with the IBM Selectric typewriter, it boomed in the late 1970s and 1980s, at first in the form of dedicated machines (microcomputers or minicomputers), although now it is more often found as a separate package on a general-purpose microcomputer, or as part of an integrated office system. In 1986, it was estimated that 70 per cent of microcomputers were used exclusively for word processing. Over the years, there have been changes in the structure of word processing as the early centralized 'pools' of specialist operators often resulted in a lack of personal contact and poor coordination with their distant users, as well as a growth in monotonous keyboard jobs. Now, with fewer people frightened by the mystique of computers, word processing has become the preserve of secretaries, clerks and even (some) managers themselves. Although it can be argued that managers might spend their time more effectively on 'management' activities, rather than on typing, some managers prefer to create reports straight onto a word processor, interacting directly with the document, and thus reducing the barriers of dictation and proof-reading.

Arguably, much of word processing's success was due to its conceptual simplicity and obvious benefits. These include the ease of amendment (without retyping the whole document), and the ability to 'cut and paste' large blocks of text to improve a document's structure or to facilitate the production of personalized standard letters. The WYSIWYG (what you see is what you get) nature of most packages allows users to judge the presentation before printing. The large range of facilities, such as spelling checker, thesaurus and foreign language character sets, and ease of use, takes much of the drudgery out of typing without degenerating into unbridled complexity. Word processors have increased the productivity of many experienced typists (with gains of more than 30%) and significantly improved the performance of non-expert typists. There are very few medium or large offices where word processing is not used and it is becoming increasingly common in small businesses and even in the home.

Despite this success, word processors do have some significant potential drawbacks. Firstly, the ease of document amendment may actually encourage changes, especially where managers do not process their own documents. Apart from allowing a slapdash approach to letter composition, there is a danger that either final editing will be omitted or confusion will result from the number of versions of a particular document. Similarly, the ease of producing standard letters increases the likelihood that the wrong letter will be sent inadvertently. Where the material is of a sales and marketing nature, this is usually harmless but where the letter refers to contractual, accounting or the more sensitive aspects of business, the consequences can be devastating. For example, a poorly prepared standard letter of recommendation for the promotion of a member of staff may create the impression that the person is not worth an 'original' letter. Similarly, care must be taken regarding standard price quotations or contract terms, although, fortunately, the informal links between companies can often identify and rectify this type of error before the parties slide into litigation.

Although basic word processing software and a minimum level of hardware are obtainable at a relatively modest price, sophisticated packages and the concomitant laser printers are costly, especially when multiplied throughout the organization. Word processors have evolved from simple text editors to systems approaching the capability of desktop publishing, comprising a large range of fonts, styles, graphics facilities and formats etc., albeit at the cost of a loss in conceptual simplicity. It has been claimed that word processing has deskilled typing, taking over many layout functions, but this fails to consider the opportunities offered for developing rather different presentation skills. Other problems include the implications for management–staff relations, given the potential use of packages for the close monitoring of staff performance. File management can also be problematic as the growing numbers of files precipitate difficulties in storage and retrieval (due to the limitations of text retrieval) and in the increased demands made on safeguards for the security of this electronic information. Furthermore, where files are accessible by many users, individual users may not relish the loss of access control over their files.

Although early word processors quickly achieved acceptance for the production of routine letters and memoranda, they could not then offer the quality of presentation needed for major company documents, such as annual reports. Desktop publishing systems, representing a convergence of word processing and commercial printing (typesetting) technologies, emerged in the mid-1980s to meet this demand. These systems comprise advanced page layout software, supported by high resolution monitors and laser printers. Desktop publishing can improve the presentation quality of documents by easing the merging of text and graphics, and considerably increasing the range of layouts, fonts, type styles and special presentation effects available. In theory, the user can control most of the printing cycle, rather than using external typesetters and printing companies. Unfortunately the range of facilities inevitably makes packages complex to learn and use, so that they often become the preserve of specialists.

However, attractive presentation involves more than just sophisticated technology; it requires certain design skills, most of which are not possessed by the average knowledge worker. All too often, naive users exceed even the realms of readability with a profusion of different fonts and special effects (*fontitis*). More serious is the danger of excessive emphasis on presentation, at the expense of a concern with content. Desktop publishing may raise the expectations of users and managers, who then demand a similarly high quality over an increasing range of documents, without realizing the time and effort involved in its production. The organization can easily be left in a situation of diminishing returns.

From document production to knowledge work

Office work is obviously much more than just document manipulation and production, but attempts to automate or support the intellectual and managerial aspects have been conspicuously less successful. Despite the large amount of research effort expended on systems for use in decision-taking, relatively little has emerged in the shape of tangible operational systems. However, this lack of success has provided useful insights into the limitations of IT.

Decision support systems

The move towards decision support systems (DSS) in the mid-1970s represented, in many ways, a healthy reaction against earlier centralized, monolithic information systems. Through the provision of appropriate software tools and decision models, DSS explicitly aim at [1]:

- Supporting human decision-making, where the problem is of a semi-structured or unstructured type (e.g. market planning), rather than automating highly structured, deterministic algorithms, such as payroll calculation;
- Decision-making rather than transaction processing;
- The individual user with a specific problem, rather than a long term function involving multiple users;
- A user-friendly, interactive mode, as the user is expected to work closely with the system to explore alternative solutions.

These characteristics implied an important change in the development philosophy, towards a greater involvement of the user in the development process through such techniques as prototyping. This served to question the traditional software engineering life cycle (see Chapter 10), with its emphasis on the structured design of robust, '*idiot proof*' systems. The target became much more flexible systems, built to be changed. The aim of user-friendliness implied microcomputer-based systems, with extensive use of graphical presentation techniques. In certain cases, approaches based on simulating processes have been adopted, where the intention is to learn more about the interrelationships between assumptions about a situation, specific decisions and their outcomes. Particular DSS appeared, such as the Hertz Fleet Planning Model to optimize that company's acquisition and organization of rental cars. More general DSS 'generators' were developed, such as portfolio management systems (concerned with optimizing the holdings of stocks and shares), that could be used to produce individually tailored DSS.

Despite these non-technical, managerial sentiments, the models underlying DSS are mostly rigid operational research models (such as linear programming) with a statistical, quantitative basis. These can be successful in certain situations, such as production management and financial planning, where quantitative modelling for efficiency optimization is an important decision criterion. However, in practice this represents only a fraction of managerial decisions, and thus the range of DSS use has been much less than anticipated by their supporters. There is considerable evidence that decision-makers rarely optimize by using deterministic formulae. Organizational decision-making is more often characterized by individual 'satisficing' or 'muddling through' in situations of considerable uncertainty, where combinations of bureaucratic, serendipitous or political factors displace simplistic economic rationality. Whereas DSS may be suitable where there is little goal ambiguity and a large measure of certainty over cause and effect relationships, such situations are rarely encountered. Where the DSS attempts to impose its designer's optimistic, deterministic rationality onto a complex political situation, it is likely to be rejected. Acceptance is much more likely where the system genuinely provides an appropriate level of quantitative support for the user's intuitive decision processes. Because of the type of models used, DSS appear to be suited to resource allocation problems but, on the other hand, it is just this type of problem that is usually the most politically loaded.

Achieving the right quantity and level of information is another problem. Information overload is not only irritating for decision-makers, it has also been implicated in the slow response to a warning system at a chemical plant that led to a dangerous explosion. The cost of developing DSS means that they are only suitable for decisions repeated fairly frequently or perhaps for major 'once-off' decisions involving very significant investments. In the latter case, such decisions normally depend more on qualitative information and intuition, rather than on 'hard' statistics. There is usually considerable uncertainty in long term planning, so that precise models are inappropriate and computer support might more usefully take the form of a simple spreadsheet. In fact, the use of spreadsheets for 'what-if' calculations is the most common manifestation of DSS theory and practice. Many highly sophisticated DSS just comprise an underlying spreadsheet structure supplemented by complex built-in statistical forecasting models.

Although many DSS concepts are now commonplace, there are relatively few non-trivial DSS in actual use in organizations. This practical failure has led to an updating and repackaging of the underlying concepts. The realization that many major decisions are not taken by a single decision-maker, but are rather the concern of a group of managers, led to the development of group DSS (see below), and the failure of senior management to use CBIS resulted in the emergence of executive information systems.

Executive information systems (EIS)

Executive information systems, such as Comshare Commander and Metapraxis Resolve, are aimed specifically at senior management, who proved to be particularly successful in avoiding conventional CBIS. EIS seek to provide the senior executive with user-friendly access to multiple data sources (both internal and external databases), together with models and tools relevant to the analysis of that data. They aim to support the identification of problems and opportunities through exception reporting, trend analysis, and the capability for senior managers to take summary information and then 'drill' more deeply into the databases. Supporters argue that advances in user-friendly interfaces, the growing computer literacy of executives, and the realization that managerial work can be supported by IT, will lead to their acceptance by senior management.

However, our lack of knowledge of the largely intuitive decision processes of senior managers, and problems with database systems themselves, do not provide a very solid foundation to achieve these goals. Also, considering the varying concerns of senior managers and the widely differing business environments, it seems unlikely that any general purpose system can succeed. If easy access to detailed operational data is achieved, senior managers may have to resist the temptations of becoming too involved in low-level operations, which may both waste their valuable time and provoke resentment and mistrust among key middle managers. Apart from a minority of analytically minded managers, many senior managers are unlikely to invest the time needed to discuss their requirements in sufficient detail for relevant systems to emerge, or to expend time learning in depth how to use these systems, unless there is an obvious tangible pay-off. In this light, there are serious impediments to the progress of EIS although, as we have argued repeatedly in discussing other technologies, in certain cases they may prove to be beneficial.

Expert systems

With their background in artificial intelligence (AI), much was expected from so-called expert systems, but to date, relatively little has been delivered in the way of relevant systems. This was despite considerable enthusiasm and investment from both governments and corporations, including the huge Japanese Fifth Generation project begun in 1981. Early claims that computers would soon be able to think, plan, learn and make human-like judgements proved to be unattainable. Writers such as Weizenbaum [2] and Winograd and Flores [3] have provided detailed critiques of the fundamental misconceptions surrounding artificial intelligence. Psychologists and researchers in linguistics still have a long way to go before they can fully explain human thought and language processes; extending these processes to machines clearly remains 'pie in the sky': "Despite what you may have read in magazines and newspapers, regardless of what politicians were told when they voted on the Strategic Computing Plan, twenty-five years of artificial intelligence research has lived up to very few of its promises and has failed to yield any evidence that it ever will" [4].

Expert systems aspire to contain the knowledge and expertise of an expert (in a specific subject area) and hold this knowledge in such a way that the system can offer sensible advice. However, there are various levels of human expertise [4] and, whilst the lower levels contain much knowledge that can be systematically stored, at the upper levels, where the recognized human experts reside, the expertise is largely intuitive and non-formalizable. Furthermore, individual experts may disagree on certain non-trivial problems, and it is not clear how such dissenting views can be incorporated into a knowledge base. It is equally hard to accommodate the more social issues of fallibility and liability for mistakes that are associated with human experts. Thus, the idea of distilling the knowledge of experts into an expert system is misconceived for all but highly formalized knowledge, no matter how sophisticated the knowledge acquisition techniques employed. However, it is a mistake to pillory expert systems excessively, despite their obvious failings. Just as DSS have given us additional insight into decision-making and managerial information systems, so the work on expert systems has produced certain useful by-products. For example, the notion that systems should 'explain' their reasoning by listing the rules used to reach the solution is a useful idea. Another helpful notion is that systems should be flexible so that users can change their stated goals or strategies during a session. Furthermore, research in artificial intelligence has produced certain novel representation schema (e.g. semantic nets, frames) and control mechanisms (e.g. forward and backward chaining), which, while failing to replicate or explain human thought processes, may still be worthwhile in other areas.

Expert systems have found limited success in a few niches; for example, the PROSPECTOR system in geology, DENDRAL in chemical analysis, and MYCIN in medicine. The XCON system is reported to be used at the Digital Equipment Corporation's factory to configure computer systems for customers' orders, although it was largely ignored by the sales force. For certain narrow domains, where the vocabulary is limited and clear, and where there is no ambiguity regarding goals and intentions, expert systems can be useful 'assistants' to experts, rather than their replacements. In most organizational situations, dominated by organizational politics and the vagaries of business policies, these conditions are likely to be very much the exception to the rule. Commentators and developers should recognize the limitations of 'machine intelligence': "Management scientists must learn to live humbly, within the constraints imposed by their inability to model situational understanding" [5]. A panel of IS 'experts' recently predicted [6] that both expert systems and generalized decision support systems would only have a limited impact in the 1990s.

Bearing in mind the relative lack of success of both expert systems and DSS, proposals to combine them to form expert decision support systems seems more likely to produce *megahype* rather than a beneficial synergy. In theory, explicit domain knowledge, held in the expert sub-system, is used in conjunction with the DSS models and tools. However, it is difficult to see how these can be any more successful than their constituent parts.

From integrated office systems to computer-supported cooperative work

In addition to the document production activities, handled by word processing and desktop publishing systems, and the more intellectual decision support tools, office information systems usually incorporate a number of software tools:

Text retrieval software	– for text documents
Structured databases	– for ordered records
Spreadsheets	– for data analysis and computational tasks;
Business graphics tools	– for chart and graph production;
Calendar and diary managers	– for the setting up of meetings and other activity management.

Offices have a major communications function and thus many of the networking tools and technologies discussed in Chapter 8 are seen as an integral part of OISs. Mail distribution may be handled by electronic mail or FAX, telephone communication can be improved by PABXs and voice messaging; and traditional meetings may be augmented or replaced by teleconferencing. In addition to conventional workstations, other hardware devices are becoming increasingly common: laser printers, optical scanners and various networking devices (e.g. PABX, gateways). With such a large range of disparate hardware and software tools, one key aim is integration: the desire to fit the various tools seamlessly together. For instance, it should be an effortless process to input documents through an optical scanner, edit them with a word processor and then dispatch them by electronic mail, but in reality this often involves complex reformatting.

Integrated office systems, such as IBM's PROFS and DISOSS and Digital's All-in-One, do provide a set of interlinked software tools. However, although these first generation, centralized systems have been popular in the USA, sales have been disappointing in the UK. Many such systems were perceived as unfriendly, ungainly and suffering from performance and compatibility problems. The latest IBM offering, OfficeVision, announced in the Spring of 1989, promises a consistent interface across a range of machines, and improved functionality and user-friendliness; the extent to which this will be realized in practice is not yet clear.

An alternative approach to integration is provided by document image processing systems, such as Olivetti's Filenet or Kodak's KIMS, which manipulate documents as images, input through optical scanners. Scanning technology, both image digitization and character recognition, has gradually improved, allowing graphics images to be input, and avoiding the rekeying of large quantities of text. They mostly address the document storage and retrieval function and can be useful where large quantities of documents, diagrams or original signatures, that are not machine-readable in any other way, constitute a key requirement. However, they remain constrained by the difficulties of text retrieval, exacerbated by the problems of indexing and cross-referencing graphics images, and their high prices limit them to large users (e.g. banks and building societies). Although some systems offer more facilities than simple storage and retrieval, they have yet to be integrated with conventional office systems.

A more radical approach to integration is that of computer-supported cooperative work (CSCW). This approach, which includes group decision support systems and electronic meeting systems, focuses more on the human aspects of office information systems. An inherent characteristic of office work is its interactive, group nature; office workers rarely carry out single tasks in sequence like assembly line workers. Rather, office work comprises individuals communicating together frequently to resolve problems or exchange information. This communication includes formal and informal meetings as well as telephone conversations and the exchange of written memoranda. The organization of office work hinges largely on groups and group interaction. CSCW, which attempts to support these group processes, owes much of its power to the recognition of the importance of groups. A variety of experimental systems have been produced, each emphasizing a particular form of CSCW.

Electronic meeting systems are aimed at solving the problems experienced with conventional meetings, such as the lack of creativity, information, participation, focus, and follow-through. This lack of 'productivity' in meetings costs organizations millions of dollars in salaries, travel, administration etc.. Electronic meeting systems are often located in custom-built electronic boardrooms, with sophisticated audio-visual and computing facilities. As well as a large shared display screen, forming a WYSIWIS (what you see is what I see) electronic 'chalkboard', participants may be provided with individual networked workstations with both public and private 'windows'. The supporting software comprises conventional database, communications, word processing and outlining packages, plus DSS modelling facilities. In addition, specialized software supports agenda setting, voting, weighting (preference formation), the input of anonymous ideas, and the production of a final 'action plan', showing responsibilities for following up specific items. The systems are supported by facilitators, who may be expert in the technology, the decision models, or group interaction. However, not all meetings are for decision-making; some are primarily for information exchange, negotiation, brainstorming, morale building. Xerox's COLAB [7] is aimed at design meetings of working groups by providing tools, such as advanced outliners, that support the hierarchical structuring of ideas and a more qualitative discussion, as opposed to the quantitative optimization of conventional DSS.

It is claimed that electronic meeting systems improve conventional meetings because they allow more alternative solutions to be considered (through the DSS modelling tools) and improve the mechanics of the processes of meetings, such as consensus formation, the recording of decisions, the input of information and ideas, as well as increasing participation and group cohesion. However, research results have been very mixed [8], showing, in some cases, little advantage over pencil and paper. Although more alternatives may be considered, participants may have less confidence in both the final decision and the overall process. Without ignoring the failings of conventional meetings, in many cases it is hard to see how computer-supported meetings will fare any better, without much greater formalization, which could equally be achieved with traditional meetings if the will to do so existed. Such systems require the motivation of a considerable level of felt need, for which there is little general evidence. Furthermore, in the case of most organizations, where IT skills are not equally distributed, computer supported meetings favour those participants with highly developed IT skills, leading to their likely domination by the more technologically minded. Also, the technical demands, in terms of display technology, networking and sophisticated software, make this a decidedly non-trivial technical problem. Our understanding of the nature of decision-making remains exceedingly crude, implying that the installation of large amounts of technology is a high-risk gamble.

However, the underlying concepts of CSCW are not confined to the context of meetings. The Information Lens system [9] comprises a sophisticated electronic mail network, based on the automatic processing of semi-structured message templates. Incoming messages are filtered and outgoing messages triggered, according to user-initiated rules. Rather than decision-making, the aim is effective information exchange between group members. Some CSCW software supports real-time conferencing ('group chats') through the real-time exchange of messages between group members at their desks. Other software focuses on the management of shared files or the location of particular expertise within the group. Software to support CSCW, known as 'groupware', currently includes packages such as Higgins and Office Works.

An interesting function within CSCW is that of scheduling group meetings, by accessing individuals' calendars in order to determine a free time. If a meeting has to be scheduled between a large number of people with very full calendars, this process performed manually can be very frustrating and time-consuming. However, the automatic scheduling of meetings depends crucially upon individuals keeping their calendars both accurate and up-to-date. Also, it is too easy for the software to be open to manipulation by unscrupulous individuals who call meetings at unpopular times (late afternoon on Christmas Eve?); some systems do not even include an explicit 'confirmation' procedure. There is also the temptation for individuals to 'invent' appointments, in order to safeguard times that are less convenient, for them or to utilize explicit privacy locks on calendars. None of this really encourages group cohesion and harmony and is likely to only work well with groups that are already successful. Such groups are likely to operate equally effective informal procedures for scheduling meetings.

Compared to traditional integrated office systems, the key advantage of CSCW is that it at least attempts to be people-centred rather than machine-centred. Where all members of the group are sufficiently expert and understand the limitations of the systems, in terms of information storage and retrieval, message filtering etc., such systems can be effective. Where that expertise and understanding is missing, the technology is likely to act as a serious barrier to the complex social interaction that sustains the work of most organizations.

Opportunities

According to their supporters, OIS can be distinguished from 'ordinary' data processing (DP) systems along the lines of figure 9.1. The benefits accorded to OIS in the figure are very much ideals, rarely totally achieved in practice. There is something very glib about the comparison, especially when almost identical figures are produced to promote other fashionable technologies, such as decision support systems and expert systems, again with DP set up as a 'straw-man'.

Depending upon the circumstances and the implementation, OISs can indeed display some of the characteristics accorded to them in the figure, but they can equally take on those of the right-hand DP column.

Office Information System	Data Processing System
Aims at effectiveness	Aims at efficiency
Provides personal tools	Automates manual tasks
Develops skills in users	Deskills
Adds value	Reduces costs
For unstructured tasks	For structured tasks
Provides management support	Provides management information

Figure 9.1 A (biased) comparison of OIS and Data Processing Systems

It has been claimed that major improvements in productivity can be achieved through better (electronic) communication and the saving of time from fewer meetings, less travel, and fewer unproductive telephone calls. Many unproductive functions, such as manual filing, could be eliminated. Just as industrial productivity was seen to increase through the introduction of large amounts of capital equipment, so it might be thought that similar results could be achieved in offices. Productivity improvements raise the prospect of savings, not only in salaries through a reduction in staff, but also in the ever-increasing costs of office space and support (cleaning, heating, security, and supplies). This line of argument is all the more attractive in the light of the increasing number of office knowledge workers, as we enter the *Information Society*. Depending upon the method of counting, the majority of workers in advanced economies may already be termed office workers. Offices are certainly the crucial pivots for information handling, and productivity improvements in offices are thus a central concern. However, as discussed below, the difficulties in measuring office and managerial productivity, mean that measurable gains are hard to identify. An exception is the case of word processing, where measurement is somewhat easier.

Strassmann [10] found that organizations with successful manual systems gained from computerization, whereas many unsuccessful organizations declined still further with the introduction of information technology. IT is not the solution for a fundamentally ineffective administrative structure. In one of his successful cases, much of the improvement came about simply through rethinking and re-structuring the work patterns, and not its automation.

Other, more qualitative benefits have been postulated for OISs. Information stored on a network should become more accessible, and also, through electronic mail, people should become more accessible. Knowledge workers can gain increased control over their work tasks, as individuals become responsible for their own document production, publishing, filing etc. Thus, there should be fewer delays and errors through failures in communication. It is claimed that jobs will become more rounded, as workers, skilled in the use of the new tools, will make an increased contribution. The net result could be increased coordination and control, with quicker and better decisions. Finally albeit superficially, the modern office, replete with ranks of microcomputers, can form a powerful marketing image (*modernism*), regardless of whether the machines are serving any useful purpose. However, such an advantage is very temporary, and the image, together with the machines, will need frequent and continuous updating for it to retain any power whatsoever. Despite such qualifications, and the overriding problems of measurement, some significant improvements have been achieved in a number of organizations. However, without the prop of quantitative measures, managers must make a broader assessment of the opportunities, taking care not to be seduced by the velvet sales pitch of the vendors.

Risks

Despite the impressive arguments for office information systems and the huge potential benefits, to date OISs have achieved mixed results. Whereas some tools (e.g. word processors and spreadsheets) have been highly successful, others (e.g. electronic mail, calendar systems) have enjoyed only patchy acceptance.

The integrated, 'all-singing, all-dancing' OIS has not been achieved in the vast majority of organizations. The UK Department of Trade and Industry's pilot schemes of the early 1980s were not particularly encouraging. Sixteen of the twenty sites retained the system (well, it was free!), but one of the four to scrap the system was the Department of Trade and Industry itself. The scheme failed to stimulate the UK OIS industry; shortly afterwards eight of the thirteen suppliers either closed down, moved out of the business, or underwent significant changes of ownership. The systems appeared to have little effect on the user organizations, who mostly used just the word processing facilities. The problems experienced were based partly on the technical shortcomings of the early systems and difficulties with the suppliers, but included more fundamental problems such as inadequate requirements specifications and evaluation difficulties.

Technical problems

As a super-set of various component technologies, OISs inherit many of their individual technical problems. The extra problem of incompatibility remains a headache, despite moves towards standardization in networks and document formats. The technical demands of supporting multi-media communication remain awesome in an environment lacking standards. In addition, the problems of text storage and retrieval limit the effectiveness of the electronic document base. Compared to manual offices, OISs are vulnerable to failure; if the entire system crashes, the users may be left without an adequate back-up system and the office potentially ceases to function. Many of the systems are highly centralized, and overload at peak working times, frustrating users as response times deteriorate. Finally, the environmental demands can be costly and disruptive, including the cabling for networks, the provision of power supplies, and in some circumstances, air conditioning. However, many studies have shown that non-technical issues outnumber the technical as the main cause of failure.

Economic problems

Even with the generally falling price of IT, OISs are expensive; high performance integrated systems, such as OfficeVision, demand sophisticated and costly workstations. Furthermore, the implementation and support costs (e.g. training, file conversion, maintenance) can be up to three times greater than the cost of hardware and software. These costs might be acceptable if they could be justified through increases in productivity or through reduced salary costs. Benefits have been achieved, but they are extremely difficult to measure. Despite some successful cases, there is no evidence of increased productivity across the board. Rather, there is some evidence that the reverse may be the case: in 1988, the American Productivity Association recorded a slight *fall* in the average output per hour for the non-manufacturing sector over the previous decade.

It is, however, extremely difficult to measure the productivity of knowledge workers; it is too easy to adopt facile methods, such as merely counting the number of pieces of paper moved daily, or telephone calls made or not made. The difficulties in evaluating their effectiveness render traditional cost–benefit studies almost meaningless. Although office salary costs have escalated, it is the salaries of managers and professionals that make up the highest proportion of the salary bill. It is unlikely that current OISs, with their emphasis on automating clerical functions, can achieve significant savings at the management level. Marginal savings might be realized amongst lowly-paid clerical or secretarial staff, but even this is somewhat doubtful. It may be that, in order to obtain the maximum benefit from information technology, the number of office workers will actually have to increase, at least in the short term. The notion of savings in paper and storage space with the onset of the 'paperless office' is no longer a serious proposition; if anything, the use of IT, with its ease of printing multiple copies of documents, has increased the amount of paper used.

Social, organizational and development problems

Despite the claims of their supporters, it is possible that OISs will reduce the quality of working life through a greater formalization of jobs and an element of deskilling, reducing individual discretion as tasks become more programmed. There is also the danger of reduced social interaction, following the introduction of electronic communication technologies. It may be a matter of the individual implementation as to whether control is further centralized or whether the autonomy of individual workers is increased. Tools become more sophisticated, and jobs are likely to become more specialized, reducing the much-touted benefits of independence and variety.

Furthermore, the health and safety dangers that appear to be associated with the use of technology remain a potent issue. Optical and muscular problems have been traced to the inappropriate use of terminals, leading to compensation settlements in the courts. Despite earlier scares, it is now generally believed that screen radiation is (probably) not harmful to pregnant women. However, the use of IT often seems to lead to increased stress in jobs, producing a greater incidence of heart and nervous problems. These important problems, common to most computer-based information systems, are not going to disappear overnight.

Organizational problems are likely to be provoked by a wholesale introduction of OIS. Changes to organizational structures, the functions and activities of both groups and individuals, career paths, and the access to information, may not meet with the approval of powerful groups within the organization. The goals and objectives of those who sponsor and develop these systems may not match those of the intended users.

In addition, there are considerable development risks as organizations need to steer away from both the dangers of incompatibility, associated with an ad hoc piecemeal approach, and the risk of relying on the development of an accurate 'grand plan' at the first attempt. Following the widespread introduction of word processing, further significant gains may require corresponding new ways of working. Such changes may not be acceptable to today's knowledge workers.

Office information systems, with their ease of access and operation, may also compromise security considerations. Towards the end of 1989, the UK Foreign Office finally stopped development work on a £4.5 million, supposedly secure, OIS. Development was running one year late due to technical problems, but the project was finally abandoned because sufficient security for diplomatic information could not be provided without making the system unusable.

Conclusion: understanding the office

"Whereof one does not understand, one should not speak"
Ludwig Wittgenstein.
"Whereof one does not understand, one should not automate"
Michael Hammer.

Of all the problems, perhaps the biggest concerns that of understanding the nature of offices and office work. A number of misconceptions have to be laid to rest before significant progress can be made.

Firstly, traditional offices are not necessarily disorganized, paper-processing operations where documents risk being lost or delayed as they wend their way through various clerical functions. Obviously, inefficient offices do exist, but IT is not a panacea. A fundamental review of the functions and procedures of an office should be undertaken prior to any consideration of new technology. A preoccupation with the 'paperless office' is a red herring that is likely to lead to the support of inefficiency with expensive technology. Traditional documents are usually more aesthetically pleasing, portable (they can be read on trains), and often less vulnerable to loss or corruption than electronic documents.

If offices are not paper-shuffling organizations, it could be argued that many offices resemble social clubs, in that people appear to spend much of their time chatting, and even those that do want to 'work' are frequently interrupted by telephone calls or meetings. On the other hand, man is a social animal and much business and many office tasks depend upon coordination and trust; this is best supported by a social network maintained by social interaction. The maintenance of this network depends upon frequent, often informal, social contact.

Another misconception is the assumption that offices are homogeneous; the classification in figure 9.2 demonstrates that this is far from the case. All these different types may be termed offices, but they clearly vary considerably in function, activities and general character. Offices are usually related to a particular management level (operational, management control or strategic management), implying different time horizons and different concerns. Office work varies in its degree of structure, and the interaction needed to carry out its functions. The office may be inward-looking, concerned with internal operations, or it may have an external bias, being more of a 'shop window'. Office workers are as diverse as the offices themselves. The traditional classification into management, professionals, clerical staff, and secretaries and typists conceals a considerable variety of different jobs. For example, the secretarial group includes both the managing director's personal secretary and the lowest grade copy typist, whose jobs differ enormously in terms of responsibility, job content, and skills. Similar situations exist in the other groups.

Transaction offices   concerned with large numbers of simple operations (e.g. sales accounts).

Casework offices
  where a much smaller number of cases (e.g. social security claims), are
  dealt with, each requiring perhaps many hours attention from a number
  of specialist staff.

Working professional office   an office that supports professionals, such as doctors or lawyers.
Engineering office   where the main activity is technical design and draughtsmanship.
Management support   mostly concerned with supporting coordination activities of managers.
Machine rooms   (e.g. typing pools).
Physical handling   (e.g. mail rooms).

Figure 9.2 A classification of office types [11]

Another dangerous misconception is that office work is standardized and predictable, and thus easily automated. Many offices, especially those acting as shop windows or management support centres, have to be extremely flexible, dealing with highly variable demands and enquiries. Much office work is interactive, group work, requiring the coordination of different workers, perhaps in different places at different times. Innovation and initiative are rightly seen as important virtues that should be encouraged, rather than swept away with standardization and automation.

As well as being a complex concept, the familiar office can be looked at in a number of ways. A different understanding may emerge depending upon how the office is viewed; Hirschheim [12] identifies seven 'views' of offices:

- Office activities
  This view comprises the examination of low-level activities, such as typing, telephone calls etc., regardless of their purpose. This simplistic approach is easy to carry out, and is appropriate for those who merely wish to mechanize such activities.

- Office semantics

  A deeper view is accorded by considering the reasons behind these activities and the goals of users.
- Office functions

  These may be fairly specific sets of activities (e.g. invoicing) or much more general (e.g. the negotiation and implementation of contracts).
- Office roles

  Roles include the beliefs and values usually associated with particular jobs.
- Decision-making

  In this view, decisions and decision-makers are placed at centre stage, including the various factors (e.g. cognitive style) that influence decision-making.
- Transactional

  Based on institutional economics, this view examines the contractual arrangements regarding information exchange and the appropriate type of organization for different situations.
- Language action

  This approach views office behaviour in terms of communication acts, seeking to remove barriers to communication.

The first three views take an 'objective', analytic perspective, that assumes there is no ambiguity about the goals of the office and its staff. The last four views are much more interpretivist, attempting to incorporate the informal, subjective, political and social aspects of office life. They view the office more as a culture than as a structure, and try to include the covert activities and goals as well as the overt. Additional views can be added to Hirschheim's list; for example, an extensive use of desktop publishing systems may mean that the office should be viewed as a 'publisher'.

Each view has its advantages and disadvantages; our task is not to evaluate the alternatives, but to demonstrate that there are a number of ways of understanding offices. It is thus extremely hard to approach completeness in understanding, although the interpretive views are likely to be more complete than the blinkered analysis of office activities. Depending upon the view taken, different models and development methodologies are likely to be adopted, leading to a different final solution. Thus, we would argue that the development of OISs has largely foundered on the difficulties of understanding the office, difficulties that are clearly conceptual rather than technological.

Discussion issue

Discuss whether the introduction of word processing requires only an analysis of 'office activities', whereas computer-supported cooperative work systems need a more interpretive approach.

Exercises

1. Try to compare the user-system interfaces of a number of software tools (packages) that are likely to be found in offices; e.g. word processing packages, electronic mail systems, spreadsheets. In what ways are the examples you chose similar; i.e. how much extra learning is required in order to use a new tool?

2. If you have any integrated software packages available, compare the functionality (e.g. range of functions) of one part of the integrated package (say, word processing) with that of a sophisticated word processor. What are the trade-offs between the generalized integrated package and the specialized, single-function package?

Suggested reading

Office information systems

Freeman, H.A. & Thurber, K.J., *Tutorial: office automation systems*, 2nd edn., IEEE Computer Society, Washington, D.C., 1986.

Hirschheim, R.A., *Office automation: concepts, technologies and issues*, Addison-Wesley, Wokingham, UK, 1985.

Hirschheim, R.A., *Office automation: a social and organizational perspective*, Wiley, Chichester, UK,1985.

Long, R.J., *New office information technology: human and managerial implications*, Croom Helm, London, 1987.

Decision support systems and expert systems

Rockart, J.F. & DeLong, D.W., *Executive support systems*, Dow Jones Irwin, Homewood, Illinois, 1988.

Harmon, P. & King, D., *Artificial intelligence in business*, Wiley, New York, 1985.

Computer supported cooperative work

Kraemer, K.L. & King, J.L., Computer-based systems for cooperative work and group decision making, *Computing Surveys*, 20 (2), 1988.

References

1. Keen, P.G.W. & Scott Morton, M.S., *Decision support systems: an organizational perspective*, Addison-Wesley, Reading, Mass., 1978.
2. Weizenbaum, J., *Computer power and human reason*, Freeman, San Francisco, 1976.
3. Winograd, T. & Flores, F., *Understanding computers and cognition: a new foundation for design*, Ablex, Norwood, NJ., 1986.
4. Dreyfus, H.L. & Dreyfus, S.E., *Mind over machine*, Free Press, New York, 1985.
5. Dreyfus, S.E.'Formal models vs. human situational understanding', *Office: Technology and People*, Vol.1, 1982.
6. Straub, D.W. & Wetherbe, J.C.,'Information technologies for the 1990s: An organizational impact perspective', *Communications of the ACM*, 32(11), 1328-1339, 1989.
7. Stefik, M., Foster, G., Bobrow, D.G., Kahn, K., Lanning, S. & Suchman, L., 'Beyond the chalkboard: Computer support for collaboration and problem solving in meetings', *Communications of the ACM*, 30 (1), 32-47, 1987.
8. Dennis, A.R., George, J.F., Jessup, L.M., Nunamaker, J.F. & Vogel, D.R., 'Information technology to support electronic meetings', *MIS Quarterly*, 12 (4), 591-624, 1988.
9. Malone, T.W., Grant, K.R., Turbak, F.A., Brobst, S.A., & Cohen, M.D., 'Intelligent information-sharing systems', *Communications of the ACM*, 30(5), 390-402, 1987.
10. Strassmann, P.A., *Information payoff: the transformation of work in the electronic age*, Free Press, New York, 1985.
11. Gunton, T.,'Moving fast up the learning curve', Computing Special Report on Office Automation, June 1983.
12. Hirschheim, R.A., *Office automation: a social and organizational perspective*, Wiley, Chichester, UK, 1985.

10   Information systems development

- *The traditional systems life cycle*
- *Critique of the life cycle model*
- *Software engineering*
- *The specification problem*
- *The programming problem*
- *IS development methodologies*
- *The project management problem*
- *Computer-aided software engineering*

Like all other man-made artifacts, the quality of a computer-based information system is highly dependent upon the production process. This process, often known as the information systems development cycle, has been at the centre of IS research and practice for more than twenty-five years. Despite the introduction of a host of new development tools and techniques in an attempt to improve productivity and quality, scarcely a week passes without headlines proclaiming another IS development failure. The development of major systems can run years behind schedule and millions of dollars over budget, and even then still fail to satisfy user requirements when eventually installed.

Many difficulties relate to the production and maintenance of software, as can be seen in the dramatic shift in costs, so that now software often accounts for eighty-five per cent of total development costs. Poorly developed systems have exacerbated the growing software maintenance burden, whereby now the majority of applications programmers (up to seventy per cent) have to be employed in correcting, updating and refining existing software. Culminating in a backlog of up to two or three years, this serves to choke off any new software development.

The causes of this recurring crisis are rooted in a complex interaction of factors that we shall examine in terms of the three 'wicked' problems of IS development: the specification problem; the programming problem; the project management problem. The *specification problem* refers to the difficulty in situating the problem domain, capturing the user requirements for the new system, and representing them in a formal specification or blueprint for programming. The *programming problem* concerns the difficulties in preparing

166

accurate and reliable programs cost effectively. Finally, the *project management problem* concerns the control and coordination of the whole complex IS development process so that projects are completed within deadline and budget.

Before discussing these problems, we shall briefly summarize and criticize both the traditional systems life cycle and the philosophy behind the emerging discipline of software engineering.

The traditional systems life cycle

The life cycle model, which has been the basis of research and practice since the 1960s, comprises a sequence of stages (figure 10.1). The number and naming of the stages differ slightly between the numerous textbooks, but the underlying assumption is of a steady uni-directional progress through the stages, without going back and repeating stages. This is unrealistic in practice, as problems encountered at any one stage (e.g. programming) may force developers to backtrack and repeat activities from a previous stage (e.g. physical or logical design). The 'waterfall' variant [1] recognizes the need for iteration, but such iteration still has to struggle against the strong forward momentum of the project, just like a canoeist paddling *up* the waterfall.

Phase	Stage
Problem definition	Realization of need Preliminary analysis Feasibility study
Analysis	Requirements analysis Logical design Specification
Construction	Physical design Programming & Testing Installation
Operation	Maintenance Post-implementation evaluation

Figure 10.1 The traditional systems life cycle

We have grouped the stages into four phases: problem definition, analysis, construction, and operation. The first two phases treat the new system in fairly abstract, 'logical' terms, while the later phases are concerned with the physical implementation of the system. The cyclical nature of the model occurs because after a period of operation, there will be an inevitable realization that further new systems will be required, and so the cycle is repeated.

The first phase, problem definition, starts with an awareness of the need for a new system, which may be triggered by the recognition of a particular problem or opportunity. Typical problems include organizational operating difficulties, and market pressures for improved cost-effectiveness, while opportunities may include technological advances or business initiatives. The preliminary analysis should include a broad statement of the objectives and constraints for the new system. These may be financial (e.g. return on investment) or technical (e.g. performance levels). Alternatively they may be organizational (e.g. increased decentralization) or social (e.g. improved staff morale). The proposal for the new system should be related to the organization's overall IS strategy and plan, and a relative priority assigned in the light of competing developments.

The feasibility study starts with the generation of a number of alternative, fairly broad options for the new system. The feasibility of each is examined to determine the extent to which it is financially viable, technically implementable and organizationally acceptable. The complex problems surrounding evaluation (Chapter 11), together with the vagaries of forecasting, mean that feasibility studies rely fundamentally upon guesswork and rules of thumb, in their search to select the best option with which to proceed to full development.

The analysis phase comprises a determination of the users' requirements, and their refinement into a logical design. This design is a statement of *what* the new system will do, avoiding the physical details of *how* it will be implemented. The design is represented in the form of a specification, which, after approval by the users, is passed over to the system constructors. Construction involves the translation of the specification into a working system. A more detailed 'physical' software design is prepared, from which the program code is written and then verified through some agreed testing procedure.

Installation comprises a number of preparatory activities, such as the setting up of new computer hardware and network connections, as well as environmental facilities such as air conditioning, fire protection, and additional power supplies. Data collection or file conversion should ensure that files in the new system are complete and up-to-date. At the same time, the documentation and the design of manual procedures are finalized. Both user staff and IS support staff must be trained, either in-house or externally. Eventually, at the end of an often lengthy development cycle, the new system is judged to be ready for operation, when it is 'cut-over' and the old system discontinued. The new system has to be maintained throughout its operation; i.e. residual errors are corrected and changes made to reflect changing requirements.

The proportion of the total project effort that goes into each stage varies considerably (figure 10.2). Small projects are dominated by programming and testing (up to 75 per cent of the effort), while larger projects spend more effort on analysis and design. Some would argue that a 40-20-40 distribution would be most effective, with emphasis given to the early stages of analysis and logical design and the later stages of testing and installation. It should be noted that, over the lifetime of a system, operation and maintenance may cost anything between four and fifty times the development cost.

	%
feasibility study	3-10
requirements analysis	10-20
logical design	3-7
physical design	18-47
programming & testing	20-40
installation	12-26

Figure 10.2 Proportion of the total effort
for a medium-large project devoted to each stage [2]

Critique of the life cycle model

Despite its continuing wide acceptance as the basic model for IS development, there is a growing body of opinion that believes the life cycle model is out-dated. It is argued that, while it may have been appropriate twenty years ago for developing relatively straightforward and isolated systems in 'green field' situations, the life cycle model contains a number of fundamental assumptions that no longer hold in today's environment.

Firstly, it is basically a linear, sequential model, where one stage follows another; each stage should be completed before the next is started. This assumes that developers will 'get it right first time', which is unrealistic in a complex uncertain environment. There may be uncertainty as to whether the requirements have been correctly interpreted or whether the whole development effort is going into solving the wrong problem. Typically, there is uncertainty with regard to the final shape and impact of the new system, not to mention total costs and the projected completion date. This uncertainty, felt both by users and developers, is prolonged by deferring any implementation until the end of the cycle.

Closely related to uncertainty is the notion of change. It is implicitly assumed that the requirements remain constant, and yet, in many cases, nothing could be further from the truth. During the months or years of development, the underlying business activities may well change radically, at worst rendering the new system obsolete even before its introduction. There is a difficult trade-off to be made between incorporating changes during development, at a cost of increasing the development time, and catering for them after installation through the already hard-pressed maintenance process.

In the model, the distinction between logical and physical phases has certain attractions, but is often unrealistic as developers intuitively have physical solutions in their minds from the very beginning of the project. Additionally, the early decomposition of the system, into detailed functions and processes, encourages a reductionism that can lead to a loss of understanding of the whole system. Another key characteristic is the project-based nature of the model; IS development is seen in terms of projects that have a start and an end. A further assumption, dating from the early years of IS development, is that the new system is to replace an existing manual system. These assumptions are not applicable to the huge number of situations where an existing computer-based system is being extended or replaced, or where the organization is proposing new activities or functions for which there is no existing system. Another assumption is that IS development mostly consists of software production, a difficult and error-prone activity that should be minimized rather than encouraged.

The final implicit assumption is that users have little or no IT knowledge and their involvement is thus not useful. Users are interviewed during requirements analysis and then merely 'sign-off' the specification and the final system. This is clearly false in the case of end-user computing. Many users now have a considerable amount of expertise, and their involvement is not merely helpful but often essential. They contribute not only knowledge, but also their values, and many would argue that it is their 'democratic' right to participate in the design of their working environment. At the same time, it should be recalled that IS development can be seen as a political process, where control may be a political prize that the IS department wishes to retain. The discussion of end-user computing will not be repeated here, but it should be noted that the life cycle is an approach suited to specialists, an approach that will have to change in the face of the inexorable march of end-user computing.

Many other criticisms have been levelled, not so much at the model itself, but rather at the tools and techniques used for the various activities within the model; for example, the programming languages and testing procedures that are employed. Certainly, in the early days, languages and procedures were very crude and were applied in a rather *ad hoc* fashion. A huge number of solutions have been proposed, and these are discussed below in terms of the three highlighted 'problems'. Many of these ideas have been incorporated into Barry Boehm's spiral model [3], which also includes a major risk assessment function. It is appropriate, before describing the three problems in detail, to introduce briefly the discipline of software engineering that seeks to address these problems.

Software engineering

The origins of software engineering can be traced back to the late 1960s as a response to the '*software crisis*'. Commentators began to realize that, to succeed, large software development projects needed more than just an army of craft programmers. Such projects require tight control and standard working practices, if they are not to degenerate into chaos. The key notion of software engineering is the application of engineering principles and systematic techniques in an attempt to achieve correct, reliable and maintainable software through a cost-efficient production process. Efficient production and quality assurance became the twin goals of software engineering. The scope of these goals has gradually been extended, beyond the initial concern with coding and testing, to the earlier stages of program design and requirements specification.

Some writers have argued for a highly formal approach based on logical or mathematical techniques, using such methods as the Vienna Development Method [4]. These formal methods offer clarity, precision, accuracy and certainty through mathematical verification. They have been found to be useful in the development of some real-time software and are now compulsory for certain aspects of UK defence software development. However, developers need a strong mathematical background to understand and use such methods. It is debatable whether a rigid, formal approach can provide the flexible tools needed for creativity in the complex and uncertain development environment. For most users, such formality adds to the impenetrable mystique of IS development, and is likely to reduce participation. Although useful in certain areas, much of IS development comprises learning, communication and negotiation; it is thus immune to formalization but rather requires a behavioural approach.

The application of engineering principles is not straightforward; compared to most engineered products, software is in essence much more abstract, with the possibility that the underlying system is in one of an almost indeterminate number of states. As with management and office work, discussions of productivity run into measurement problems; the most common measure, the crude 'lines of code', takes little account of programming style or language characteristics. Although many of its techniques are fairly novel, software engineering remains rooted in the traditional life cycle model, concentrating on the relatively technical aspects of producing software. It is important to note here that the production of well-engineered software is just a subset, albeit a key subset, of the total activities of developing an information system. In the final analysis, information systems are social systems that cannot be engineered completely or formally.

The specification problem

Basically, computers only carry out tasks for which they have been programmed and so it is necessary to specify the requirements in minute detail. However, the starting point is typically a business problem situation, where the problem itself may not be clear, where there is considerable ambiguity regarding the objectives and processes, but where there is a sense of crisis, reflected in poor performance and soaring costs. Somehow, this crisis situation, amplified by the political and emotional feelings of the participants, has to be translated into a precise blueprint for a new system. The elicitation of user requirements and their representation in a formal specification is an intractable problem and yet it is a key stage on which much of the final success of the whole project depends. Errors may be very costly to rectify later; in some cases, up to 95 per cent of the software has had to be rewritten.

Requirements analysis

Because the requirements for the new system are not easily obtained directly, the existing system is analyzed, typically using the following techniques. Many user jobs are documented in terms of a job description, and so a starting point may be to examine the 'rule book' that states how these tasks should be carried out. This may reveal the original logic of the current work organization, but rarely represents what happens in practice. People tend to develop short-cuts so that working according to the rule book (*working to rule*) is in reality an effective form of industrial action, that can bring organizations swiftly grinding to a halt. Alternatively, analysts can set themselves up in the user's department and observe operations, but people tend to behave differently when they know that they are being watched, and furthermore much 'knowledge work' is not susceptible to observation. In addition, many functions are subject to monthly, seasonal or annual peaks and troughs, that are likely to be missed during a few days of observation. Questionnaires can be distributed to users, but success depends on the selection of respondents, the clarity and completeness of the questionnaire, the frankness of the respondents, and their willingness to spend sufficient time in answering the questionnaire fully. As such, questionnaires are not suitable for obtaining precise or procedural information about users' tasks or requirements.

The most common technique is that of interviewing users, but this often suffers from communication problems and misunderstanding, stemming from the different backgrounds, values and technical jargon of the user and analyst. For example, the phrase 'customer sales next year' may seem perfectly innocuous but could contain a minefield of semantic difficulties. Firstly, it may not be obvious what constitutes a 'customer'. If the firm sells goods to a chain store, the customer could be conceived as the client's head office that pays the invoices, the store that orders the goods, or the distribution depot to which the goods are delivered. Similar problems exist with the concept of 'sales'. Should these be shown at current prices? Should they include sales taxes and discounts? Should they be based on orders or payments? Finally, there are difficulties with the concept of 'next year'. This could be interpreted as the next financial year, the next calendar year, the next twelve months, or the next 365 days.

These problems might be more easily surmounted if the user and analyst shared common objectives and worldviews (*Weltanschauung*). However, the user probably wants a system that is easy to learn and use, but also adds to their status and the control they exert over their work. On the other hand, the analyst may prefer a system that is either easy and quick to build, or else is technically elegant, thus improving their career prospects. The analyst may not fully understand the subtleties of the user's job or the importance of the system to the user's working environment. Similarly, the user may not understand the techniques used by the analyst or appreciate the importance of the requirements analysis for the development of the final system.

Other, more novel, elicitation techniques include the use of 'brainstorming' sessions amongst groups of users, which can be useful unless they become dominated by the more vociferous users, or alternatively, everyone lapses into self-conscious silence. Another alternative is the 'Delphi' technique of circulating questionnaires so that users can see the responses of other users and amend their own comments accordingly. Finally, protocol analysis can be used, whereby the user 'talks through' their actions for either a typical or unusual task or case. These novel techniques and the more conventional ones are well described in the literature (e.g. [5]).

The problems of requirements elicitation are exacerbated by the climate of uncertainty and the changes in requirements that occur during the development process. In many ways, requirements elicitation has been neglected by researchers [6], who have become fixated with the representation of the specification. Elicitation is much more than just the first informal step towards specification. The social nature of information systems, where different groups may have very different requirements and expectations, means that it is impossible to specify requirements objectively. Furthermore, the excessive emphasis on technical requirements has led to the neglect of the more qualitative users' demands that affect the usability of the new system. These may include job design, office layouts, training needs, documentation and screen designs. Such issues are often treated as afterthoughts, if at all, being addressed only when the technical system is nearly complete and it is too late to incorporate major improvements.

Logical design and specification

Developers arrive at the specification by refining the vast amount of data collected during the requirements analysis, through the process of logical design. The physical detail of current operations is factored out, leaving just the logic of the current system as a basis from which to create the new logical design. Because of the ambiguity and verbosity of natural language, the process uses mostly graphical and analytical tools favoured by software engineering. These include entity-relationship modelling to model the data, data flow diagrams to represent the information flow between functions, and decision tables to show the combinations of relevant conditions and actions. In addition, data dictionaries are used to store data definitions, and 'structured' English (a form of pseudo code) is used to describe processes. Research into formal specification languages (such as Z [7]) has aimed at removing ambiguity, furnishing the automatic detection of *some* inconsistency and incompleteness, and the production of executable specifications. However, these specification languages cannot identify all inconsistencies or all the functions and data that have been omitted.

In addition to software and data designs, the specification should include the hardware and network configurations required. Thus, the specification for even a medium-sized system is usually a bulky document, containing upwards of 100 pages of text, 150 pages of lists and tables, and a further 50 pages of diagrams.

As well as its sheer size, the specification has a serious defect, in that it should ideally serve two functions. On the one hand, it is a sign-off document for user management to authorize the next stage of construction, and thus should be readily understandable to users. On the other hand, it should act as a blueprint for the programmers and program designers, which is facilitated by using a relatively formal language in which they are fluent, but which is thus unlikely to be understandable to the user. This 'schizophrenic' feature is far from satisfactory and the end result is often that the specification satisfies neither party.

As well as the software engineering approach of increased formalization, the specification problem has been addressed somewhat differently by prototyping, which seeks to improve requirements analysis and evolutionary systems, which recognize that the task is often hopeless.

Prototyping

Prototyping can be described as the construction of cheap, flexible and simplified systems for exploration and experimentation, often directly with the user in an operational environment. Like other industries (e.g. car manufacture), prototyping is becoming a popular alternative to the life cycle. It has become feasible in IS development through the availability of modern software tools such as fourth generation languages. Although it can be incorporated within the traditional life cycle [8], the approach is fundamentally different; prototypes are built to be changed, and development is iterative not linear. Any number of prototypes can be built; the first prototype is usually very simple, exploring basic assumptions about the problem situation, and then each additional prototype becomes a little more complex, incorporating more and more realism.

Prototyping reduces uncertainty by demonstrating the overall shape of the new system early on. It acts as a concrete vehicle for user involvement; users can relate more easily to a physical system, rather than to an abstract model represented by data flow diagrams. Therefore, it can reduce the divide between user and developer, generating confidence and facilitating learning by both parties. It should clarify requirements by highlighting misunderstandings and omissions, and the consequent ease of making changes should encourage developers to test alternative designs.

The disadvantages lie mostly in its implementation. Firstly, there is a danger of 'more haste, less speed', as developers, in their rush to build the first prototype, may skimp on the requirements elicitation. Secondly, prototyping requires new skills and attitudes, from both users and developers. Users should learn to become involved with development and not to expect developers to produce the ideal system at the first attempt. Similarly, developers need to develop the skills both to build prototypes and to interact with the users. While prototyping should reduce the risk of failure in the long run, it can increase costs in the short run and delay a project. Furthermore, the translation from the final prototype to the production version often involves rewriting the software in a more machine-efficient language. Fresh errors may creep in and users may be disappointed that the production version is not as flexible as the prototype. On the other hand, users may opt to keep the final prototype, which may cause operating problems, especially if it is insufficiently robust in terms of security and recovery. Finally, in the case of large systems, it may not be feasible to prototype the whole system at once , and there are risks that prototyping various parts of the system in parallel will result in these sub-systems diverging from each other. Nevertheless, the approach is widely used.

Evolutionary systems

Instead of a finite project delivering a completed system, there are occasions when a more evolutionary view is preferable. This portrays an installed system that evolves over time as it is extended and changed in the light of experience or environmental changes. This may be appropriate for large-scale complex systems as well as for individuals with a general requirement for microcomputer use. The latter may prefer to start with a few basic packages and allow their more sophisticated needs to evolve with usage. This notion thus refutes the project-based life cycle, preferring to emphasize the maintenance activities caused by changing circumstances. It is related to prototyping, in that systems are designed to be changed; the main difference is that evolutionary systems evolve in use not in experimentation, and the timescales are thus much longer.

This approach explicitly addresses the problems of uncertainty and change in requirements analysis, by denying the feasibility of any 'final' specification. It permits much scope for user involvement by allowing time for the users to learn the evolving system. However, it may suffer through its own inherent insecurity and uncertainty, in that developers and users cannot know how long the particular version will survive before it is changed. Even more troublesome is the case where the lack of planning has meant that there is insufficient flexibility (or upgrade path) for the system to evolve, and so developers must start again from scratch. However, despite these objections, it is an approach that is becoming attractive in an increasing number of situations.

The programming problem

This problem is not just that of preparing accurate and reliable programs that work according to specification. Programming needs to be carried out at consistently high levels of productivity, and the resulting software must be maintainable. The costly spectre of maintenance includes rectifying errors, accommodating changes in the environment, and enhancing and optimizing the code. The cost of maintenance, which usually exceeds the original development cost, is further increased by poorly designed, written and documented software. The first time a US social security payment of over three digits was required, the necessary rewriting of software cost more than $30 million. Cases have been reported where software that cost $30 per line of code to develop has cost up to $4000 per line to maintain over its lifetime. Thus, software flexibility, the notion that software can be changed easily, is mostly mythical. Ideally, maintenance should be undertaken by the best programmers in the organization, but this is very rarely the case in practice. It is a low status task, too often delegated to junior or second-rate programmers, who are unlikely to be well motivated by a task that is usually less than satisfying. They probably did not write the original software, and their difficulty in reading and understanding the program logic is likely to be reflected by introducing even more errors and by poorly documenting any changes made. Naturally, this makes maintenance even harder next time, and so the effort needed spirals upwards. At worst, organizations may become maintenance-bound, such that new developments are postponed indefinitely because development resources are tied up on maintenance.

Program design

Before programmers can start writing code, the specification must be translated into a detailed software design. Originally, this process was very much *ad hoc*, but with the advent of software engineering, it has become more formalized.

'Modular' design supports maintainability by aiming at the production of independent program modules that can be changed without causing unpredictable repercussions elsewhere in the software system. This is achieved by repeatedly decomposing the system through top-down stepwise refinement into simple low-level elements. These elements may be based on processes or data structures. The 'hard engineering' face of software engineering can be seen in the quantification of this modularity through measures such as *cohesion* and *coupling* [9].

The preoccupation with producing elegant code may result in *gold-plating*, where excessive effort is expended in dressing-up simple routines in shrouds of technical elegance, whilst simultaneously neglecting other important areas of design, such as the user–system interface. No matter how well the underlying software has been engineered, the system is likely to be a failure if the user finds it difficult to use. Thus, more attention should be given to designing for usability, through improved dialogue, and screen design including, where appropriate, the use of WIMPS (windows, icons, mice, and pull-down menus).

Programming

Programming languages, the principal tools, have multiplied and become much easier to use and more 'English-like'. Popularity has shifted away from the classic third-generation languages (FORTRAN, COBOL and BASIC) towards languages that emphasize the structuring of procedures and data (e.g. C, Ada). However, the huge maintenance burden of old systems ensures the survival of the older languages for the foreseeable future. Increased formalization can be seen in the use of languages with a stronger formal theoretical base, such as logic programming languages (e.g. Prolog) and functional languages (e.g. LISP).

Ease of use reached a peak with fourth generation languages, such as FOCUS, which have been credited with five-fold gains in programming productivity. Lacking the breadth and flexibility of more complex languages, they are most suitable for small applications or prototyping. A rather different direction is that of object-oriented programming (e.g. Smalltalk and C++). Instead of writing programs in terms of procedures, programmers define 'objects', their values and operations, and the messages that pass between these objects. This approach is inherently modular as each object possesses its own private memory and methods that are inaccessible to other objects. The programming effort can be reduced through the reuse of objects, and the classification of objects into object types that allows the inheritance of common characteristics.

In order to limit the idiosyncrasies of individual programmers, the way programs are written has become increasingly standardized and controlled through the enforcement of well structured and clearly documented programming styles [10].

Testing

The number and complexity of activities involved in software development make it a fundamentally error-prone operation, and place considerable reliance upon the testing stage. Despite the advances of formal mathematical methods, most software is still tested by 'throwing data' at the programs, and checking whether the results are those expected. This is a laborious and painstaking process, but the number of IS failures resulting from software bugs testifies to both its necessity and its shortcomings. Testing should be carried out in stages, starting with individual program modules, and building up to testing the entire system. A proper test plan, with a wide range of test data, should be prepared and adhered to, avoiding the temptation to skimp testing in order to catch up on the project schedule. Having discovered the existence of errors, it is up to the debugging process to identify and correct the errors. Whereas testing is a fairly systematic task, debugging remains largely an art.

The concept of testing has been largely subsumed into the more extensive one of quality assurance (QA). Many argue that QA should be rigorously applied throughout the development process; for example, by carrying out extensive design and code inspections. This may involve a separate QA group working together with the development team with the aim of combining the objectivity and expertise of the QA group with the application experience of the developers. The recognition by both IS management and staff that errors are inevitable, because of the complexity of the process, should reduce the potential for conflict between the two groups.

However, two key features remain largely impervious to the various mathematical, logical and statistical techniques employed under the banner of quality assurance. Firstly, the huge number of different paths through the network of a complex piece of software means that not every combination can be tested. Whilst the most common are checked, testing is necessarily incomplete, and some errors are likely to remain. Secondly, the test data is usually selected, consciously or unconsciously, to conform to the specification, but the specification itself may be *wrong* because of errors in the analysis phase.

Application packages, reusable code, and reverse engineering

These represent three different approaches to the programming problem. The purchase of pre-written application packages is a widely-used alternative to developing in-house software. For most applications, a wide range is available, of varying cost and capability. This approach virtually eliminates program design and programming, and is thus usually cheaper, faster and more reliable. However, packages are not tailor-made, and need varying degrees of customization to match the organization's requirements. The lack of access to the original program code may mean that it is impossible, either to alter the code to interface with adjacent systems or to cope with changing requirements. Packages do not obviate the need for the other stages of the life cycle: in particular, the feasibility study, requirements analysis, database design, configuration testing, and training.

A variation on this theme is that of reusable code, in the shape of a library of well-documented standard program modules. Like packages, compared to repeatedly 'reinventing the wheel', the reuse of modules offers considerable savings in cost and time, and also gives the security of using proven reliable modules. However, there are a number of highly pragmatic problems [11]. Firstly, there is the problem of 'fit'; it is not obvious how many truly generalizable modules exist that will fit a range of problems, apart that is from certain low-level mathematical routines. It is not clear what size of module should form the basis of the scheme, or how the libraries should be organized and indexed so that modules can be found quickly. Finally, there is the increased investment in the extra care in design, testing and general housekeeping required to guarantee the quality of these standard modules, especially if they are to be portable across a wide range of hardware and system software.

Where the documentation is poor and the system has been considerably changed since installation, reverse engineering is an alternative maintenance approach to patching the already fragile code. This involves the automatic analysis of existing code in order to distil out the underlying structure. It represents the life cycle in reverse, as the current design and specification are produced from the existing code. They can then be modified, and new efficient and reliable code produced. With appropriate tools, this seems a feasible approach, but it does raise serious implications for software copyright if it is applied to commercial packaged software.

IS development methodologies

A valid criticism of the traditional life cycle is that it basically comprises a collection of *ad hoc* development techniques. Development methodologies simply provide a systematic approach and a set of interlinking tools and techniques, all held together by a common perspective. As an aside, this terminology is a classic example of the tendency in IT to create an unnecessary mystique: in the IS world the term 'methodology' means nothing more than 'method'.

By providing standard techniques and documentation, a methodology increases IS management's control over projects, and provides 'hooks' for project management. They reduce management's dependence upon the ingenuity of individual developers, and facilitate the exchange of staff between projects. Furthermore, systems developed using the same methodology are likely to be easier to interface together.

A large number of methodologies grew out of the computer systems analysis techniques of the late 1960s and early 1970s. Individual methodologies tend to differ in their assumptions about the development process and hence the priorities they give to various aspects. Early methodologies (e.g. ADS, SOP), largely based on forms or checklists, were superseded during the late 1970s by structured methodologies. Some of these emphasized structure in terms of functions (e.g. [12]) while others gave priority to data structures (e.g. [13]). More recently, methodologies have taken a more balanced approach, including the UK Government standard, SSADM [14], which has grown into a comprehensive but highly complex methodology, with a large number of tools and techniques. The adoption of SSADM by the Government has, in many ways, stifled further debate through the politics of force. Eager for Government contracts, developers have rushed to embrace (or at least *appear* to embrace) the standard.

Most methodologies are technically oriented with an inherently analytic, rational perspective that takes little note of the people involved. On the other hand, ETHICS [15] emphasizes user participation and a socio-technical approach. The participative approach has many advantages, but has been largely overtaken by the more direct participation of end user computing. The Scandinavian ISAC methodology [16] attempts to combine both the technical and the more problem-oriented aspects of development.

Often the most tricky problems occur in the early stages of development, when it may not be clear how to even conceptualize the problem. The Soft Systems Methodology [17], resting on a strong theoretical base of Systems Theory, provides some useful tools and techniques that facilitate a systemic approach to the problem situation. It aims at a clearer understanding of the problem and a reconciliation of the conflicting views of the participants, rather than a formal specification of requirements or elegant program code. This approach has proved to be effective in a large number of real problem situations. However, it does require a commitment to understanding, as opposed to systems development, by both the analyst and the problem owners.

Suffice to say, despite the assertions of those with heavily vested interests, there is no best IS development methodology. Much depends upon the nature and context of the problem in hand, and on the expertise of the developers.

The project management problem

The management of programmers

The important place of people in the overall scheme of things is discussed further in Chapter 12, but it is appropriate to mention here the particular problem of managing programmers, as traditionally this has had an unhappy impact on project management in terms of planning, estimation, and project control. In the early days, programmers were of very variable quality, highly mobile and well paid, and there was high turnover of staff. Managers had little experience of supervising programmers, who considered themselves to be individual craftsmen, and thus not subject to conventional management techniques. This situation led to problems of recruitment, training, and evaluation, with consequent difficulties of control. Staff turnover still remains a problem for many organizations, but the growing expertise and professionalism of both IS management and staff, together with the increased formalization and standardization of the IS discipline, have reduced the craft aspects considerably.

As programmers typically work in project teams, their organization is important. The notion of *egoless programming* [18] involves treating programs as the product of the group, in order to overcome the resistance of individual programmers to the correction or modification of *their* programs by others. Alternatively, *chief programmer teams* have been instituted that relieve senior programmers of their administrative responsibilities, allowing them to design and code the key program modules, while supported by a small team of junior programmers. Although this arrangement ensures that the expertise of senior programmers is fully utilized, the raising of a few select programmers to the status of chief programmer may cause resentment amongst the others.

When projects start to run late, it is very tempting to add extra programmers unthinkingly: the *Mongolian horde* principle. Based on his experience with thousands of programmers developing the IBM OS/360 operating system, Brooks [19] formulated his well-known law: *Adding staff to a late software project makes it later*. The extra coordination and training of the new programmers can dramatically reduce the potential additional output.

However, the emphasis on standardization, aimed at the development of *software factories*, is not without its drawbacks. We still have relatively little knowledge of the cognitive processes behind programming, and managers must beware the loss of programmer creativity attendant upon uniformity and the de-motivating features of factory life.

The management of projects

IS development methodologies provide a basic management framework, as to a lesser extent does the life cycle itself; however, an additional layer of external project management is required to prevent projects from drifting out of control, under the self-perpetuating pressures and complexities of development.

Project management is qualitatively different from other IS management functions, as each project is unique, with its own highly specific demands and constraints. The project manager is given a particular set of resources to produce a specific system, within fairly rigid budget and time constraints. The resources comprise mostly people with highly varied but expensive skills, who must be combined and coordinated to produce the required deliverable, a project compl-eted within tight constraints. The project manager has to transcend the multitude of individual functions in order to control the project as a whole. He has to create the necessary working environment in order to gain a high sense of commitment towards the project from the various specialists in the team. Project managers must try to steer their projects through the minefield of uncertainties, and, while support tools are available, much still depends upon their experience and particular managerial and social skills.

The basic tenet of project management is the staged approach, which prov-ides the foundation for project planning and control. Large complex projects are decomposed into manageable parts, as that 'great leap forward' is in practice best achieved in 'short comfortable hops'. Thus, at the first level, the project is broken down into stages, roughly corresponding to those of the life cycle, and then each stage is further decomposed into activities. Each stage should produce a signif-icant and identifiable deliverable (e.g. the requirements specification), which becomes the subject of an end-of-stage review. Project control is effected through these reviews, where all parties, including users, can reassess progress of the project. The review may lead to some minor rescheduling of subsequent stages, or even a major change of plan. Each stage is made up of a number of activities, and these activities should be treated in a consistent fashion. Ideally, each activity (e.g. writing a particular group of code modules) should be small enough (perhaps less than ten man-days) to control tightly. It should be specified in advance, and should produce an identifiable deliverable that can be reviewed by the project manager. Where appropriate, the deliverable should be validated as part of an overall quality assurance programme.

Project planning is one of the most important, and yet most difficult, areas of project management: the old axiom that 'if you can't plan it, you can't do it' haunts project managers. Planning should satisfy the project deadlines and ensure that the appropriate resources are available when, and only when required. For example, specialists (such as networking experts) may only be needed for parts of the project, but should not be under-utilized for days, awaiting their turn to contribute. The project plan attempts (often vainly) to control the prevalent uncertainty, and acts as the yardstick against which the project is monitored and controlled. Plans are formulated at two levels: a broad plan for the whole project in terms of stages, and detailed plans for the activities of the current stage. For each stage, the activities and their dependencies need to be determined, and the appropriate resources estimated and scheduled. These operations can be supported by the diagrammatic techniques of critical path analysis, PERT (program evaluation and review technique), and Gantt charts [20].

Estimation remains the Achilles' heel of planning, since it is very difficult to estimate the amount of work required for a particular stage in advance. The methods used are professional judgement (rules of thumb), the 'historical' approach (a comparison with past projects), or a formal mathematical approach (e.g. COCOMO [21]). Results are obtained from the latter by inserting values for a number of carefully chosen parameters, such as estimated program size, complexity, and personnel capability. The formal approach has had mixed results, comparing well with the judgements of inexperienced project managers, but in many instances it has not proved as accurate as experienced judgements.

The production of documentation should proceed steadily in the background throughout the development process. It is a myth that the end product of software development comprises only the software, for it disregards the crucial importance of documentation in making complex software at all usable. Documentation, in the shape of installation, reference, tutorial and operating manuals, is required by both users and IS staff. In addition to current specification and designs, the project manager should also have an up-to-date project history, in terms of changes made to the original specification, and the designs rejected as well as those accepted. The poor readability of most documentation attests to the low priority given to it by many organizations. Few IS staff are taught how to write technical manuals, and there is often a complete absence of standards. However unexciting, good documentation is essential; large numbers of systems are operating with hardly any documentation, rendering maintenance a nightmare.

As things start to go wrong there is a general feeling that the project is sliding out of control, manifesting itself in the handing over late of intermediate deliverables, or escalating costs. The causes are likely to be many and varied, representing a particular combination of unforeseen human and technical problems. In such a case, the project manager should rework the plan, reorganize individual priorities, redeploy resources and try to increase motivation. Too often, in the desperate race to finish the project, the response is one of cutting corners on the apparently unessential tasks such as planning, documentation, and testing. Such action has the predictable consequence that the final system is incomplete, and contains a high in-built maintenance overhead.

Project management faces two unmistakeable forces that are very difficult to reconcile. On the one hand, there is an increasing formalization, reflected in the growing popularity of mathematical models for estimation, and the use of software tools and IPSEs (integrated project (programming) support environments). On the other hand, project management is people management, requiring a more sensitive, interpretive approach. The project manager has to manage and coordinate a mixed team of various specialists, who may be used to a considerable amount of freedom regarding how they carry out tasks: "The central question in how to improve the software art centres, as it always has, on people" [22].

Computer-aided software engineering

IS development is a complex and data-intensive activity, and large quantities of information have to be manipulated throughout the development cycle. Much of this was in real need of computer support, but, until recently, the old adage that 'the cobbler's children are always the last to get new shoes' was applicable to IS development. However, considerable attention is now focused on computer-aided software engineering (CASE) tools and IPSEs. There is some confusion regarding the terminology, but in general CASE tools can be regarded as relatively independent workstation tools, whereas IPSEs are basically mainframe-based integrated toolkits, although there is clearly some overlap between these two notions.

Complete automation of IS development is infeasible, due to its complexity. However, for very simple or tightly constrained tasks, software tools known as application generators (e.g. Ideal) and program generators (e.g. IP3) have been successful. The former produces object code, while the latter produce source code (e.g. COBOL). However, their limited application potential has made them appropriate in only a relatively few cases.

CASE tools comprise a variety of software tools, applicable to most stages of the life cycle [23]. For analysis and design, a number of tools (such as Excelerator and Information Engineering Workbench) have appeared that offer high-quality graphics capabilities to support the creation and manipulation of software designs in the form of data flow diagrams, structure charts and other diagrammatic representations. Supporting the symbol conventions used by a number of the more popular IS development methodologies, they allow such diagrams to be drawn and changed very quickly and simply. They also provide enhanced data dictionary facilities that maintain up-to-date definitions of database components, such as record and field formats. As such, they provide various validation checks, automate the production of documentation, and act as a database for the development process.

Tools that support the coding process include sophisticated compilers and linkers, as well as code, screen and report generators. These generators can also be used for the production of prototypes. Other tools support testing and debugging, such as test data generators; static data analyzers that examine code structure; and test harnesses that provide a simulated environment. There are also graphics-based tools to support project management activities by facilitating the otherwise laborious tasks of drawing and amending PERT and Gantt charts.

CASE tools potentially represent important productivity aids by improving the speed, accuracy, flexibility and consistency of IS development, including the production of documentation. A drawback is that many are single-user micro-based tools, that are of limited value for large teams building mainframe systems. Potential users, faced with the number, diversity and limited scope of many tools are not helped by the lack of standardization. Furthermore, the tools need to be used together with an IS development methodology if they are to be used rigorously, and this implies a need for compatibility with the methodology.

Integrated tool-sets are available in the shape of IPSEs such as Maestro II (from Philips) and Perspective (from SD-Scicon). The origins of IPSEs can be traced back to the Stoneman specification of the US Department of Defense's requirements for the Ada programming language. IPSEs are mostly complex, expensive, mainframe-based environments aimed at large software projects such as real-time military systems. In this regard, they emphasize project control, standardization, quality assurance and coordination between team members. They are mostly firmly rooted in the traditional life cycle with little regard for prototyping, user involvement, or IS development methodologies. Research [24] has suggested that individual, social and organizational factors are more important than technical ones for the successful implementation of IPSEs. Thus, they need to be more flexible to fit into a variety of organizations, and more supportive of individual creativity, rather than being a vehicle for rigid project control.

Conclusion

Considerable ingenuity has been applied to the problems of IS development and much progress has been made. However, there is no 'silver bullet' that will solve all the problems and finally kill the 'werewolf' of IS failures [22]. Additionally, throughout the various stages of the development cycle, there is a noticeable tension between increased formalization and a 'softer', more qualitative approach. Whilst the main 'populist' trend is towards a more formal approach, propelled by the momentum of the software engineering movement, those who distrust formalization have considerable evidence to support their case. Again we would argue for a balanced position, as a monopoly for either school of thought would be disastrous. IS development is a highly complex activity; some areas should be formalized and others should remain the prerogative of interpretation and subjective judgement. The mapping out of their respective territories will surely be a major part of the research agenda for the next decade.

Discussion issues

1.   Can IS development methodologies stimulate creativity, or are they just vehicles for standardization and control?

2.   Discuss ways of integrating the various development cycles (the traditional life cycle, prototyping, evolutionary systems, end-user computing) so that each is available for the IS department of a large organization.

Exercises

1.   For a simple case (e.g. the planning of the end-of-term party or staff party), carry out a requirements elicitation exercise, using the common techniques of gathering information.

2.   Take the case of the admissions procedure for your university or college, or staff recruitment procedure for your company, and apply the analysis and/or design tools from either one or two IS development methodologies.

Suggested reading

Life cycle model

   Burch, J. & Grudnitski, G., *Information systems: theory and practice*, 5th edn., Wiley, New York, 1989.

Software engineering solutions

   Boehm, B.W.,'Improving software productivity', *Computer*, 20(9), 43-57, 1987.

   Brooks, F.P.,'No silver bullet: essence and accidents of software engineering', *Computer*, 20 (4), 10-19, 1987.

Pressman, R.S., *Software engineering: A practitioner's approach*, McGraw-Hill, New York, 1982.

Formal methods

Hoare, C.A.R.,'An overview of some formal methods for program design', *Computer*, 20 (9), 85-91, 1987.

Requirements analysis

Galliers, R. (ed.), *Information analysis: selected readings*, Addison-Wesley, Sydney, Australia, 1987.

Land, F.,'Adapting to changing user requirements', *Information and Management*, 5, 59-75, 1982.

Prototyping

Naumann, J.D. & Jenkins, A.M.,'Prototyping: the new paradigm for systems development, *MIS Quarterly*, 6 (3), 29-44, 1982.

Testing

Abbott, J., *Software testing techniques*, NCC, Manchester, UK, 1986.

Myers, G., *The art of software testing*, Wiley, New York, 1979.

IS development methodologies

Avison, D.E. & Fitzgerald, G., *Information systems development: methodologies, techniques and tools*, Blackwell, Oxford, 1988.

Project management

Gildersleeve, T.R., *Data processing project management*, 2nd edn. Van Nostrand Reinhold, New York, 1985.

Keen, J., *Managing systems development*, 2nd edn. Wiley, New York, 1987.

CASE tools

Gibson, M.L.,'The CASE philosophy', *Byte*, 14 (4), 209-218, 1989.

IPSEs

Dart, S.A., Ellison, R.J., Feiler, P.H. & Habermann, A.N.,'Software development environments', *Computer*, 20 (11), 18-28, 1987.

References

1. Boehm, B.,'Software engineering', *IEEE Transactions on Software Engineering*, December, 1976.

2. Davis, G.B., & Olson, M.H., *Management information systems: conceptual foundations, structure and development*. McGraw-Hill, New York, 1984.

3. Boehm, B.W.,'A spiral model of software development and enhancement', *Computer*, 21 (5), 61-72, 1988.

4. Jones, C.B., *Software development: a rigorous approach*, Prentice-Hall, Englewood Cliffs, New Jersey, 1980.

5. Licker, P.S., *Fundamentals of systems analysis*, Boyd & Fraser, Boston, 1987.

6. Hirschheim, R.A. & Schafer, G.,'Requirements analysis: a new look at an old topic', *Journal of Applied Systems Analysis*, Vol.15, 101-118, 1988.

7. Spivey, J.M., *Understanding Z: a specification language and its semantics*, Cambridge University Press, Cambridge, 1989.

8. Dearnley, P.A. & Mayhew, P.J.,'In favour of system prototypes and their integration into the systems development cycle', *Computer Journal*, 26 (1), 36-42, 1983.

9. Stevens, W., Myers, G. & Constantine, L.,'Structured design', *IBM Systems Journal*, 13 (2), 115-139, 1974.

10. Kernighan, B. & Plauger, P., *The elements of programming style*, McGraw-Hill, New York, 1974.

11. Geary, K.,'The practicalities of introducing large-scale software re-use', *Software Engineering Journal*, 3 (5), 172-176, 1988.

12. De Marco, T., *Structured analysis and system specification*, Yourdon Press, New York, 1978.

13. Jackson, M.A., *System development*, Prentice-Hall, Englewood Cliffs, New Jersey, 1983.

14. Downs, E., Clare, P. & Coe, I., *Structured systems analysis and design method: application and context*, Prentice-Hall, Hemel Hempstead, 1988.

15. Mumford, E. & Weir, M., *Computer systems in work design: the ETHICS method*, Associated Business Press, London, 1978.

16. Lundeberg, M., Goldkuhl, G. & Nilsson, A., *Information systems development: a systematic approach*, Prentice-Hall, Englewood Cliffs, New Jersey, 1981.

17. Checkland, P., *Systems thinking, systems practice*, Wiley, Chichester, 1981.

18. Weinberg, G., *The psychology of computer programming*, Van Nostrand Reinhold, New York, 1971.

19. Brooks, F.P., *The mythical man-month*, Addison-Wesley, Reading, Mass., 1975.

20. Yeates, D., *Systems project management*, Pitman, London, 1986.

21. Boehm, B.W., *Software engineering economics*, Prentice-Hall, Englewood Cliffs, New Jersey, 1981.

22. Brooks, F.P.,'No silver bullet: essence and accidents of software engineering', *Computer*, 20 (4), 10-19, 1987.

23. Avison, D.E. & Fitzgerald, G., *Information systems development: methodologies, techniques and tools*, Blackwell, Oxford, 1988.

24. LeQuesne, P.N.,'Individual and organizational factors and the design of IPSEs', *Computer Journal*, 31 (5), 391-397, 1988.

11   Evaluation, monitoring and control

- *Evaluation*
- *Measurement and subjective judgement*
- *Evaluation techniques*
- *Understanding evaluation*
- *Risk analysis*
- *Computer-based monitoring*
- *Control*

Evaluation

Over the last ten to fifteen years, the evaluation (or assessment) of information systems has become an increasingly key issue, as significant amounts of scarce capital are poured into CBIS and as the headlines fill with tantalising stories of their successes and failures. It is hardly surprising that organizations, their management, workforce and shareholders, are all eager to determine whether the investment has been worthwhile. Evaluation is perceived as an essential part of the management process; an evaluation of the current position, in respect of past policies, forms an important input to contemporary planning and decision-making. In systems terms, evaluation provides the crucial feedback function, helping to prevent the repetition of the same costly errors; and so the organization learns. While there is a strong argument for evaluation to be carried out carefully, in a professional fashion, the evaluation of information systems is an area full of potential pitfalls. We shall argue that formal evaluation studies cannot be as objective and rational as most of their supporters imagine, and that organizations, which are striving for more precise 'harder' measures of their performance, are in reality seeking a *philosopher's stone*.

    The term 'evaluation' has been used in a number of contexts, but in this book we are referring to the notion of judging the value of a system, or part of a system. This can be thought of in monetary terms (both benefits and costs), or in terms of usefulness or success (as opposed to failure). We therefore focus on the organizational impact, rather than on the purely physical performance of the equipment; for example, we are not concerned with aspects such as the ratings of computer power in millions of instructions per second.

Organizations are normally concerned with two questions of evaluation: firstly, the viability or usefulness of a particular investment; and secondly, the relative merits of a number of alternative proposals. These questions usually appear at two distinct points in the systems development life cycle. During the early stages, they appear within the feasibility study when decisions are taken as to which development option, if any, should be pursued. This decision is severely constrained by the need to predict the future within a climate often characterized by considerable uncertainty. However, we shall argue that the second stage of evaluation, the post-implementation evaluation of an operational system, is nearly as problematical, even though largely freed from the indeterminacies of future speculation. In this chapter we shall concentrate mostly upon this *post facto* evaluation. The difficulties attached to this evaluation of consequences will clearly demonstrate that even more formidable problems face the estimation of the value of systems in advance.

Formal evaluation is becoming increasingly fashionable in more and more aspects of our working life and leisure, perhaps reflecting the science-based optimistic rationality of the age. This can be seen in the increasing pressure to use management accounting principles to measure the productivity of both individual departments and entire organizations. It is also apparent in the application of cost benefit analysis to social policy and the provision of social services, and even in the popularity of 'unbiased' guides to consumer products, based on extensive laboratory tests. Certain indicators of this quantitative evaluation, such as the unemployment rate within the economy, the rate of inflation, the petrol consumption of cars, and the dollar exchange rate, bask in a mystique of sublime omniscience: "which responds to numbers as though they were the repositories of occult powers .... [it] is an exaggerated regard for the significance of measurement, just because it is quantitative, without regard either to what has been measured or to what can subsequently be done with the measure. Number is treated as having an intrinsic scientific value." [1]

Such confidence in quantitative measurement is totally unjustified, when one considers that for the most part, the measures are crude, transient indicators of highly complex social situations. For example, the size of a database may not have any relationship with its usefulness. An impressively large database, running to many gigabytes of data, may have vast numbers of redundant records simply because one group of data collectors was rewarded on the basis of the number of records accumulated. Despite the difficulties, organizations, governments and individuals have a strong desire for objective, systematic, and formal evaluation studies. Accountability is an important ingredient in modern organizations; how can individuals be accountable without some form of objective evaluation? These pressures now apply not only to commercial organizations but also to schools, universities and hospitals. Politicians, the electorate and consumers seem to want to know, in quantitative terms, how well these organizations are performing.

This desire for formal evaluation is felt particularly strongly in the case of information systems. This may be due to the size of the investment they require, or their potentially wide-ranging impact, their general unfamiliarity, and their potential for conspicuous success or disaster. In these circumstances, where organizations have to justify their huge investments, it is easy to dismiss the opinions of the more 'intuitive' managers and rely instead on those who appear to be controlling the organization in a rational scientific manner. Thus, formal evaluation studies are set up with the express purpose of determining an objective, accurate measurement of a system's 'success'. They frequently involve teams of evaluators, and rely upon relatively systematic techniques to produce a result largely expressed in precise quantitative terms.

However, we would argue that there are fundamental difficulties with the formal evaluation of information systems, that render many studies totally worthless. These difficulties mostly stem from two factors discussed in previous chapters: the principle that information systems are social systems, and the difficulty of placing a value on information itself. Rather than being interested in the laboratory evaluation of a particular computer or piece of software, we are concerned with the evaluation of information systems as they operate within organizations. The complexity and ambiguity inherent in organizations, when considered as social and political systems, implies that simplistic notions of objective measurement and positivist causality are quite inappropriate.

Furthermore, individuals within the organization have a powerful instinct to carry out their own 'informal' evaluation. We all intuitively evaluate everything of interest that we come into contact with during our daily lives. Almost subconsciously, we evaluate people, events, and artifacts according to our own personal system of values; it is hard to think about anything without simultaneously evaluating it in some way. On the one hand, this urge to evaluate may increase our desire for formal evaluation, especially if we believe it will support our informal judgements, but, on the other hand, it can render such formal approaches superfluous. Informal evaluation can be highly effective and cost-efficient compared to the resources allocated to a formal study and its associated bureaucracy. Both formal and informal evaluation, carried out after implementation, are likely to be muddied by the *post hoc* rationalization, where mistakes are concealed and lucky successes are attributed to good planning.

Critics would argue that such informality naturally makes the evaluation subjective, hasty and inaccurate. However, for those most concerned with a new system, because of drastic changes to their working methods or redundancies, this informal evaluation can reach a surprising depth, whether carried out individually or with their colleagues in the canteen. Thus, formal evaluation studies necessarily take place in an environment of powerful subjective value judgements of individuals and groups, operating within a lively political system.

Formal studies are further hampered by the economic nature of information, in particular the problems of measuring the amount of information and attaching values to it. Information does not behave like other economic resources and attempts to fix dollar values are highly arbitrary. These doubts about the effectiveness of formal evaluation are reflected in the results of a recent survey [2], which indicates that many organizations give little credence to evaluation studies made after the implementation of an information system. Although such studies are widely practised, they are mostly carried out immediately after system cut-over, and are dominated by members of the development team. The evaluation criteria are mostly confined to aspects of the information provided by the system (accuracy, timeliness etc.), with the impact on, and consequences for, the user and the organization being rarely studied. This suggests that the main reason for carrying out the studies is project closure, i.e. to mark formally the end of development projects, rather than any attempt at organizational learning.

Measurement and subjective judgement

"You cannot measure what is not defined. You also cannot tell whether you have improved something if you have not measured its performance" [3]. Formal evaluation relies upon the measurement of various factors, but there are many problematic subjective aspects to this 'objective' measurement, especially regarding the treatment of intangibles, such as quality and satisfaction. Measurement can be seen to comprise three steps [4]: the identification of an underlying dimension, its definition into units and scales, and finally the execution of the measurement. The first two steps are clearly judgemental, "based on the values, beliefs and concerns of those involved in defining the measure". While there may be little contention or ambiguity in the laboratory measurement of the performance of a computer against accepted benchmarks, this is not the case with a complex operational information system, comprising hardware, software, data, documentation and procedures.

The evaluation of information systems should be related to the requirements of the individual organization and its users, but it is often far from clear which factors should be measured, how they should be measured, and why those factors are selected and not others. In this situation, there is a strong temptation to measure either that which is easiest to measure, or that which is most likely to produce the desired result. Evaluation studies may be carried out for a host of reasons: as justification for extensions or replacement systems; as part of the planning or resource allocation process; in order to 'tune' a system; as part of the internal marketing of a system; or as a more political allocation of credit and blame. Thus, evaluation in terms of 'objective' measurement depends throughout on subjective judgements; much depends upon *who* carries out the evaluation, *why* they are carrying it out, and for *whom* the report is prepared.

Considerable choice exists regarding the judgement of *what* to evaluate:

accuracy	quality	usability
flexibility	relevance	user satisfaction
functionality	reliability	utilization
productivity	security	volume
profitability	speed	

Each one of these aspects of a system may be more or less relevant to the situation, but each is a hazy ambiguous concept that has to be broken down for the purposes of measurement. In each case, there are many possible ways of breaking down the concept. For example, functionality may comprise both the range of functions and the effectiveness of performing each function. Usability may comprise one or more of the following: the ease of learning, the ease of retention, the probability of errors, the speed at which the task can be carried out, and the ease of recovering from errors. User satisfaction may be viewed as expressed satisfaction (through a questionnaire survey) or in terms of staff turnover statistics. Similarly, security can be examined in terms of system failures, back-up and recovery; the ease that intruders can penetrate the system; or the effectiveness at identifying or disabling intruders. Any attempt to circumvent this problem by discussing the 'quality' of information systems runs very quickly into exactly the same difficulties.

Having subjectively selected which aspects (and sub-aspects) should be evaluated, the issue of *how* they should be measured arises. This comprises the selection, again subjective, of particular measures that appropriately represent the aspect in question; for example, the mean time to complete a task as opposed to the median or maximum. Similarly, profitability can be represented through cost benefit analysis or through the various financial ratios, such as proportion of turnover or return on investment. Finally, an appropriate method of actually obtaining the measurements has to be determined; for example, self-timing, the timing of keystrokes by software or by an observer with a stopwatch. Having carried out such procedures for all the various aspects, some form of weighting scheme may be required to reflect the relative importance of each measurement, in order to arrive at a final combined result. This again is highly subjective.

Similarly, the judgement of *when* to carry out the evaluation can make a considerable difference to the result. Immediately after installation, users and developers are at the start of their learning curves and are bound to find the system strange and awkward. Further along the curve they will become more accustomed to the new system and it might seem that the system is working well. Further still, when users normally start to employ the more peripheral functions, fresh problems and opportunities start to emerge. Both in terms of learning and in terms of upgrades and extensions, the system is an evolving and consequential entity. From the perspective of evaluation, it constitutes a moving target, and moving targets are notoriously difficult to hit. Similarly, the business and technological environment may be highly changeable, again affecting the results of any evaluation. A long term perspective may even be able to accommodate today's successes that become tomorrow's failures (and vice versa), but organizations cannot afford to wait forever to pronounce a verdict. Furthermore, the performance evaluation of a system that is subject to dramatic traffic peaks poses additional problems, as to when to carry out an evaluation. Thus, when to evaluate is a key judgement, and a highly subjective one.

Finally, having struggled to assemble some form of quantitative results, these must be compared against certain criteria, which are equally subjective. The results of IS evaluation studies should be seen as highly relative. Rather than firm technical benchmarks, they are compared against the expectations of individual users, based on their current knowledge, the previous system and the alternative designs rejected during development. Underlying these judgements are the different individual value systems, originating from the norms of the conflicting groups that they represent. All the common evaluation techniques, described below, are equally riddled with subjectivity. Evaluators may have considerable freedom in respect of what is evaluated and how it is evaluated; their decisions, based upon their own subjective perceptions, will obviously have a significant influence on the final result. The evaluation of an information system cannot be an objective, deterministic process based on a positivist 'scientific' paradigm. Such a 'hard', quantitative approach to social systems is misconceived.

This subjectivity also applies to the evaluation of the effectiveness of organizations themselves. Concerning commercial organizations, profit figures are just one element; they need to be balanced against market share, return on capital, and long term prospects, as well as the more qualitative aspects of staff morale and customer goodwill. The case is put even more starkly in regard to non-commercial organizations. It is not at all clear how to measure 'objectively' the performance or quality of schools, universities and hospitals. The number of examination passes, the number of scientific papers, and bed occupancy ratios only demonstrate partial aspects of such organizations' performance, and it is all too easy to examine them out of context. Much of the evaluation of police forces in the UK traditionally focused on the tidy, single figure of the clear-up rate for crime, but the limitations of this approach have at last been recognized and future evaluation is to be based on some thirty indicators, including response time to emergencies, public complaints and the utilization of manpower.

In the evaluation of social policy, Legge [5] identifies three 'crises of evaluation', which apply equally to information systems. The *crisis of utilization* concerns whether the results of the study are actually used by decision-makers. The *crisis of verification* refers to the difficulty in judging whether the methods used have produced valid results. Verification refers to truth or correctness, while validation refers to soundness. Finally, the *crisis of accreditation* refers to the effect of the underlying values of the evaluator and the evaluator's sponsors.

Evaluation techniques

We shall examine the commonly used evaluation techniques in terms of a framework of three 'zones' [6]: efficiency, effectiveness, and understanding. The classification is based upon the assumptions underlying each technique regarding their objectivity/subjectivity. Efficiency-based techniques assume that objective, rational measurement is feasible, while techniques for understanding rest on assumptions that evaluation is totally subjective or political. Techniques that address effectiveness tend to have elements of both objectivity and subjectivity.

Efficiency

Efficiency is concerned with the relatively low-level aspects of optimizing the way predetermined tasks are carried out. The objectives are unambiguous and, as such, the evaluation of efficiency is relatively objective, lending itself readily to a more positivist approach, with the intention of a greater precision of measurement. Examples of such evaluation concern the technical performance of computers in terms of speed, capacity and reliability, with the implicit assumption that faster, higher capacity and more reliable computers are the unshakeable objectives. This technical performance can be measured by hardware or software monitoring devices recording the performance of operational systems, or they can be simulated off-site. The testing of software to determine whether it meets its specification is another form of efficiency evaluation; of course this assumes that the original specification is correct. As in production management, where such techniques originated, the evaluation of efficiency has very much a technical flavour, and is concerned mostly with correctness and optimization. This type of evaluation is essential for functions such as quality assurance (QA) and capacity planning, but it does not address what must be our main concern, the questions of whether the system is successful, and whether the original investment is worthwhile. Even the concept of 'quality' is used very narrowly to mean a conformance to the specification, an attitude we would consider highly suspect.

Effectiveness

The measurement of effectiveness is currently of great concern to organizations; it involves taking a broader view, removing the assumptions of unambiguous objectives and predetermined functions. According to Drucker [7], efficiency refers to 'doing things right', and assumes that the 'things' in question have to be done, while effectiveness refers to 'doing the right things'. To quote Strassmann's example [3]: "Driving a car that gets 100 miles per gallon is not *effective* if you are driving around without purpose". Effectiveness is much more difficult to measure than efficiency as it involves subjective context-dependent interpretation. Both efficiency and effectiveness have their place; usually certain tasks are essential and should be carried out as efficiently as possible, others may turn out on closer inspection to be redundant and should be discontinued.

The notion of productivity is an important component of effectiveness, but the measurement of office and management productivity is extremely difficult. In a manufacturing context, productivity is much more straightforward; inputs can easily be related to outputs, where both raw materials and labour (inputs) and finished products (outputs) are relatively simple to measure. In the office or management context, it is not meaningful to try to measure the inputs and outputs of information, decisions, control and coordination. Strassmann [3] criticizes traditional approaches to productivity, and proposes the notion of 'value added' by management, which he calculates from the residue from turnover after the costs of raw materials, operational labour and financial capital have been deducted. This value is then compared against the cost of management salaries and overheads. In some cases, this approach can be useful, but it implicitly attributes all changes in turnover to the actions of management, whereas they may be caused by any number of other factors, such as market, legal or fiscal changes, or just 'dumb luck'. Similarly, this calculation implicitly assumes that particular actions of management directly produce effects within a certain time frame; for example, the same financial year. These assumptions are untenable in many cases. There is evidence within industry that these problems are widely recognized, and that many organizations do not even attempt to measure office or management productivity.

One relatively simple technique for measuring effectiveness is to try to measure the amount of usage of a system. This assumes that a useful system will be used extensively, whereas a poor system will be used very little. This assumption may be meaningful for evaluating airline routes (in terms of seat occupancy), but this proposition does not often hold for information systems. It is more often the case that usage is mandatory; i.e. no matter how bad the system is, it has to be used. For example, there is usually no alternative to particular transaction processing systems and central database systems. Furthermore, some information systems may appear to be used extensively, but, on closer inspection, such usage turns out to be nominal, as the users continue to rely on traditional methods based on 'black books' in 'bottom drawers'. Other systems, by their very nature, may not be used very often, but when they are used, they are virtually essential; for example, annual planning systems, and virus hunters.

One of the most familiar techniques for the evaluation of effectiveness within organizations is that of cost–benefit analysis, whereby the success of a system is based on the amount (if any) that the benefits exceed the costs. Originating in the field of economics, the technique has become well established in many fields, but it is still highly subjective, as to which costs and benefits are included in the analysis, and how they are valued. The complexity of organizations and of organizational information systems is such that the evaluation of an individual system in isolation becomes meaningless, unless adjoining systems are also considered. Similarly, this complexity implies that simplistic notions of causation should be viewed with extreme scepticism. For example, an increase in revenue may coincide with the introduction of a new system, but this could equally be attributed to market changes. Intentions and actions may be followed by desired consequences, but that does not imply causation. For example, the British computer manufacturer ICL's expansion in Eastern Europe took place after their use of decision support systems, but another likely cause may have been the US embargo on IT exports to the Eastern Bloc. 'Dumb luck' can turn even the most misguided into successful conclusions, purely by chance.

Thus, there is considerable scope for the evaluator to include or exclude elements, depending upon the desired outcome. Intangible costs and benefits tend to be either ignored altogether, treated as a side issue, or given some arbitrary valuation. In the UK, the Roskill Commission's cost–benefit analysis for London's third airport was bitterly criticized: "It is just possible that cost–benefit exercises have some utility as supporting evidence for certain kinds of decision, but when the art is elevated to the level of a comprehensive framework for decision making, the cost of cost–benefit becomes severe indeed, amounting almost to actual vitiation of proper professional and political procedures." [8]

The difficulties of placing a value on information render the benefits side of the equation very shaky ("ill-conceived, unsound, or even fantastic" [9]), but, on closer examination, the determination of costs is almost as difficult. Various cost conventions can be used, based on actual expenditure, resource usage or opportunity cost, and the treatment of inflation and depreciation provides further scope for variation. The human costs, in terms of user and management time and overheads, are usually open to interpretation, while the more indirect costs in terms of staff morale, resistance, absenteeism and general uncertainty are rarely considered at all. Similarly, third party costs in the shape of customer inconvenience and lost business are frequently ignored. While some improvement may be shown in terms of quantities (e.g. the number of customers served by each staff member), the quality of service may have deteriorated. Furthermore, 'savings' can often be shown by shifting work to another department under cover of the general reorganization; in other words, 'robbing Peter to pay Paul'. Potential benefits, in terms of reduced staffing or overheads may be achievable, but may not actually be realized, as staff and offices are retained for any number of reasons. From the perspective of evaluation, introducing the notion of 'value-added' may be little more than just a fashionable change of terminology for 'benefits'; for there is little real insight into how to measure the value.

Thus, even without considering the thorny issue of the value of information, the process is wide open to interpretation and exploitation. Cost–benefit analysis is not a precise science; according to Tapscott's *First Law of Cost-Justifying Office Systems* [10]: "The probability of a chooser accepting a cost–benefit analysis is directly proportional to the degree to which s/he is favourably inclined to the technology anyhow."

An alternative approach to ascertaining the success of a system is to compare it against its original objectives. Although an apparently straightforward method for defining success, there are severe practical difficulties even with this approach. In many cases, the original objectives are not formally stated, and even where objectives can be unearthed, they may not have been quantified; for example, 'an improvement in customer service', with no mention as to how such improvement should be measured. In other cases, the formal objectives may hide covert political aims, such that although the formal objectives may have been achieved, the system may not be acceptable to users because the anticipated political gains did not materialize. The original objectives for certain highly novel systems may have been unrealistically high or low, but, on implementation, the system is evidently successful. In many cases, the objectives change during development; in which case, it is not clear which objectives should be used for evaluation. Considering the organization as a political system, it is unlikely that the original objectives represented a real consensus, and this raises the question of *who* set the objectives, and *how* they were set. Also, the original objectives may not have been consistent with the objectives of the organization or particular individuals and groups. Objectives are man-made; they are not etched in stone, and they are usually open to subjective interpretation. It may be difficult to separate perceptions of the original objectives, and how reasonable they were, from perceptions of their achievement and the success that this represents.

Many organizations, mindful of the views of users, prefer some form of questionnaire survey. The rationale is that the system is considered to be successful if the staff believe it to be so, as when staff productivity or job satisfaction has improved. This approach means that organizations face problems of wording the questionnaire in such a way as to obtain relatively unbiased results, as well as dealing with the problems of non-response and the preservation of anonymity. Such questionnaire evidence can be criticized as subjective, flimsy and uninformative, falling into the 'is everybody happy?' category [11]. However, this should be viewed in the light of the subjectivity inherent in the apparently objective methods discussed above; such surveys do at least give the users some chance to express their opinions. Much depends upon the expectations of those surveyed; unrealistic expectations are likely to result in an initial dissatisfaction, but this may be tempered over time. A key difficulty is selecting who should be surveyed, given the likely variation of views between different groups. Also, where different groups are polled (for example, senior management, middle management, office staff, customers and IS staff), it is by no means clear how to cope with any inter-group variation.

Understanding evaluation

The evident inadequacies of the above techniques imply an urgent need to re-examine the evaluation situation, in order to gain a fresh understanding. Thus, we would advocate that evaluation should be approached in terms of understanding organizational situations, systems and events. This means attempting to understand the social and economic context of the information system, the reasons why the system performs in a particular way, and why individuals reach particular opinions regarding the worth of the system. This does not mean totally discarding the familiar techniques, discussed above, but it does mean being in a position to interpret their results in the context of the organizational and social reality. This includes relating the results, not only to the stated aims of the organization, but also to the unstated objectives of the various groups within the organization. The complexity of organizations and the importance of local contingencies means that a good understanding of the specific situation is essential; formal frameworks are frequently wrong-footed by the subtleties of real situations. An emphasis on understanding legitimizes the powerful informal evaluation of the key actors, linking it to the more systematic elements of formal studies. Informal evaluation is too potent and too valuable to remain covert.

This brings us to the 'understanding' zone of the framework. This zone is qualitatively different to the others; it refers to techniques that attempt to explain the evaluation process, rather than aiming at any measurement as such. Such evaluations must take into account the subjective, social and political factors within the situation and, towards this end, techniques such as role-playing or management games may prove useful. Much of the theoretical work developed within cognitive science, with regard to the way individuals build different mental models of their worlds [12], could be adapted to the evaluation problem. Similarly, there have been a number of studies of organizations that attempt to encompass the political aspects [13]. However, such efforts remain largely within the confines of research establishments.

Understanding evaluation must include an appreciation of the social nature of evaluation, as both informal and formal evaluation are social activities. As we have argued in preceding chapters, information systems are not 'objective rational' systems created and operated to further the goals of the organization. Rather, both in development and operation, they reflect the organization's culture and internal political system, and are evaluated by the organization's members accordingly. Formal evaluations usually involve *inter-group* interaction, while informal ones comprise *intra-group* discussions. Formal evaluation teams are often made up of individuals from a number of departments and will probably involve canvassing the opinions of many others. Similarly, informal evaluations are not merely personal reflections, they involve much informal discussion within groups, where opinions are formed collectively.

A formal study adds a new political forum within which groups can interact. Where the system has obvious failings, this interaction is likely to take the form of conflict. If there are no appropriate existing forums, a formal evaluation study may be a relevant approach but, in many cases, existing mechanisms will prove to be adequate. Therefore, the need for a formal study and a specially selected team will depend upon the circumstances: the type and severity of problems; the importance of the system; and the existence of alternative channels for discussion. Thus, a formal evaluation is not an objective piece of scientific measurement, it is an organizational social action. Formal evaluation does not replace political conflict in organizations with some form of rational solution – the opposite is more likely, in that it may add to political conflict. A particular recommendation from the evaluation study may be a significant political prize, conferring legitimacy on a group's political objectives. En route to this prize, there may be certain tactical positions to be won, in terms of the membership of the evaluation team and the setting of terms of reference. However, it is all too often impossible to separate the rhetoric of rational evaluation from the underlying political motives: "Key actors used the language of efficiency to push the CBIS in a direction that increased their own power and control in the organization" [13].

Our critique of formal evaluation techniques should not be seen as an attempt to discredit evaluation altogether, but as another example of our general call to balance opportunities and risks. The desires and needs of both the individual and the organization to evaluate systems are too powerful to dismiss, even bearing in mind the difficulties discussed above. Furthermore, our view of organizations, in terms of systems, intrinsically includes evaluation as a feedback mechanism. Our objection is to the mindless quantification of complex social events that can only be interpreted in a qualitative sense. We wish to avoid evaluation studies, where considerable effort and talent are wasted in chasing the 'Holy Grail' of a single figure solution, the *right* answer. There is a misplaced desire to collapse all our intuitive understanding of a situation into a single (if possible, linear) scale where: "The answer to the Great Question .... Of Life, the Universe and Everything .... Is Forty-two" [14].

The aim should be to increase the richness of our understanding with a broader contextual approach, rather than to concentrate on the detailed development of particular techniques. We need to take an eclectic approach by employing a range of techniques to evaluate the various aspects of operational information systems. There is no single best technique, and the selection of techniques requires expertise and understanding. In most cases the mixture should include both quantitative and qualitative, formal and informal techniques, as they tend to tell different parts of the story. Wherever possible, a longitudinal approach, involving either a study over a period of time or repeated studies at intervals, is advisable to overcome the problem of when to carry out evaluation.

However, to achieve this breadth of evaluation may demand a paradigm shift, away from the objectivist, positivist approach, towards a much greater acceptance of the qualitative interpretivist position. Whilst a positivist, 'scientific' approach is appropriate for the physical sciences, it is clearly inappropriate for information systems considered as social systems. Such a paradigm shift is not trivial, the values of the 'scientific method' are deeply embedded in the fundamental beliefs of many managers. They are also highly convenient: "Positivistic [evaluation] designs prosper largely through acting as a rhetoric for an evaluation ritual whereby the lack of rationality of actual decision making and the accountability and responsibility demanded of the idealized decision maker, are reconciled" [5].

Managers need to understand the severe limitations of evaluation, without discrediting or dismissing it entirely. Thus, senior and middle management, both from user departments and from the IS department, should try to evaluate as much as is appropriate, according to their particular circumstances. Those people perhaps most concerned, the users, will almost certainly evaluate the new system in considerable depth. In the light of the intrinsic subjectivity of this task, any further concentration on perfecting the minutiae of the tools and techniques of measurement is clearly inappropriate. It is highly likely that it will lead to yet more reductionism, such that the point of *what* is being evaluated is lost all together: "We tend to spend more and more time and use even more refined technological tools for solving the wrong problem more precisely" [15]. We may end up in a situation, just as problematical, where we descend into a maelstrom of ever decreasing circles, measuring more and more of less and less.

Risk analysis

Throughout this book, we have emphasized the problem of risk that is intrinsic to information systems development and operation. The most obvious operating risks are probably those concerned with security, such as hacking and fraud, but they also include risks arising from faulty or inappropriate hardware, bug-ridden software, and the vagaries of careless operation and misuse. With regard to development, the problems of uncertainty make development a risk-laden activity; we cannot predict either the future in terms of the requirements for the new system, or what the new system will look like. There is the risk that changes in the business environment may render the system obsolete, or perhaps the general requirements were misunderstood from the start so that the system solves the wrong problem. Risks abound, and projects, especially large ones, will tend to run out of control, precipitating a never-ending spiral into budget over-runs and delivery delays. Organizational risks arise where the system does not match the existing skills, management or organizational structure, or runs foul of political conflict or resistance. The development of a new system may cause adverse knock-on effects on adjacent systems, or on parts of the overall network or data infrastructure; such as overloading parts of the network or causing inconsistency in the data. In business terms, there is a risk in disturbing the status quo of the market, and provoking a savage response from competitors. Finally, there are technical risks of an excessive reliance on either an old technology that has become obsolete, or on a new, unproven technology.

Many organizations and their insurers typically clutch their rabbit's foot, wrapped in an 'all risks' insurance policy, and trust to good fortune. However, such insurance policies rarely cover much more than the value of the hardware, ignoring both the potential information loss and the resultant damage to the organization. In other fields, ranging from capital investment to the siting and construction of safety critical installations (such as nuclear power plants), the pressures to examine the risks formally has led to the development of a large body of theory known as risk analysis [16]. In information systems, similar pressures have persuaded a number of writers explicitly to incorporate some form of risk analysis procedure into IS security, the IS development cycle, and evaluation studies. By its nature, this analysis is forward looking and is clearly relevant to feasibility studies, carried out early in the development cycle. Even the post-implementation evaluation must have some future orientation and thus some form of risk analysis may be appropriate.

Risk analysis takes a number of forms including a simple sensitivity analysis to clarify the dependence of the predictions on certain assumptions. Using a spreadsheet or simulation package, particular assumptions (e.g. regarding traffic levels or operational procedures) can be changed, and the effect determined. Alternative futures and alternative decision strategies (e.g. maximize profit, minimize regret) can be examined using decision matrices. Another systematic approach is to use fault tree analysis, to detect potentially fatal combinations of circumstances, but the complexity of many situations is such that the analysis is infeasible without computer support, which itself may be less than totally reliable. A popular approach to risk analysis is to try to quantify risk in financial terms through the use of a formula such as:

$$R = P \times C$$

where R = a particular risk, expressed in dollars per annum
       P = probability of that risk occurring
       C = cost of exposure to that risk

This approach can be used to rank individual risks as a basis for prioritizing their control; i.e. a large value for R suggests that some form of control is definitely required to overcome the risk, whereas a small R value may suggest that this risk can be lived with. However, adherents of this theoretically tidy approach rarely recognize the considerable problems involved in practice [17]. The estimation of both the probability and the cost of exposure are highly subjective, which in line with the principle of *GIGO* (*Garbage In – Garbage Out*), makes the resultant figure for risk highly unreliable. There is usually little past experience on which to base estimates, such that risk analysis becomes an exercise in guesswork, masquerading as a scientific technique. The complexity of modern organizations and the continual changes in the environment render the technique simplistic at best and often misleading. The subjectivity of the estimates leaves the approach wide open to political exploitation; it may take only a limited manipulation of the figures to render an infeasible project feasible or vice versa. There is usually very limited feedback regarding the effectiveness of the risk analysis process or the controls themselves. Disasters may be avoided, but whether avoidance was due to good fortune or to the effectiveness of the controls is rarely debated. When disasters do occur, they may be typically attributed to bad luck or an unfortunate combination of circumstances. Alternatively, they become a political football kicked around the organization until the blame is attached, to the guilty or the innocent, or just dissipated in charges and counter-charges. Similarly, successes are usually attributed to good management, regardless of the degree of good fortune involved. Finally, risk analysis is totally inappropriate for the relatively unlikely risks that may actually prove to be fatal. An example quoted by Newton [18] makes this point clear: the complete loss of a billion dollar organization may be a 10 million to 1 chance, implying a risk of $100 – this is clearly nonsensical.

As with the evaluation techniques themselves, formal quantitative risk analysis may have a place in IS management, but only if it is carefully executed by skilled personnel who recognize its limitations. In particular, managers must distinguish between intention and consequences: business is not deterministic. Unintended consequences may result from certain actions, regardless of the original intentions. Under these conditions, risk analysis can increase the general level of understanding of the proposed system and its environment. However, it needs to be combined with the qualitative judgements of a wide spectrum of managers and staff, if a meaningful interpretation is to be produced. This interpretation will comprise a list of the risks that the organization has decided to control (and those it has decided to mitigate) and the plans to control them.

Computer-based monitoring

An important aspect of the evaluation of operational information systems is the monitoring function. Reliable, accurate data concerning the day-to-day usage and performance can provide a valuable input to any evaluation. A key characteristic of information technology is its ability not only to process information as part of a particular function, but also to record readily and routinely these performance details. Suitably interpreted, such data can be a rich source of information.

There is nothing very contentious about such monitoring until, intentionally or unintentionally, it is extended to cover the organization's workforce. The results of using this approach in offices and factories is highly unpredictable. On the one hand, it provides an apparently unbiased record of events and people's actions, which, if shared amongst supervisors and staff, could provide a good basis for a discussion of problems and generally facilitate organizational learning. Computer-based monitoring potentially relieves management of much of the onerous supervisory role. This role, usually that of a first-line supervisor, involves ensuring that each member of staff is working properly and is especially tedious in cases where the work itself is of a mundane, boring nature. The face-to-face interaction incumbent in monitoring the performance of their juniors may be highly stressful for both first-line supervisors and more senior managers. Depending upon the personalities of the people involved, the embarrassment of visibly observing a person's behaviour, and perhaps reprimanding that person, may be nearly as stressful as being on the receiving end of the reprimand.

However, there are strong objections to the use of technology to monitor and supervise people, both in terms of effectiveness and ethics. Where the machine completely takes over supervision, this can lead to a dehumanizing of the roles of both supervisors and supervised. The discomfort of human supervision may be eliminated, but this may reduce social contact [19], so that supervisors and supervised may never communicate face-to-face. Clearly this cannot produce a cohesive, organic organization. Unlike traditional monitoring, individuals may not realize that they are being watched, and thus monitoring becomes surreptitious and can easily be perceived as infringing the individual's basic right to privacy. A vice-president of a large American bank, commenting on his methods for evaluating the productivity of employees, is quoted as saying: "I measure everything that moves". This type of attitude demonstrates a lack of respect for the workforce that is hardly likely to engender trust and responsibility. It is more likely to encourage cheating and fraud as employees play the game of trying to beat the system. Zuboff [19] describes the ease with which both management and the workforce can abuse the monitoring system, either by circumventing it altogether, or by entering fake information. This could be just the first step towards alienation, absenteeism, fraud or worse.

Traditional supervision does not consist solely of disciplining staff or urging them to greater output; it comprises a strong element of maintaining a social relationship. This relationship, apparently based on a 'how's it all going, how's the wife' chit-chat may be essential to the functioning of the organization. The traditional supervisory relationship provides a channel for explaining sudden changes in output. For example, a relationship of trust is likely to uncover cases where performance has declined due to domestic problems, and then the welfare function of the organization can be alerted. Supervision should focus on teaching and quality, rather than monitoring and judgement. Such human subtleties are inappropriate for computer-based monitoring. As with all aspects of evaluation within an organization, a good understanding of the specific situation in terms of the organizational culture and history will suggest the limits within which such monitoring should be constrained. There is a significant danger that arbitrary monitoring will alienate the workforce, without providing any useful data.

In some of Zuboff's cases, middle management were content to utilize information systems just to monitor their staff, but were most unhappy when headquarters used similar techniques to monitor their own performance. In the USA, a national organization has been formed to identify cases where employers are abusing employee monitoring; this is seen as a first step towards legislation. As with much of information technology, in the right hands it can provide beneficial information as a prelude to discussion but, implemented without care, there is a risk of significant damage to the organization.

Control

In systems terms, the control activity completes the cycle of execution and feedback (evaluation), such that the understanding gained from evaluation can be used to redirect effort, both within the organization as a whole and within the IS function. Regardless of IT, information systems are channels through which control is directed. The growing centrality of information systems to the organization means that senior management has to ensure that the systems are integrated with the rest of the organization. The huge investments in IT imply that senior management must consider the efficient utilization and management of expensive resources; without it, IT becomes a 'black hole' that sucks in investment without producing any noticeable benefit. Thus, there is a need for some form of external control over IS development and management. Senior management require a means to monitor the performance of the organization's information systems, and a channel both to feedback comments, complaints and ideas, and to discuss issues and problems on a regular basis. Chapter 4 examined the alternative IS departmental structures, and nothing more will be said here about the internal control mechanisms. We shall instead focus upon two important external control mechanisms: the administrative control provided by steering committees, and the financial controls made available through chargeback mechanisms.

Steering committees

At the highest level of the organization, there is usually some form of policy-making steering committee that plans, monitors and controls IS activities. It will typically be made up of a number of senior managers from user departments, as well as the CIO or IS manager. In many senses, IS management, formally or informally, reports to this committee. Similar committees may exist at departmental level, others are responsible for the development of particular systems. However, our concern is with the higher level committees, whose functions typically include strategy formulation and planning, resource allocation, the approval of major projects, and various aspects of performance review. The committee may also act as a forum for the discussion of the various issues surrounding the organization's information systems and technology.

Such steering committees aim to coordinate information systems operation and development across the organization. They provide both the opportunity for senior management to become involved in the policy making and control of information systems, and the opportunity for the IS department to obtain senior management support for particular initiatives. The potential thus exists for a two-way exchange of ideas and influence, although there are dangers that such a committee can become a 'star chamber' to castigate IS management, or alternatively a tame body that merely rubber-stamps IS demands. Thus the selection of its members, especially the chairman, and its terms of reference need some care. The skills and expertise of its members, particularly regarding IT, require a careful balance between 'experts', who may be tempted to acquire every fashionable technology, and 'Luddites', who may attempt to scuttle every initiative, regardless of its merits. Similarly, the management level of the members of the committee has to be such that, on the one hand, they possess real influence, but on the other hand, they are in close touch with the operational requirements of the organization. It is particularly important for the committee to have effective links with the rest of the organization to ensure that it both receives reliable information regarding the current and future situation, and has the political clout needed to implement its policies and decisions.

Even once the membership issue has been settled, steering committees are still prone to a number of tensions. Like any other such forum, they may become a battleground for the various warring factions within the organization. This may be functional, if such conflict is contained within the committee and does not totally paralyse it. Another tension refers to the underlying functions of the committee: the extent to which committees are decision-making bodies, focusing on the executive function; 'talking shops', providing a forum for discussion; or working groups, producing a particular deliverable such as a plan. Each of these functions has its own relevance and its own demands; care must be taken that committees do not drift into unforeseen directions. Decisions must be taken as to whether the committee is permanent, in which case thought must be given as to its evolution as conditions changes, or whether it has a fixed lifetime. Also the procedures for creating the agenda and appointing the officers should be regarded with care, to prevent political hijacking. Furthermore, it must be decided how open the discussions should be, and hence to whom the minutes should be circulated. The frequency of meetings is an important aspect that can threaten its effectiveness; too frequent meetings demand an excessive contribution from their members, encouraging boredom and absence, whereas too few meetings render the committee increasingly redundant, as its decisions come to be taken elsewhere.

Chargeback mechanisms

There is increasing discussion within organizations as to how to account financially for the IS function, a problem that is growing as the IS budget grows. Software packages can monitor system usage on a departmental basis, and these costs, together with those of development, can be 'charged-back' to user departments. This should not be seen as an esoteric accounting activity. For where users 'pay' for IS services from their own budgets, internal market forces may provide users with considerable control over the IS function. However, the problems of identifying and allocating costs, highlighted in the above discussion of cost–benefit analysis, applies equally to chargeback schemes. In addition, as will be shown through the following description of the four main techniques, a significant problem is to balance the conflicting objectives of efficient resource utilization and the encouragement of IT usage [20].

Under the first technique, the *Service Centre* scheme, IS costs are charged as organizational overheads (an unallocated cost centre), rather than being debited against user departments. This method involves relatively little bureaucracy and generates little conflict. IS services become 'free' to users, encouraging their usage, but making no contribution to efficient resource utilization. As they are free goods, departments may well inflate their demands for technology and systems, with no mechanism to choke off demand. Without the discipline of costs and budgets, resources may be allocated on blatant political grounds, rather than through financial justification. With little control over the IS budget, there is nothing to discourage IS department inefficiency.

The second method, of *Cost Centres*, involves charging user departments according to the cost of providing the services. This should reduce the more unreasonable demands of users, as well as provide some form of financial control over the IS department. The accounting procedures are relatively simple, but the allocation of costs may appear to the users to be arbitrary and unpredictable, and may merely have the effect of discouraging usage. Charges are made *post facto*, determined by factors on the supply side, over which users have little or no control. This unpredictability is likely to lead to frustration on the part of the users and perhaps increased conflict. This cost-based approach, as well as ignoring any benefits, is also likely to penalize innovatory demands of users; the risk of such systems 'going through the ceiling' in terms of costs may become too great. This approach does little to discourage IS department inefficiency, as charges can always be passed on to users, and the IS department's failings are effectively covered up.

Under the third technique, of *Profit Centres*, users are charged according to an agreed price, rather than according to costs, with the IS department becoming a full profit centre. The IS department might be rewarded on their profit figures, and are thus encouraged to become more efficient as cost over-runs can no longer be passed on. This also encourages the growth of a service culture, with the IS department providing a service to users at an agreed price. From this, the IS department may be encouraged to form partnerships with users and to market its services both within the organization and externally. However, this type of approach may go against the underlying values of the organization; it may be deemed inappropriate for a mere service department to engage in such entre-preneurial activity. The IS department may gain certain kudos from external sales, which might be pursued at the expense of the organization's own needs. This approach may well discourage innovation and potentially profitable, but risky, development, should the IS department imitate one of the more conserv-ative commercial software producers. Perhaps the organization needs the IS department to lead innovative development, even if at times it is unsuccessful. Also, significantly, if there is an excessive profit component built into the price, then the overall costs to the organization of carrying on their mainstream business may increase unnecessarily. Service levels for 'uneconomic operations' may worsen and conflict between users and the IS department becomes more likely.

The final technique, a variant on the profit centre approach, involves charging the users at cost, but crediting the IS with a profit component, debited against a central overheads account. This should motivate both users and the IS department, but may degenerate into artificiality and complexity. In any case, the setting of the internal prices (transfer prices) required for profit centres is not trivial. A 'cost plus' formula may make both the IS department and users more cost conscious, but the 'plus' element is highly arbitrary. Similarly, a market-based approach is likely to be equally arbitrary; there are likely to be few external services or standards against which to relate the internal prices. Excessive arbitrariness in setting prices is more likely to provoke conflict than efficiency, effectiveness and innovation.

These 'pure' alternatives can also be combined together, such that for some services, the IS department is treated as a service centre, and for others, either a cost centre or profit centre. The financial controls are thus tailored to suit the particular service. Clearly, there will be certain services, including the enforcement of standards and certain 'help' and fault-fixing services, for which the IS department is highly unlikely to wish to charge users. However, taken to extreme, this hybrid approach is likely to lead to increased complexity, with too much scope for cross-subsidies and 'playing the system'.

Earl [20] relates chargeback schemes to the position of the organization on McFarlan & McKenney's Strategic Grid. He suggests that service centres are appropriate for turnaround organizations, cost centres for factory organizations, hybrid centres for strategic organizations and profit centres for support organizations. This can also be related to Nolan's Stage Model, such that the organizational accounting systems for IS evolve and become more sophisticated in parallel with the evolution of the use of the technology. This is an attractive argument, although constrained by the inherent limitations of underlying models.

The key questions that organizations must ask are whether they wish to encourage or discourage the use of IT, whether their concern is efficiency or effectiveness, and whether their aims are strategic or tactical. Whatever the answers to these questions, for chargeback schemes to be accepted by users, they must be understandable, fair, and predictable, as well as fitting into the organization's overall accounting ideology. In other words, to take advantage of such schemes, the notion of flexible departmental budgets should already be accepted and departments should possess the necessary expertise such that the whole scheme does not just become a huge chore. Managers should realize the limitations of IS costing, and schemes should not be so costly to administer that any improvements achieved are swallowed up by the overheads of the accounting process. Chargeback can lead to resource conservation and the reduction of wastage, but it can also lead to increased conflict and a bureaucratic nightmare, as innovative applications are strangled in squabbles over spurious costings.

Conclusion

From the above discussion, it is clear that all aspects of the evaluation, monitoring and control of information systems have a significant element of subjectivity. An objective, 'cook book' approach based on dubious measurements is evidently inappropriate. There is a definite need to understand the local situation and act accordingly, utilizing whatever techniques are available to help the manager paint a richer picture. However, it is important to note in carrying out a post-implementation evaluation, that just because we cannot measure changes objectively or quantitatively, this does not mean that no changes have occurred. Similarly, the search for increased office and management productivity should not be devalued by the fact that we cannot measure such productivity reliably. Organizations and their managers should be made aware of the problems of evaluation and, for those engaged in evaluation exercises, the time is ripe to evaluate the evaluators.

Discussion issues

1. Why do you think that formal evaluation has become so fashionable in so many different areas?
2. Compare and contrast computer-based monitoring of people with traditional supervision in a context with which you are familiar.

Exercise

Take a piece of software with which you are familiar, and carry out a personal evaluation of it. You will need to draw up the aspects that you feel the evaluation should address, e.g. usability, speed, etc. Compare your results with that of others who evaluated the same software independently. After a gap of at least a few days, try to evaluate your own evaluation: which points did you miss, or over-emphasize? Ideally, this exercise should be repeated after one month and then again after six months.

Suggested reading

A collection of papers concerning various aspects of measurement.

> Mason, R. & Swanson, E., *Measurement for management decision*, Addison-Wesley, Reading, Mass., 1981.

The proceedings of a conference concerned with evaluation.

> Bjorn-Andersen, N. & Davis, G.B. (eds), *Information Systems Assessment: Issues and Challenges*, North Holland, Amsterdam, 1988.

Steering committees (Chap.7), Evaluation & control (Chap.8)

> Earl, M.J., *Management strategies for information technology,*, Prentice-Hall, Hemel Hempstead, 1989.

Evaluation of Information Technology

> Clegg, C., Warr, P., Green, T., Monk, A., Kemp, N., Allison, G. & Lansdale, M., *People and computers: how to evaluate your company's new technology*, Ellis Horwood, Chichester, 1988.

References

1. Kaplan, A., *The Conduct of Inquiry: Methodology for Behavioural Science*, Harper & Row, New York, 1964.

2. Kumar, K.,'Post implementation evaluation of computer-based information systems: current practices', *Communications of the ACM*, 33(2), 203-212, 1990.

3. Strassman, P.A., *Information payoff: the transformation of work in the electronic age*, Free Press, New York, 1985.

4. Mason, R.O.,'The role of dialogue in the measurement process', in: Krippendorff, K. (ed.), *Communication and control in society*, Gordon & Breach, New York, 1979.

5. Legge, K., *Evaluating planned organizational change*, Academic Press, London, 1984.

6. Hirschheim, R.A. & Smithson, S.C.,'A critical analysis of information systems evaluation', in: Bjorn-Andersen, N. & Davis, G.B. (eds), *Information systems assessment: issues and challenges*, North Holland, Amsterdam, 1988.

7. Drucker, P., *The Effective Executive*, Heinemann, London,1966.

8. Self, P.,'Nonsense on stilts: cost-benefit analysis and the Roskill Commission', *Political Quarterly*, 41(3), 249-260, July 1970.

9. Machlup, F.,'Uses, value, and benefits of knowledge', *Knowledge, Creation, Diffusion, Utilization*, Vol.1, No.1, 62-81, 1979.

10. Tapscott, D., *Office automation: a user-driven method*, Plenum Press, New York, 1982.

11. Suchman, E.A., *Evaluative research: principles and practices in public service and social action programs*, Russell Sage Foundation, New York, 1967.

12. Johnson Laird, P.N., *Mental models: towards a cognitive science of language, inferences and consciousness*, Cambridge University Press, Cambridge, 1983.

13. Laudon, K.,'Environmental and institutional models of system development: a national criminal history system', *Communications of the ACM*, 28(7), 728-740, 1985.

14. Adams, D., *The Hitchhikers Guide to the Galaxy*, Pan Books, London, 1979.

15. Bjorn-Andersen, N.,'Challenge to certainty', in: Bemelmans, Th. (ed.), *Beyond productivity: information systems development for organizational effectiveness*, North Holland, Amsterdam, 1984.

16. Hertz, D.B. & Thomas, H., *Risk analysis and its applications*, Wiley, New York, 1983.

17. Baskerville, R.,'The frailty of risk analysis and ambivalence toward professional certification: two mutually resolvent problems', *SUNY Working Paper*, State University of New York, Binghampton, New York, 1989.

18. Newton, T.,'Strategies for problem prevention', *IBM Systems Journal*, Vol.24, No.3/4, 248-263, 1985.

19. Zuboff, S., *In the age of the smart machine: the future of work and power*, Basic Books, New York, 1988.

20. Earl, M.J., *Management strategies for information technology*, Prentice-Hall, Hemel Hempstead, UK, 1989.

12   Managing function and phenomena

- *Information technology, uncertainty and the manager*
- *An explanatory analogy*
- *Measures or managers?*
- *So who takes decisions?*
- *'Control' and human resource management*
- *Summary*

Information technology, uncertainty and the manager

Given the profound uncertainty they face, senior management must now question whether the use of IT is an appropriate universal response. For uncertainty does not conform to a neat computational logic, it is a foreboding, where the surprise of imminent change is outside of our control. Human responses in this situation are insecurity, stress, fear, panic, immobility, but also trust, confidence and courage. Personal characteristics, needs and aspirations, social integration, quality, motivation, loyalty are all relevant for the evaluation and significance of such uncertainty. Decision-taking under these circumstances is, even more than usual, a social phenomenon. It becomes meaningful only in a manager's relationship to his environment, and thus, it is part of his self-determined personal reality. As such, it eludes any generalizing characterizations. Complex theories, which claim to grasp at the concept of uncertainty, and at its significance to managerial reality, are more pseudo-scientific than real. It is experienced as an integral part of the total managerial reality; it is subjective, individual and perpetual. Any framework that claims to deal with uncertainty in a formalized way is bound to lead to dilemmas. Therefore, trusting completely in a computerized response to uncertainty is nonsensical.

Simply conceptualizing the reality of business as a sequence of 'antiseptic' laboratory problem situations, and dealing with each in a generalized way, is not enough. Nevertheless, many managers seem to prefer to trust in machines and formal methods, because these are seemingly more controllable than people, with all their human idiosyncrasies. It seems to be a cultural preference in Western societies, that the stability of impersonal concepts, even if not particularly applicable, is to be trusted in preference to the 'awkwardness' of people.

213

Computational methods are so appealing and comforting, because of their conceptual clarity and their apparent lack of ambiguity. But a manager's job is characterized by ambiguity. Faced with uncertainty, a manager cannot know what might crop up, when and from where. He has to assess the past, the present and the future, free from any limitations that impede his competitiveness. Probabilistic market research is insufficient to indicate emergent effects. Take for example the success of the Sony Walkman. No amount of brainstorming or market research could have predicted its success. In fact Akio Morita had to push its development through against considerable resistance [1].

Unless managers are aware of its limitations, the probabilistic treatment of a critical situation can even lull them into a false sense of security and control, because it focuses by definition on the measurements and assumptions of the past, and substitutes the unknown future with an elaborate extrapolation of past trends. Yet a manager's job is characterized by uncertainty, not only about the known variables of his environment, but also about the unknown, and the unknowable. This is the fundamental difference between 'probabilistic uncertainty' and an 'emergent uncertainty' that is symptomatic of so much decision-taking in management. Against such a background, information technology has permeated the infrastructure of international business. Whether we like it or not IT is now essential for commercial survival. Everywhere, management perceive information technology as central to doing business and building their organization. No matter what the sector: public or private, media or mining, every organization has to develop a variety of strategies in order to cope with the impact of information technology.

An explanatory analogy

But with this recognition comes the realization that expertise in electronics and computing is not enough, indeed these may not even be the most important skills. Instead, what is essential is a comprehension of the 'nature of the beast', of the behaviour of the technology in an organizational context. What is immediately apparent is that technical issues alone rarely feature in the success or failure of a system; the critical determinants are the socio-cultural phenomena within the organization itself. There is an understandable discomfort and confusion within 'scientific management' about a situation where technological determinism does not dominate. We find it useful to illustrate this predicament with a well known analogy. However, we must stress that this analogy is meant, not as a denial of the value of information technology, but as a recognition of its limitations and the problem of its management. It is intended to reflect the consequences of applying IT, and to highlight the dangers of overconfidence in the merits of technology.

This analogy is the *Universal Roach Exterminator*[1], sold by mail-order in the USA to solve the problem of cockroach infestation. The product consists of hardware (a mallet and a block of wood) and software (the list of operating instructions – *1:catch the cockroach; 2:place it on the block; 3:hit it with the mallet*). Step 3 is relatively straightforward, but of course it does depend to a certain extent on step 2. For if the operator is too slow the cockroach will escape, too fast and he will hammer his thumb. Therefore, operational guidelines must be assembled; and naturally the equipment has to be purchased, maintained, stored and transported; carcasses must be removed; hygiene procedures must be developed. No doubt, further tools will be produced to deal with each of these new situations. But it does not end there. The use of the tool may have unforeseen consequences: neighbours may complain about the noise; animal-rights activists may demonstrate; nightmares about giant cockroaches beckon. As with the case of every other technology, before we know it, the implications are running riot, and a highly complex social system has exploded onto the scene. Welcome to the real world of phenomena, a world incapable of naive description in terms of functionality and mechanistic procedures.

Of course, this particular 'mallet technology' is ridiculous, because nothing has been gained by its application. All along the real solution was not killing a cockroach but catching it in the first place, a reality quietly hidden away in the first step of the software. But no doubt some 'trap technology' can be developed to overcome this, so that step 2 can begin. Laughable as this example may be, it does have parallels with technology in general, and with information technology in particular (see Figure 12.1), and it does teach some salutary lessons. In a problem domain, before all else, the problem has to be sensed, and solutions/actions situated (step 1). Then a great deal of 'housekeeping' must be done (step 2), before we can apply the tools of the technology (step 3). This example also reveals that a technological solution is not applied in a vacuum. Granted it has to be properly managed in order to achieve its intended functional aims. But at the same time management must deal with any implications of its use, avoiding any emergent hazards while profiting from any unexpected opportunities that may arise (back to step 2). These risks and opportunities must be sensed as problems, and subsequently solved (back to step 1): and the feedback loop, which carries the potential of opportunity and risk, is closed. Some loops will imply risk, and these must be intercepted and curtailed. Even the

---

1   It has recently been brought to our attention that a slightly different form of this analogy has been used by D.C.Gause and G.M.Weinberg in their excellent book, *Exploring Requirements: Quality before Design*, to explain why CASE and CAD tools will not eliminate people from the design process.

feedback loops that enable commercial opportunities must be monitored, to ensure that they do not oscillate into positive feedback. Every organization must face up to the problem of keeping the commercial and social feedback from information technology under some semblance of control.

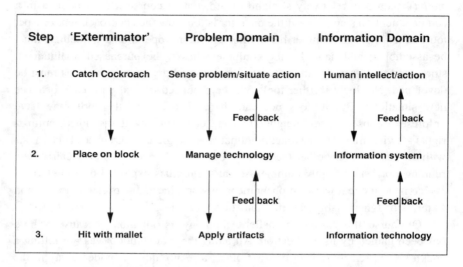

Figure 12.1 The three step application of technology

Dealing with technology in these abstract terms, we can see that what is commonly referred to as information technology actually only relates to the production and application of tools and artifacts (step 3). Managing both the functionality of the technology and the phenomena of complex systems that spontaneously manifest themselves around information technology is the domain of information systems (step 2). However, prevailing over them both is the dominant requirement of intelligent human response, to sense a problem and to distinguish between what is appropriate and inappropriate action (step 1). Our 'mallet and block' approach is obviously inappropriate. A version of the commercially available 'roach motels' is perhaps more suitable, where a box, open at both ends, emanates an odour attractive to roaches. As a roach enters, it gets glued to the box. Once full, the box is incinerated, roaches and all. Of course the 'motel' raises its own questions, as for example about the suitability of the chemicals being used. Only the user, on the basis of personal criteria, can decide which method is more appropriate. The question we have to ask is, "are the tools of information technology of the 'mallet and block' type, or of the 'motel' type?". Our warning to anyone too confident in the applicability of a particular product of information technology, is "think again, think 'cockroaches'".

In a 'scientific society' such as ours, the dominant paradigm is to formulate every new solution in terms of technology, even to sense the situation as being a problem specifically because of the potential of that technology. *"Give a boy a hammer, and he will look for nails"* (although our example has introduced a technology-inspired paradigm shift, so that now the boy will also look for cockroaches). Our predominant 'information ideology', of aiming yet more information technology at any or all of our three steps, will only expand each step into a further three corresponding steps. This will introduce more complexity to an already complicated situation. Thus, arguably, the most general successful applications of information technology have been

(a) where there is a real need, and the sensing of the problem and the situating of the solution (step 1) are reasonably straightforward (there have probably been well structured manual systems previously in place), and

(b) where the technology is reasonably stable, and not too complex to manage (step 2) (because of (a), and because the inevitable extra effort is more than compensated by savings in managing the old manual system), and

(c) where the technology itself (step 3) is non-problematical and appropriate;

(d) the consequences of applying the tools are limited, and the feedback loop is broken so that few further management problems are introduced.

However, initial success with IT can induce managers to introduce more and yet more layers of technology. To justify the extra effort and expense, they will look around for partners in search of that mystical pot of gold, 'synergy', that they read about in management books. With our 'mallet technology', they could look to the kitchen and use a meat mallet and a cheese board as the tools; but would you eat food prepared in that kitchen? The implications of using each new layer of technology will feed back in the forms of new questions about the appropriateness of solutions, and of new management problems. The original clear demarcation of three steps collapses in a confusion of multiple overlapping systems. Complexity increases to a point where utility turns into reliance, reliance becomes dependence, and the *Law of Diminishing Returns* precipitates a descent into a management nightmare. Ultimately, within this feedback loop, the self-serving logic of technology will take on a significance far greater than the original problem. Both the sensing of problems and the situating and managing of solutions becomes impossible, and the whole edifice of this 'information ideology' falls apart.

Given the enormous changes we are facing, it is evident that, in order to achieve any long-lasting utility from information technology, organizations require a new approach, which will involve a fundamental change in attitude towards skilled individuals, their education and motivation. Even if we emphasize the relative dominance of communication over computerization, the problem still remains. It is self-evident that it is not the channel of communication that is significant (step 3), but the information that is being transmitted and the reasons for its transmission (step 1), and how that information is being used (step 2). To date, computer education and business applications have concentrated on the last of the 3-steps in our 'information domain', when it is apparent that the seeds of both success and failure germinate in the first two steps. Future emphasis should be placed on the commercially and organizationally 'appropriate'. This necessitates the development of an IS strategy for the place of information technology within the organizations. It can only be in relation to that strategy that the idea of appropriateness has any legitimacy. Then, and only then, can tactical decisions be made about the purchase of equipment and the production of business applications.

Measures or managers?

Worldwide, we see a trend towards the unquestioned investment in new technology, especially hi-tech, in preference to a balanced, sensitive and rational assessment. In fact, there is even a tendency to search for new ways of satisfying technical preconditions just in order to apply the technology; solutions looking for problems. A consequent numerical bias leads to dubious attempts at mapping social phenomena into numbers and functions. The lust for numerical solutions and the 'bubbleware' of developmental methodologies is spreading. In many cases, commonsense has been abandoned in favour of mathematical sophistication. Such simplistic, though mathematically elaborate, conceptualizations are a threat to managerial responsibility. This has come about, not least through the enthusiastic self-promotion of the information systems community. But "complete information" [2] about any situation is only possible within simplistic conceptualizations of reality. The fact that we are charmed and fascinated within this self-delusion, should prompt uncomfortable questions about its feasibility, justification, likelihood and desirability.

Numbers are presumed autonomously and uniquely meaningful. Numerical measurements are assumed to be capable of representing human and social phenomena. A case in point is where managerial responsibility is supposed to consist of a succession of problem situations, each adequately expressed numerically. Numerically derived results are taken to be good approximations to the solutions of managerial problems, if not *the* solutions. Reality is assumed to be equivalent to, and treated as identical with, the information that represents it. Thus, it is claimed that optimal actions are possible using the power of an information system. It is easy to forget that so much of management is not looking to optimize, but to compromise.

The perspective of 'control', driven by numbers, projects its limited certainty about the future into strategic planning, and comes up with precise solutions that can only be of limited validity. The pitfall of computerized information systems, not being able to assess reality other than by numbers, is mirrored in the IS approach to strategy. In fact, the forecasting techniques of IS are merely an assignment of numbers to the future. That these numbers can be at best as adequate or as inadequate as the input, points to the poverty of this approach. Using such forecasts as a strategic tool is, therefore, only the belief that numbers are meaningful in relation to the future. Strategy becomes a matter of controlling the future by labelling it, rather than continually re-evaluating the uncertain situation. This approach, searching for the right numerical label to represent the future, is more akin to numerology or astrology. Of course we would agree that there are many problems where numerical data is of paramount relevance for a decision maker. However, we do maintain that numerical data by itself cannot suggest an appropriate course of action. No number of 'what-if' simulations on spreadsheets, taken in isolation, can tell a manager what the future holds.

Paradoxically, even though these numerical computer solutions may have a questionable basis, they can nonetheless prove extremely useful. Only after accepting this unscientific, yet opportunistic application of computers in search of a tactical payoff, can the real advantages of computerized information systems be found. The perversity of consequence turns design logic on its head. Commercial success will only be found if the industrial and educational infrastructure is expanded beyond the design of technological systems, to a sympathetic understanding of what is appropriate and inappropriate action. This will require a strategic attitude and a continuous experimental stance aimed at minimizing the inevitable risks that surround information technology, whilst making the most of its potential. Information systems are steeped in a culture of 'optimistic rationality', that by rational understanding things will get better. Bitter experience undermines this confidence. It is a common feature of management literature that, whilst managers usually act rationally, this may not coincide with acting for the benefit of the organization as a whole. There is considerable evidence of departments or groups acting in their own interests, attempting to increase their share of organizational resources and status. The prospect of a new information system may represent a rare opening for significant political manoeuvres as large amounts of 'territory' come 'up for grabs'. The arbitrariness of cost–benefit studies in search of efficiency, unquestioned in the euphoria of computerization, provides a golden opportunity for the shrewd political operator.

Senior management must relinquish any expectation of 'being in control', even with the methods of 'scientific management'. We can only control in the sense of formulating and precipitating actions or intentions, but this is not being in control of consequences. It is a delusion both to assume that we are in control of the application of information technology, and to conclude by extension that organizations can be controlled accordingly. Horror of not being in control, and the ensuing insecurity, can propel the terrified businessman into the hands of unscrupulous consultants, sophisters selling 'the quick fix' and certainty. But sadly the problems will not go away. Paradoxically, it is because of this very lack of control that information technology has a major role to play. The future applications of information technology must be as the means of enhanced communication, so enabling organizations to maintain flexibility and to adjust tactical intention to making short term gains, while relating consequences to perceived strategic aims in the long term. It is, therefore, essential that we emphasize information and its communication among people, and separate it from technology. We must see information, not as a commodity, but as a consequence of context. Systems must be continuously updated, based on learning from on-going experimental observation of behavioural feedback within each organization. Future success will depend on the right management skills linked to a broad understanding of the place of information systems in both local and global situations. And this is only possible by employing the best quality 'thinking managers', who must be thoughtful in, and responsible for, both their actions and those of their colleagues.

So who takes decisions?

Yet major investment is being made in information technology. Businessmen and politicians, who really should know better, line up to call computer specialists, geniuses or whiz-kids, probably because of their own ignorance of the confusing collection of trivia that is so much of information technology. There are far too many inarticulate exponents of low-level IT skills around, for them to be credited with the label 'genius'. The present-day and short term skill shortage shrouds the low intellectual content in a mystery that has no inherent value. The skill that should be valued is the ability to understand and manage the obscurities of effectively applying this technology. Simplistic methodologies for systems development are supposed to encapsulate expertise, but they fail to cope with the kaleidoscope of subtlety and intrinsic singularity of each particular business situation. Expertise just cannot be separated from experience.

Whether a manager goes about his decision-taking by formulating a problem and consulting solely numerical information, or whether he really does take decisions, is rarely on the agenda. Mary Douglas [3] argues that really important decisions are not taken by people at all, but by the institutional framework (an organization's disposition). By the same token, the approach of W. Edwards Deming [4], although aimed primarily at the management of production, could be relevant to the management of information systems. His theory of quality control via statistical inspection, indicates that much of the variation in performance of workers within a system is actually a product of that system itself. Thus his conclusion is that bonuses for best performance are ill-conceived. According to Deming, it makes no sense to reward or blame someone for the arbitrary nature of a system: that today your journey to work was ten minutes less (or ten minutes more) than usual had more to do with the railroad system than with the train driver. That such variation is possible means there is room for improvement in the system. This does not mean that individuals cannot make a difference. However, it is essential to judge how much of a good run of results is a product of an individual's talents, and how much is just being in the right place at the right time.

It is the same with the management of systems, whether of the information system or the organization it serves. All too frequently, individuals take the credit for benefits accruing from 'dumb luck', and deny responsibility for failure, blaming it on 'bad luck'. For luck, both good and bad, can be interpreted as arbitrary random variation within a system's interaction with its environment, and mediated by its disposition. In their arrogance, the self-styled 'Masters of the Universe' fail to see that the effects of much of their particular decisions are made marginal, when the consequences of a system's performance bypass their intentions. For so many decisions originate in a cultural mind-set, and in organizational and environmental constraints, and are fuelled by the timely arrival of information. Often an organization's performance succeeds or fails despite management decisions; decisions cannot circumvent the inevitable. Computerized information systems can reduce freedom in the decision-taking role even further. The manager may be effectively prevented from responding creatively, for computers limit him from the very start, not only to a certain conceptualization of a problem, but also to a certain conceptualization of what constitutes a problem. A bias towards numbers and measurement, which led him to use computerized information systems in the first place, leads him to presume that forced and contrived probabilities are valid representations of reality. As a consequence, tensions arise that are created by the very use of the computerized system.

So when managing systems, it is essential for managers to recognize that the systems themselves will play a role. Attributes of information systems such as timeliness, content, relevance, exhaustiveness, redundancy, level of detail and format, can both compel and constrain decision-taking [5]. It is the job of management to ensure that the system operates in a manner appropriate for their company, making the most of opportunities and minimizing risk. They must change, develop and enhance their systems, by linking their individual talents to a sympathetic observation of, and experimentation with, the behaviour of their system. The lessons learned must be incorporated in modifications to the system artifacts and mechanisms. Continual observation and experimentation of the ensuing new line of evolution must be fed back into further change.

'Control' and human resource management

There are no universal laws for explaining the behaviour of information systems, only general principles. So a 'thinking manager' needs to develop an approach which will deal with the observed consequence of technology as embodied in his organization, his information system and society at large. This approach must be predicated on the limited applicability of computers, and grounded in perpetual observation and experimentation, in contingencies, and in a sympathetic reaction to the disposition of the social and commercial environment. A manager needs to know what computers can and cannot do, and what they can do well. But his must be a sceptical approach, not based on a naive belief that a description of the situation via models and structures will enable the manager to be 'in control' of consequences. He must not get bogged down in the many introverted disputes which dominate IT thinking, but instead continuously maintain flexibility and adjust tactical intention, so as to relate consequences to perceived strategic aims. That is why some form of continuous experimental feedback is essential within each organization, as some form of incremental prototyping, in order to cope with unpredictable, unintended consequences of system behaviour. This new attitude is needed in order to overcome the cynical opportunism widespread in many IT stakeholders, who are profiting by their promotion of 'confidence through information technology', as they prey on a business world racked with doubt and uncertainty. Management must shoulder the responsibility for tangible adverse commercial consequences of their systems, they cannot shift the blame onto a technology that ultimately cannot be culpable or accountable.

Unfortunately, the penetration of the managerial environment with IS leads more and more managers instead to try some 'what-if' scenarios with the computer. Each time these systems are used, the manager should ask himself, whether the implicit concepts of the machine procedure are adequate to the situation. There is a great temptation to get an 'independent' output not tainted with human bias, especially in opaque situations. That this independence is highly dependent on choices, assumptions and beliefs is possibly not apparent. Besides, using the machine is so convenient and fashionable. But it is exactly these situations that call for the manager's qualities to steer the enterprise. Management is not just a matter of 'machine minding'. Grasping the place of IS within the business reality is a never-ending process. It is the manager's decision, and he should choose carefully, whether to apply computer power, man power or a thoughtful mix.

It is highly amusing that a technology, which it was claimed would replace human intellect, *"computers will keep us as pets"*, turns out to be critically and pivotally dependent on people. The sheer volume and complexity of expertise needed by today's company has culminated in 'the rise of the expert individual'. Companies that had hoped to reduce their dependence on 'the expert', perversely are even more dependent than ever. Every company needs experts who are alert to every opportunity and have the skills to plan strategically for the future. These are the experts who are unwilling to accept conventional wisdom, who not only look to the future, but who have developed their hindsight to interpret the past and are the first to take tactical advantage of opportunistic trends that they sense in the changes around them. This new breed of manager is crucial to the innovation necessary for commercial success. But innovation is not a secret to be found in text books or high-powered seminars, it is a frame of mind. The people with the skills to handle this new responsibility are in very short supply. Companies must value this 'social capital', perhaps more than 'financial capital'. Such top quality human resources, 'gold collar workers', do not depend on the accumulation of vocational skills, at best a short term gain, but on a long term and continuing investment in education at all levels of management. Vocational skills may look into the closed technological environment, but it is education that gives an intellectual platform on which to base decisions in these times of change.

There are many interesting books on human resource management well worth reading; within the IS world the work of J. Daniel Couger [6] and colleagues may be singled out for attention. They stress certain key characteristics that can make jobs interesting, and thus motivate staff.

- *Skill variety*: the extent to which carrying out a job involves different activities, each requiring different skills and talents of the staff.
- *Task identity*: the extent to which a completed job is identifiable as a 'whole'.
- *Task significance*: the extent to which a job has an impact on the lives and work of other people, both inside and outside the organization.
- *Autonomy*: the extent to which a job provides independence, discretion and freedom, in scheduling and determining of work practices and procedures.
- *Feedback*: the extent to which the job results in the staff obtaining information about the effectiveness of their performance.

They also consider a *motivating potential score*, which measures the potential in a job for eliciting positive motivation towards the work. Also stressed are certain personal characteristics on the part of staff, including:

- *Individual growth need strength*: a scale measuring an individuals need for accomplishment and for learning and developing skills.

- *Social need score*: a scale measuring an individual's social skills and need for social interaction.

All these factors are mapped onto numerical scales and used for comparative analyses. Although overly numerical to the tastes of the present authors, their work does include some very subtle and profound insights into the workings of the information systems community. Using the Delphi procedure [7] they asked US Chief Information Officers (CIOs) to rank 'Dominant Human Resource Trends' for the coming decade [8], resulting in the following priorities:

- Acquire stronger business orientation.
- Prepare strategy to transfer certain IS tasks to the user.
- Define skill requirements for the future IS environment.
- Retrain personnel.
- Encourage managers to be businessmen rather than technologists.
- Emphasize creativity and innovation.
- Find new ways to motivate employees.
- Provide training in communication and behavioural skills.
- Develop better measures of performance.
- Provide for technical specialists.
- Reward principal contributors.
- Leverage the capabilities of people through the use of technology.
- Improve IS professionalism.
- Understand the changing nature of the work force.
- Re-orient managers to non-IS career paths.
- Plan for telecommuting.
- Better mental health provision.
- Use a holistic approach to people management.
- Assist employees in stress/burnout.
- Manage more effectively, contractors and contractor employees.

This list goes to show just how much emphasis is now being placed by IT managers on human resources, and how that emphasis is not merely directed at technological and methodological issues.

Therefore, success in information technology reduces to maintaining the services of a motivated broad-based educated elite, but we would stress not a 'Mongolian Horde' of programmers. No company can afford to lose such valuable assets, and high salaries by themselves will not retain quality people. Those with the 'right stuff' require a stimulating intellectual climate, not a rule-based bureaucracy. They prefer intellectual freedom to organizational constraint. The emphasis must be on human resource management to motivate staff to their full potential. Many compromises must be made to present-day 'best practices' of business, if the stagnation caused by the loss of good people is to be avoided.

Summary

Information technology is just another in a long line of technological enterprises whereby mankind feels it can subjugate nature by mere force of will. Because of this dominant mind-set, it was inevitable that organizations would find computer based information systems thrust upon them as a panacea, and all with the highest motives. For computer output carries a weight of meaning and authority that is derived from the dominating position of science and technology in Western society. The early business successes of computer installations have generated and reinforced the platform of authority for applying information technology, and have laid claim to a scientific legitimacy, from which to justify further action. Thus, the basis of decision-taking shifts from objective knowledge to a numerical justification grounded in this self-propagating consensus authority.

Despite the growing number of failures of computer systems the proselytes of information technology still whisper in our ears that computerization really is a competitive advantage. We are haunted by images of competitors gaining a commercial lead by introducing computerized systems. This undercurrent makes it easier to justify expenditure on computerized schemes, when everybody else does, rather than to explain how we should invest, and perhaps why we should not. But it is ideological blindness, and not the reality of advantage, that is bouncing us into these decisions. As a consequence, the portrayal of information technology as a controllable tool goes unchallenged in another vicious circle of the blind leading the blind. But this technology furnishes neither a prescription for, nor even a proscription to action, but merely an accepted way of interpreting the commercial environment. The legacy of applying this technology is a rigid framework of 'social engineering', forcing organizations to accommodate the requirements of information technology, and not the reverse. The mounting strain that this loads onto organizations necessitates a major rethink about the applicability of information technology. Computerization is a prisoner of societal consequences which cannot be controlled, no matter what the management regime.

The task of IT-management is to cope with the systemic manifestations and consequences of technological and organizational change. Against a background of commercial uncertainty, business decisions will require a broad-based and solid understanding. This stance must be more than just a token tribute to philosophical problems and questions of meaning. It is not good enough to respond with an anti-intellectual 'so-what?'; for that is a smug statement of complacency towards any questioning of cherished beliefs, and hardly the attitude that should be taken by a strategist in the face of profound uncertainty. In order to be strategic, understanding must be disconnected from such prevalent authority. Hence, there is a crying need for a balanced reassessment of the problems associated with the expansion of technological systems as integral parts of organizations. As new technology is confidently applied in ever more unstructured environments, the unsuitability of its instrumental rationalism brings about more frequent and increasingly disastrous consequences. The designers of grand schemes optimistically believe that, by mere intention, they can confine the consequences of using a computer installation to the achievement of a 'wish list' of their original goals.

Too often the response to commercial uncertainty is the ritual application of computerized systems that are becoming increasingly bureaucratic, forming rigid and inadequate structures that lead to deadening conformity and repression. In their models, designers (we could call them bureaucrats) include only the tidiness that they see and understand. Yet this tidiness is only a snapshot of fragments of ordered functionality and usability in a sea of misconception. Users know they are working in operational environments that are messy and vague, much of it caused by the debris of detail, that lies outside the design. This debris can be reconstituted by a particular contextual significance and relevance, and thereby form either an erratic and unpredictable nature and the potential of disorder, or the seeds of real commercial opportunities. But rather than minimizing the risks and maximizing the opportunities nourished by this systemic behaviour, many computer systems and methods are built on barren narrow intentions and simple goals that lead inevitably to counterproductiveness.

It should be clear that uncertainty is as much a hazard as it is an opportunity. The fact, that uncertainty is perpetual, supports the view that decision-taking under uncertainty is not a matter of finding the right spot to link in computer power, or of finding the right information. It is not a professional problem, but a matter of a manager's perpetual analysis, of the system, environment and himself; it is a personal affair. A strategy that supports this understanding of uncertainty has to advocate flexibility and variability, as well as the manager's responsibility to excel individually. Even with information technology, nothing has really changed. The answer to whether information technology can help managers cope with the dynamically changing business world is, as always, 'yes and no'. Information technology, and in particular telecommunication technology, does not necessarily help to maintain a stable infrastructure, for it just creates a different infrastructure by changing the way businesses communicate, and thence precipitates further transition. But since IT cannot be controlled totally, IT cannot control this transition. As ever, the availability of good people is the age-old answer. As tools in the hands of the right people, information technology can be an enormous advantage. But as a magic wand in the hands of a 'sorcerer's apprentice', IT accelerates uncontrollable change and brings certain chaos.

Discussion issues

1. Consider the evolution of systems, their intentions and consequences; in particular focus your discussion around (a) EFTPOS, (b) Computer Centres and Advisory services, (c) the microcomputer community, (d) the systems analysis community, (e) computer consultancies.

2. Follow up on the issues of human resource management. Consider Couger's list; what other concerns do you think are important? Have some issues only recently emerged? What can be done to achieve these goals?

References

1. Morita, Akio, *Made in Japan: Akio Morita and Sony*, Collins, London, 1987.
2. Lindley, D.V., *Making Decisions*, Wiley, New York, 1985.
3. Douglas, M., *How Institutions Think*, Routledge & Kegan Paul, London, 1987.
4. Deming, W. Edwards, *Out of the Crisis*, Cambridge University Press, Cambridge, 1986.
5. Ahituv N. & Neumann S., *Principles of Information Systems for Management*, W.C. Brown, Dubuque, Iowa, 1982.
6. Couger, J.D. & Zawacki, R.A., *Motivating and Managing Computer Personnel*, Wiley, New York, 1980.
7. Linstone, H.A. & Turoff, M., *The Delphi Method; Techniques and Applications*, Addison-Wesley, Reading, Mass., 1975.
8. Couger, J.D. & Zawacki, R.A.,'Dominant Human Resource Trends: Year 2000 vs. 1986', *Proceedings of the 18th Annual S.I.M. Conference.*

List of Abbreviations

ACM	Association of Computing Machinery
AI	Artificial Intelligence
ATM	Automatic Teller Machine
BCS	British Computer Society
BSP	Business Systems Planning
CACM	Communications of the ACM
CASE	Computer-Aided Software Engineering
CBIS	Computer-Based Information System
CD-ROM	Compact Disk Read Only Memory
CEO	Chief Executive Officer
CFO	Chief Finance Officer
CIM	Computer Integrated Manufacture
CIO	Chief Information Officer
CRLC	Customer Resource Life Cycle
CSCW	Computer-Supported Cooperative Work
CSF	Critical Success Factors
DBMS	Database Management System
DEC	Digital Equipment Corporation
DoD	Department of Defense
DOS	Disc Operating System
DSS	Department of Social Security
DSS	Decision support system
E-mail	Electronic mail
EDI	Electronic Data Interchange
EFT	Electronic Funds Transfer
EFTPOS	Electronic Funds Transfer – Point of Sale
EIS	Executive Information Systems
EPOS	Electronic Point of Sales
ES	Expert System
EUC	End User Computing
FAX	Facsimile Transmission
GST	General System Theory
HCA	Hospital Corporation of America
IBM	International Business Machines
ICL	International Computers Limited

ID	Identification
IPSE	Integrated Project (Programming) Support Environment
IS	Information System
ISDN	Integrated Service Digital Network
ISO/OSI	International Standards Organization /Open Systems Interconnection
IT	Information Technology
ITSEC	Information Technology System Evaluation Criteria
KISS	Keep it simple, stupid
LAN	Local Area Network
LSE	London School of Economics and Political Science
MIS	Management Information System
OIS	Office Information Systems
OSI	Open Systems Interconnection
PABX	Private Automatic Branch Exchange
PC	Personal Computer
PERT	Program Evaluation and Review Technique
PTT	Postal, Telephone and Telegraph authority
QA	Quality Assurance
RAF	Royal Air Force
RSI	Repetitive Strain Injury
S&L	Savings and Loan Institution
SDI	Strategic Defense Initiative
SHAPE	Supreme Allied Headquarters in Europe
SIG	Special Interest Group
SIM	Society of Information Management
SWOT	Strengths, Weaknesses, Opportunities and Threats
TCSEC	Trusted Computer System Evaluation Criteria
TEMPEST	Transient Electromagnetic Pulse Emanation Standard
VAN	Value Added Network
VDU	Visual Display Unit
VHF	Very High Frequency
WAN	Wide Area Network
WYSIWIS	What You See Is What I See
WYSIWYG	What You See Is What You Get

Index